Helen Hackett is Professor of English at University College London. Her previous books include *Shakespeare and Elizabeth: The Meeting of Two Myths* (2009), *Women and Romance Fiction in the English Renaissance* (2000) and *Virgin Mother, Maiden Queen: Elizabeth I and the Cult of the Virgin Mary* (1995).

I.B.TAURIS SHORT HISTORIES

I.B.Tauris Short Histories is an authoritative and elegantly written new series which puts a fresh perspective on the way history is taught and understood in the twenty-first century. Designed to have strong appeal to university students and their teachers, as well as to general readers and history enthusiasts, *I.B.Tauris Short Histories* comprises a novel attempt to bring informed interpretation, as well as factual reportage, to historical debate. Addressing key subjects and topics in the fields of history, the history of ideas, religion, classical studies, politics, philosophy and Middle East studies, the series seeks intentionally to move beyond the bland, neutral 'introduction' that so often serves as the primary undergraduate teaching tool. While always providing students and generalists with the core facts that they need to get to grips with the essentials of any particular subject, *I.B.Tauris Short Histories* goes further. It offers new insights into how a topic has been understood in the past, and what different social and cultural factors might have been at work. It brings original perspectives to bear on manner of its current interpretation. It raises questions and – in its extensive further reading lists – points to further study, even as it suggests answers. Addressing a variety of subjects in a greater degree of depth than is often found in comparable series, yet at the same time in concise and compact handbook form, *I.B.Tauris Short Histories* aims to be 'introductions with an edge'. In combining questioning and searching analysis with informed history writing, it brings history up-to-date for an increasingly complex and globalised digital age.

A Short History of . . .

the American Civil War	Paul Anderson (Clemson University)
the American Revolutionary War	Stephen Conway (University College London)
Ancient Greece	P J Rhodes, FBA (University of Durham)
Ancient Rome	Andrew Wallace-Hadrill (University of Cambridge)
the Anglo-Saxons	Henrietta Leyser (University of Oxford)
the Byzantine Empire	Dionysios Stathakopoulos (King's College London)
the Celts	Alex Woolf (University of St Andrews)
the Crimean War	Trudi Tate (University of Cambridge)
English Renaissance Drama	Helen Hackett (University College London)
the English Revolution and the Civil Wars	David J Appleby (University of Nottingham)
the Etruscans	Corinna Riva (University College London)
Imperial Egypt	Robert Morkot (University of Exeter)
the Korean War	Allan R Millett (University of New Orleans)
Medieval English Mysticism	Vincent Gillespie (University of Oxford)
the Minoans	John Bennet (University of Sheffield)
the Mughal Empire	Michael Fisher (Oberlin College)
Muslim Spain	Alex J Novikoff (Rhodes College, Memphis)
Nineteenth-Century Philosophy	Joel Rasmussen (University of Oxford)
the Normans	Leonie Hicks (University of Southampton)
the Phoenicians	Glenn E Markoe
the Reformation	Helen Parish (University of Reading)
the Renaissance in Northern Europe	Malcolm Vale (University of Oxford)
the Risorgimento	Nick Carter (University of Wales, Newport)
the Spanish Civil War	Julián Casanova (University of Zaragoza)
Transatlantic Slavery	Kenneth Morgan (Brunel University)
Venice and the Venetian Empire	Maria Fusaro (University of Exeter)
the Vikings	Clare Downham (University of Liverpool)
the Wars of the Roses	David Grummitt (University of Kent)
Weimar Germany	Colin Storer (University of Nottingham)

'Helen Hackett surprises us time and again with fresh insights. She deftly traces the roots of English Renaissance drama to the indigenous traditions of Miracle Plays and Moralities, while giving due weight to its classical forebears, particularly Plautus and Terence. She ranges right across the golden age of English drama, from its tentative origins to its flowering in Lyly, Marlowe, Shakespeare, Jonson, Middleton and Webster. She finds room to discuss Elizabeth Cary and Mary Sidney and is very good on gender issues in a theatre where the roles of women had to be acted by young men. She does justice, brilliantly, to the role of material culture in underpinning the extraordinary drama that became the jewel in the Elizabethan literary crown while seamlessly weaving accomplished close readings of the texts into a broad sweep tapestry. The result is a richly rewarding and immensely readable book by a leading Renaissance scholar at the top of her game. Hackett carries her learning lightly: there are no clichés here, and not a single pedestrian sentence. Her limpid style is the perfect vehicle for an original treatment that illuminates at every turn.'

– René Weis, Professor of English, University College London

'Helen Hackett's *Short History of English Renaissance Drama* is in fact remarkably wide ranging, inclusive and original. An exceptionally sharp eye and a clear, cool head enable her to deal beautifully with many thorny issues and challenging texts. These range from "the cultural impact of the Reformation" to the dense, learned, conflicted writing of Ben Jonson; the extreme savagery of English revenge tragedy; and slippery issues of gender raised both by Shakespeare's comedies – with female roles performed by young boys – and by less public "household" plays performed, and sometimes written, by women. Finally, the author traces continuities from Shakespeare's own age to the present day, in which, as she rightly observes, "Renaissance drama continues to thrive, enthrall and provoke". The book is underpinned by wide-ranging footnotes and a substantial Bibliography. It is a pleasure to read throughout. Students for whom this will be a first introduction to Renaissance drama are fortunate indeed.'

– Katherine Duncan-Jones, FRSL,
Senior Research Fellow in English, Somerville College, Oxford

A SHORT HISTORY OF ENGLISH RENAISSANCE DRAMA

Helen Hackett

I.B. TAURIS
LONDON · NEW YORK

For Angela Trueman and Christine Joy,
with thanks for their inspiring teaching.

Published in 2013 by I.B.Tauris & Co Ltd
6 Salem Road, London W2 4BU
175 Fifth Avenue, New York NY 10010
www.ibtauris.com

Distributed in the United States and Canada Exclusively by Palgrave
Macmillan, 175 Fifth Avenue, New York NY 10010

ISBN: 978 1 84885 685 1 (hb)
ISBN: 978 1 84885 686 8 (pb)

A full CIP record for this book is available from the British Library
A full CIP record is available from the Library of Congress

Library of Congress Catalog Card Number: available

Typeset in Sabon by Ellipsis Digital Limited, Glasgow
Printed and bound by TJ International Ltd, Padstow, Cornwall

Contents

Acknowledgements

I am grateful to the English Department of University College London for granting me a term of research leave in which most of this book was written. I would like to thank my colleagues and students at UCL for sharing with me many insights into Renaissance drama over many years. Particular thanks are due to colleagues in the UCL Centre for Early Modern Exchanges, the London Shakespeare Seminar, and the London Renaissance Seminar. I am also grateful to the staff of the British Library, Senate House Library (University of London) and UCL Library.

I have learned a lot about Renaissance drama over many years from conversations and written exchanges with the late Julia Briggs, Helen Cooper, Brian Cummings, Gregory Dart, Paul Davis, Katherine Duncan-Jones, Alison Findlay, Andrew Hadfield, Michael Hattaway, Margaret Hannay, Margaret Healy, Tom Healy, Nick Hutchison, Paulina Kewes, Eric Langley, Tim Langley, Chris Laoutaris, Elizabeth Mackenzie, Gordon McMullan, James Shapiro, Alison Shell, Nicholas Shrimpton, Tiffany Stern, Peter Swaab, Ann Thompson, René Weis, Sarah Wintle, Sue Wiseman, and Henry Woudhuysen.

I am grateful to Alex Wright for inviting me to write this book and for being such an engaged and supportive editor. The production team, especially Ricky Blue and Cecile Rault, have been a pleasure to work with.

Marilyn Corrie gave invaluable feedback on chapter 1. My greatest debt, as ever, is to Stephen Hackett, who read every chapter in draft

Helen Hackett

ciencies are of course my own. Ed and Marina Hackett also read
and commented on parts of the book in draft, put up with my
absences (physical and mental), and cheered me on. As ever I am
grateful to Birute Gelumbauskiene for invaluable domestic help.

Angela Trueman, an inspiring and outstanding teacher, introduced
me to the excitement of Renaissance drama. Christine Joy, an equally
excellent teacher, trained me in English Renaissance history and in
historical method, and dared to cast me in a play. I will always be
deeply grateful to them, and I can only hope that I have lived up
to their high standards. This book is dedicated to both Angela and
Christine as a small but sincere gesture of thanks.

In all future printings and editions of the work, full acknowledge-
ment of the provenance of unattributed copyright material will be
provided.

A Note on the Text

Original spellings have been retained in quotations, with the exception of u/v and i/j, which have been modernised. Titles of Renaissance works have been modernised. Dates of Renaissance plays are difficult to establish, since there may be no record of the first performance, and there may be a gap of some years between performance and publication. Dates given in this book are based on information from recent editions, and refer to the likely date of composition and first performance (rather than publication), unless otherwise stated. In the notes and bibliography, 'U' stands for 'University' and 'P' for 'Press', as in Oxford UP (i.e. Oxford University Press).

All biographical information is from the *Oxford Dictionary of National Biography* (Oxford: Oxford UP, 2004; online edn, Jan 2011), www.oxforddnb.com, unless otherwise stated. All references to the *Oxford English Dictionary* (abbreviated as *OED*) are to www.oed.com (Oxford: Oxford UP, 2011). All quotations from William Shakespeare's works are from *The Norton Shakespeare*, ed. Stephen Greenblatt et al., 2nd edn (New York: Norton, 2008), unless otherwise stated. All quotations from Thomas Middleton's works are from *The Collected Works*, gen. eds Gary Taylor and John Lavagnino (Oxford: Oxford UP, 2007), unless otherwise stated.

Introduction

RENAISSANCE AND REFORMATION

English Renaissance writers loved to use the image of life as a performance. 'All the world's a stage,' from Shakespeare's *As You Like It*, is the most famous example,[1] but it is found in many other places too, such as the following lines by Sir Walter Ralegh (1552–1618):

> What is our life? A play of passion.
> And what our mirth but music of division?
> Our mother's wombs the tiring-houses[2] be
> Where we are dressed for this short comedy.
> Heaven the judicious sharp spectator is
> Who sits and marks what here we do amiss.
> The graves that hide us from the searching sun
> Are like drawn curtains when the play is done.
> Thus playing post we to our latest rest,
> And then we die, in earnest, not to jest.[3]

It is not surprising that writers of the Elizabethan and Jacobean periods turned to the stage for images of human existence, since they were living through an extraordinary and unprecedented flowering of drama. This was a period of remarkable creative fertility, as the new possibilities of the commercial stage were seized upon avidly and inventively by a generation of exceptionally talented writers: not just Shakespeare, but also Christopher Marlowe,

Ben Jonson, Thomas Middleton, and John Webster, to name but a few.

In modern times, we have seen how new technologies have created previously unimagined opportunities for communication, entertainment, and artistic expression, from cinema to radio to television to the internet. The late sixteenth century was a similar period of technological and cultural innovation. England's first commercial purpose-built playhouses were constructed, presenting plays to unprecedentedly large audiences, perhaps as many as 3,000 at each performance,[4] and dependent upon pleasing that crowd to ensure financial viability. At the same time, the printing press, a fifteenth-century invention, came into widespread commercial use; now not only could plays be presented on stage to an audience, but they could also have a longer life and wider circulation as printed books. Just like the media innovations of the twentieth and twenty-first centuries, these new technologies inspired writers and performers to develop fresh and startling works of art. Inventive minds experimented with the potential of the commercial stage and of print as means of self-expression, of dissemination of knowledge and ideas, and of daring commentary upon the political, religious, and cultural upheavals of the times. They also used drama as a medium of philosophical reflection upon what it is to be human.

The cultural innovations of Renaissance drama were effected to a large extent through the skilful use of language. Visual spectacle (in such forms as processions, graphic violence, and rich and symbolic costumes) was clearly important in many plays; nevertheless, the playhouses were fairly sparse in their use of scenery, so drama was heavily reliant on skilful writing to engage the audience. It was vital that the spectators' imaginations should work in collaboration with the efforts of the actors, as the Chorus famously exhorts in Shakespeare's *Henry V*:

> Can this cock-pit hold
> The vasty fields of France? Or may we cram
> Within this wooden O the very casques
> That did affright the air at Agincourt?
> . . . let us, ciphers to this great account

On your imaginary forces work.
Suppose within the girdle of these walls
Are now confined two mighty monarchies ...
Think, when we talk of horses, that you see them,
Printing their proud hoofs i'th'receiving earth;
For 'tis your thoughts that now must deck our kings.
(*Henry V*, Prologue, lines 11–14, 17–20, 26–8)

The task of the playwright was to create a virtual reality, and to this end it was vital that he should deploy the English language with the utmost literary skill. A central component of Renaissance education was training in rhetoric – the art of using language effectively, especially for persuasion – and we see this reflected in the work of the dramatists. Moreover, most Renaissance drama was poetic drama, by which is meant not only that it was written in verse, but also that each play had poetic unity, combining themes and recurrent images to create a coherent and satisfying work of art. This, then, was a drama which used literary powers to arrest, beguile, and move its audience.

The range of tone and mood in Renaissance drama was extraordinary. Even within Shakespeare's own body of work, we move from the slapstick of *The Comedy of Errors* to the high tragedy and terror of *Macbeth*, from the exuberance of *A Midsummer Night's Dream* to the bleak nihilism of *King Lear*, from the lyricism of *Romeo and Juliet* to the scabrous satire of *Troilus and Cressida*. Add to these the epic grandeur and extreme violence of Marlowe's *Tamburlaine*, the ingenious and decadent horrors of revenge tragedy, the down-to-earth realism of city comedy and domestic tragedy, and more, and it is apparent that Renaissance dramatists were creating a multitude of diverse imaginary worlds. This is before we even look beyond the commercial playhouses to other forms of drama such as court entertainments, civic pageantry, and the so-called 'closet dramas' that were staged in aristocratic households, all of which will be considered in the following chapters.

It has been estimated that some 3,000 plays were written over the period 1560–1642. Even though only around a sixth of these survive, this constitutes a massive contribution to English culture and history.[5] The achievements of English Renaissance dramatists resound down the centuries, as their plays continue to be presented on modern stages to enthralled spectators, and to be widely studied and read. This book will survey drama from the early sixteenth century to 1642, when parliament, led by Puritans, took charge of government and closed the playhouses. It will concentrate particularly on the late Elizabethan period (*c.*1585–1603) and the Jacobean period (1603–25) since these produced most of the Renaissance plays that are well known today. Its aims are threefold: to convey the variety and richness of English Renaissance drama; to explore why and how this period produced this creative explosion; and to suggest why these plays continue to have such hold upon readers and audiences in the modern world.

WHAT WAS THE RENAISSANCE?

At the outset it is worth pausing to consider what we mean by the term 'Renaissance'. Literally it means 'rebirth', and the *Oxford English Dictionary* defines it as 'the revival of the arts and high culture under the influence of classical models, which began in Italy in the fourteenth century and spread throughout most of Europe by the end of the sixteenth.'[6] It took a little time for these developments to reach England, and therefore the English Renaissance is usually regarded as having taken place in the sixteenth and seventeenth centuries. In English drama, the period of greatest activity and artistic achievement was from the late 1580s to the 1620s, covering the last part of the Elizabethan period (Elizabeth I reigned from 1558 to 1603) and the Jacobean period (the reign of James I, 1603–25).

Fifteenth-century Italy saw an artistic and intellectual flowering which many of its participants regarded self-consciously as a movement of renewal and of the rediscovery of the classical arts and scholarship that had fallen into decay in the middle ages. Classicism became associated with purity, naturalism, and clarity, as opposed to the supposed gothic barbarity of intervening centuries. This attitude was crystallized in the term *rinascita*, or rebirth, first used by the Italian artist and critic Giorgio Vasari (1511–74) in his book *The Lives of the Artists* (1550) to describe how Italian painters and sculptors of the fourteenth to sixteenth centuries had revived classical style and techniques. The general use of the term 'Renaissance' in cultural history began later, with *The Civilization of the Renaissance in Italy* (1860) by the Swiss author Jacob Burckhardt (1818–97). For Burckhardt the cultural advances of Italy in the fourteenth to sixteenth centuries were dependent upon the existence of competing independent city states ruled by despotic dynasties, who deployed artistic patronage as a means of celebrating and promoting their power. In this culture, despots and artists alike personified the triumph of the self-interested human will: 'Despotism ... fostered in the highest degree the individuality not only of the tyrant or *condottiere* himself, but also the men whom he protected or used as his tools.' Burckhardt takes as an example Leon Battista Alberti (1404–72), an author, artist, and architect: 'an iron will pervaded and sustained his whole personality; like all the great men of the Renaissance, he said, "Men can do all things if they will."' In his mastery of a wide and diverse range of intellectual interests Alberti also exemplified Burckhardt's idea of the Renaissance man, 'the "all-sided man" – *l'uomo universale*'.[7]

Scholars of the medieval period have sometimes been resentful, not without reason, of the implication in these ideas of the 'Renaissance' that what went before was a kind of dark age of ignorance and primitivism, waiting for the rebirth of classical learning to shed light and bring progress. In England, where as I have said we tend to define the Renaissance as beginning in the sixteenth century, we should not lose sight of cultural continuities with preceding centuries, and indeed the first chapter of the present book will give some attention to the drama that came before the age of Shakespeare. Feminist scholars have also questioned whether women had a Renaissance: did the new learning reach further than a rather select community of educated men?[8] Mindful of this question, chapter 8 below will explore Renaissance drama in relation to gender, including the extent to which female performers and writers were able to participate. The Renaissance, then, is a term which has been useful to historians as a way of carving up the past into manageable sections, and indeed continues to be useful; but we need to be mindful of the extent to which it is a later construction, and of the assumptions that underpin it.

Nevertheless, many writers of this period were conscious that they were living through a period of cultural change and innovation. Erasmus of Rotterdam (c.1469–1536), the great humanist scholar, derided the elaborate intricacies of medieval scholastic debates in philosophy and theology, such as how long it took to form Christ in the Virgin Mary's womb, or whether the incarnate God could have taken on any shape such as a woman or a flintstone or a gourd, complaining that 'these subtle refinements of subtleties are made still more subtle by all the different lines of scholastic argument, so that you'd extricate yourself faster from a labyrinth.'[9]

Along with his friend Sir Thomas More (1478–1535) and their circle, Erasmus set himself to slice through these pedantic accretions in quest of truth. Meanwhile humankind's sense of its place in the world was being rocked by the discovery of new lands far beyond Europe, where people lived according to different models of social organisation and religious beliefs. Even more radically disturbing were the astronomical discoveries of Nicolas Copernicus (1473–1543) and Galileo Galilei (1564–1642) that the earth was not at the centre of the universe. John Donne wrote of what we may call the psychological effects of the new learning: 'new philosophy calls all in doubt, / The element of fire is quite put out; / The sun is lost, and th'earth, and no man's wit / Can well direct him where to look for it.' For Donne this new cosmic uncertainty has produced social and spiritual upheaval:

> 'Tis all in pieces, all coherence gone;
> All just supply, and all relation:
> Prince, subject, father, son, are things forgot,
> For every man alone thinks he hath got
> To be a phoenix, and that then can be
> None of that kind, of which he is, but he.[10]

This description of fragmentation, alienation, and individualism may strike us as eerily prescient of modern times. Then as now, rapid ideological and scientific change had far-reaching social and cultural consequences.

Erasmus was described above as a humanist. This is another

term, like Renaissance, which requires careful consideration. Today we associate humanism with secularism: the British Humanist Association, for instance, defines itself as an organisation of 'non-religious people who seek to live ethical and fulfilling lives on the basis of reason and humanity. We promote Humanism, support and represent the non-religious, and promote a secular state.'[11] This is not what humanism means in relation to Renaissance scholars. In this context, humanism is the study of what we now call the humanities – that is, literature, languages, the arts, philosophy, history, and so on – and its core was classical scholarship, based on knowledge of the writings and artworks of ancient Greece and Rome.[12] Moreover, for Erasmus, More, and their followers, the purpose of this revival of classical learning was very much the service of God. A return to a pure, classical Latin was necessary partly to cut through the accretions of commentary in medieval scholasticism so as to regain direct contact with original authorities; but it was needed also, and most importantly, to achieve a better translation of the Bible.

The Bible of the medieval church was the Vulgate, a Latin translation made in the fifth century by St Jerome. This text was found to contain a number of errors – in some cases with theological consequences – and so in 1516 Erasmus published a parallel text of two new, more correct versions of the New Testament, one a collation of the original Greek texts, the other a new Latin translation. His aim was to purify and strengthen Christianity, although in practice his translation contributed to the destabilising developments that would lead to the Reformation (of which there will be further discussion below). But this was most definitely scholarship in the service of God, as was that of More, who shared in Erasmus's criticisms of abuses within the Catholic Church, but who is well known for his rigorous adherence to Catholicism in persecuting those who left the old faith for new Protestant doctrines, and in opposing to the death Henry VIII's schism from Rome.

Even so, the revival of interest in classical authors, who were after all pagans, and in classical statuary, which celebrated the human body with such naturalism, undoubtedly brought a new consciousness of the powers and gifts of humanity within a Christian universe. Indeed, one reason why Erasmus opposed Protestantism was because

Protestant theologians maintained that people could only be saved by divine grace, not by their own efforts to be good, whereas Erasmus believed in human perfectibility. A good example of Christian humanism is John Milton's *Paradise Lost* (1667), in which Adam recalls his first awakening after his creation: 'By quick instinctive motion up I sprung, / . . . and upright / Stood on my feet . . . / My self I then perused, and limb by limb / Surveyed, and sometimes went, and sometimes ran / With supple joints, and lively vigour led.' He has all the muscular vitality of an athlete on a Greek vase or in a Roman statue, and eagerly relishes his physical prowess, but the consequence is not egotism or solipsism, but a desire to know and worship his creator:

> Tell, if ye saw, how came I thus, how here?
> Not of my self; by some great maker then,
> In goodness and in power pre-eminent;
> Tell me, how may I know him, how adore,
> From whom I have that thus I move and live,
> And feel that I am happier than I know.[13]

Adam's sense of his own extraordinary faculties leads to a celebration not of his own superiority, but of the greatness of his divine creator. For other Renaissance writers such as Marlowe, a classical education did arguably lead away from Christianity to the possibility of entertaining atheistical ideas, as will be discussed in chapter 3 below; but for the most part the Renaissance was a movement of Christian humanism, and religion continued to play a central role in society and culture, as we shall explore further shortly when we consider the Reformation.

Certainly an important consequence of humanism was the prominence of classical texts in the educational curriculum. Sixteenth-century England saw unprecedented activity in the founding of free grammar schools, mostly funded by private benefactors. By 1577, when William Harrison contributed a *Description of England* to Raphael Holinshed's *Chronicles*, he was able to write that 'there are great number of grammar schools throughout the realm, and those very liberally endowed, for the better relief of poor scholars, so that there are not many corporate towns now under the Queen's dominion, that hath not one grammar school at the least, with a sufficient living for a master and usher appointed to the same.'[14] At such schools boys would encounter the comedies of Terence, the rhetoric of Cicero, and the poetry of Ovid, Virgil, and Horace. Girls tended only to be educated if their families were wealthy, and were taught at home by private tutors, but their curricula too centred on classical authors, while omitting racier parts. Some boys went on to study at university at Oxford or Cambridge, or at the Inns of Court (the centres of legal training in London); at all these institutions the formal curriculum was rather narrow, but there was extensive extra-curricular intellectual and literary activity, in which again classical writers featured largely. Ovid was especially popular, partly because of the risqué and witty nature of many of his writings, partly because his *Metamorphoses* was such a rich source-book of narrative and images.

Important Renaissance literary influences came also from Italy. The sonnets of Petrarch became extremely influential in sixteenth-century England, where by the end of the century nearly every poet was producing a sonnet sequence lamenting his unrequited devotion to an unattainably chaste mistress. Such sonnets were less about the supposedly desired mistress than they were about exploring the subjectivity of the poet, and displaying his wit and skill as a literary artificer. Also influential was *Il Cortegiano* (1528) by Baldassare Castiglione (1478–1529), translated into English as *The Book of the Courtier* by Sir Thomas Hoby in 1561. This was a discussion of the qualities needed to be an ideal Renaissance man: he must be skilled in all fields, including rhetoric, fashion, wit, government, and love, and he must exercise his skill in all these fields with *sprezzatura*, that is, an unaffected grace which makes excellence appear effortless. *The Courtier* was particularly important in introducing to England the philosophy of the fifteenth-century Florentine neo-Platonists, who had argued that love of human beauty should be spiritual, not carnal, and could thereby lead to love of God. Castiglione borrows from Plato the image of an upward ascent to express this: the lover of a chaste and beautiful woman must 'make use of this love as a step by which to climb to another that is far more sublime', until his soul, 'consumed in this most joyous flame, . . . ascends to its noblest part, which is the intellect; and there, no more over-shadowed by the dark night of earthly things, it glimpses the divine beauty itself'.[15] This provides a note of aspiration and idealism which runs through much English Renaissance love poetry, and many depictions of love in the drama of the period too. A dark counterpoint to this idealism, however, was provided by the influence of Niccolò Machiavelli (1469–1527), especially his best known work *Il Principe* (*The Prince*, 1513), which advocated a pragmatic approach to self-advancement and politics. Machiavelli and his followers would come to be caricatured in English drama as satanic schemers. If this was an exaggerated picture, nevertheless it was true that Machiavelli argued that the successful acquisition and exercise of power may necessitate giving a low priority to moral considerations.

Some historians and literary scholars prefer to designate this period not as the 'Renaissance', but as the 'early modern period'. To some extent this is an attempt to find a more neutral term than 'Renaissance', which is loaded with potentially glorifying implications. The idea is simply that what comes between the 'medieval' and the 'modern' is the 'early modern'. At the same time, however, this phrase implies the inception of practices and beliefs that are recognisably modern. These include social structures, such as the rise of the nation state, of the middle classes, of the nuclear family, and of capitalism rather than feudalism. They also arguably include the development of a modern sense of selfhood. For Burckhardt the Renaissance was the beginning of the rise of individualism, of confident self-will and self-assertion. More recent scholars, however, have often found the sixteenth- and seventeenth-century self to be characterised by a sense of insecurity, fracturedness, and troubled self-awareness, and have found in this an incipient modernity.

In his hugely influential book *Renaissance Self-Fashioning* (1980), Stephen Greenblatt explained that he had set out in somewhat Burckhardtian spirit to write an account of 'the role of human autonomy in the construction of identity. It seemed to me the very hallmark of the Renaissance that middle-class and aristocratic males began to feel that they possessed such shaping power over their lives.' As his research proceeded, however, he found that individuals were inescapably shaped by cultural institutions, such as the family, religion, and the state.

Consequently 'there were, so far as I could tell, no moments of pure, unfettered subjectivity; indeed, the human subject itself began to seem remarkably unfree, the ideological product of the relations of power in a particular society.'[16] Greenblatt is deliberately punning on the term 'subject' here: it connotes at once a subject-position, 'I', possessing subjectivity; the subject or patient of psychoanalysis; and the subject of a state, subjugated under government authority. There is clear influence here from the French cultural historian and theorist Michel Foucault (1926–84), in the wake of whose work there has been growing and continuing interest in how the minds and bodies of individuals in the past were affected and controlled by the ideological conditions in which they lived. For Francis Barker, writing in 1995, the sixteenth and seventeenth centuries brought 'a new set of relations between state and citizen, body and soul, language and meaning'. The interventionist state which seeks to control the psyches of its citizens may be seen as exemplified in the oppressive practices of political performance and surveillance at Hamlet's Elsinore. In such conditions the individual, like Hamlet, becomes self-conscious and self-questioning; he gains sensitivity and interiority, but at a price of self-doubt and self-division:

> The subject is cast in on itself, controlled from within by its selves; crippled by struggles and anxieties inside itself; radically undermined by the loss of its own body with which it is ever in contact but whose insistent reminders of a material limit to its subjection, which it cannot quite determine for itself, it must ever attempt to quell.[17]

Barker and others have posited the kind of subjectivity that he describes here as distinctively proto-modern. This entails a far darker view of the period than the celebration and optimism implied in the term 'Renaissance'; yet it is a view in which perhaps we can more readily recognise a sense of the origins of the world that we know today.

In the present study I will continue to use the designation 'Renaissance' as the term most familiar to the widest body of readers, but with a consciousness that the period is riven by conflicting cultural forces which make it far more complex and less unified than this label might imply.

THE CULTURAL IMPACT OF THE REFORMATION

If the concept of the Renaissance has been a subject of debate, there can be no doubt that a Reformation of religion took place in the sixteenth century, and that this had a far-reaching effect at all levels of society on people's lives and their sense of themselves. The medieval church was the Roman Catholic Church; there was no other church in Europe. Hostility to abuses in the church and resentment of its power had simmered for some time, but in the early sixteenth century, as we have seen, humanist scholars like Erasmus had initiated a new critique of its intellectual and spiritual stagnation. While they tried to work from inside the Catholic Church, others were more impatient. The schism in Christianity – the birth of Protestantism – is usually dated to 1517, when Martin Luther nailed his 95 theses (arguments against what he saw as ecclesiastical malpractice and false teaching) to the church door at Wittenberg in Germany. Just as Renaissance artists and humanist scholars returned to the classical world to find models for their new departures, so Luther claimed to be returning the church to its founding principles, seeking to restore the Christian faith to the simplicity of its early years. Very often in this period, the shock of the new is in many ways the shock of a return to the old, to the forgotten or suppressed.[18]

Luther's teachings marked a radical rupture in how people thought about their relation to God and the world, and therefore had wide impact on the arts, including literature and drama. He taught that there was a 'priesthood of all believers': that each individual has a personal relationship with God, and that the church is not a worldly institution with a hierarchical structure (Pope, archbishop, bishop, priest), but the spiritual collective body of all these faithful individuals. This questioning of authority and hierarchy had implications for the state as well as the church which would reverberate through sixteenth- and seventeenth-century England. In the 1530s Henry VIII, seeking a divorce from Catherine of Aragon who had failed to produce a male heir, and also seeking more power and wealth, enthusiastically endorsed the Protestant challenge to papal supremacy, making himself Head of the Church of England. However, monarchs were understandably less enthusiastic about moves to replace orderly tiers of church government with the more local and democratic system of synods or presbyteries (councils of church elders). Early in the next century James I expressed his view concisely: 'No bishop, no king'.[19]

Meanwhile for literature the 'priesthood of all believers' had the immensely important consequence of promoting vernacular translations of the Bible, widely disseminated via the new technology of print. The English Bible was the product of the Protestant belief that each individual should have direct contact with the Word of God without needing the mediation of a priest, and that each believer should cultivate a personal relationship with God. William Tyndale's assertively Lutheran English New Testament of 1525 was followed by the first authorised English Bible, Henry VIII's Great Bible of 1539, translated by Miles Coverdale. Ensuing important translations were the widely read Geneva Bible of 1560, which promulgated puritanical Calvinist doctrines (see below), and Elizabeth I's official Bishops' Bible of 1568. These were of course followed by the landmark Authorised Version commissioned by James I and first published in 1611, now widely recognised as one of the most influential books in English.

The English Bible played a vital role in the history of English literature, not only giving Scripture a new centrality in the consciousness of the English people, but also promoting literacy and the publishing trade, since the laity had to be taught to read in order to achieve personal contact with the Word of God, and this of course created a reading public equipped to read secular books too. Crucially, the English Bible also advanced confidence in English as a richly expressive language worthy to convey divine truths. English writers began to emerge from traditional deference to Latin, Italian and French as superior languages. In the early 1580s Sir Philip Sidney (1554–86) wrote a *Defence of Poesy*, the first English work of literary criticism, in which he defined 'poesy' not just as verses, but as imaginative literature in general. Comparing English with other languages, he asserted that 'for the uttering sweetly and properly the conceits of the mind (which is the end of speech), that hath it equally with any other tongue in the world.'[20] He put theory into practice by writing the first English sequence of love sonnets (*Astrophil and Stella*) and the first English prose romance (the *Arcadia*). Edmund Spenser (*c.*1552–99) made the first attempt to write an English national epic in *The Faerie Queene* (1590, 1596), to be followed by his admirer John Milton (1608–74) with *Paradise Lost* (1667). All three of these writers were devout Protestants whose beliefs, including faith in England as God's chosen nation, run forcefully through all their writings.

Luther's central doctrine was 'justification by faith alone', meaning that the only means of salvation was by whole-hearted belief and by the workings of divine grace; human beings could not earn a place in heaven by 'good works' such as gifts of money to the church, or repeating certain prayers a certain number of times. Associated with this was the doctrine of 'predestination', teaching that only a certain number of chosen people – the elect – would be saved by divine decree, and that the rest of us were inescapably condemned to damnation. This doctrine was adopted and taken further by Jean Calvin (1509–64), author of the *Institutes of the Christian Religion* (1536), who established a Protestant city state in Geneva. Calvin laid particularly harsh emphasis on the limited number of the elect, and on the impossibility of altering one's destiny for heaven or hell by any kind of worldly action, however virtuous. However, Calvinists believed that members of the elect would feel God's grace working within them, and that they would experience joyful confidence in their own salvation. This naturally gave rise to a good deal of soul-searching and looking within to detect these signs of divine grace, and generated numerous writings in the form of spiritual autobiography or conversion narrative. Protestantism, then, made a significant contribution to a new culture of self-scrutiny, to explorations and expressions of interiority, and to the growth of autobiographical modes of writing. It is an important context for the ways in which Shakespeare's tragic heroes probe their inner selves in their soliloquies.

Protestantism also brought fundamental changes in how people thought about forms of representation. According to the Catholic Church, the consecrated bread and wine of the Eucharist underwent transubstantiation, whereby they were transformed into the physical body and blood of Christ. Luther had challenged this, preaching instead consubstantiation: that is, a spiritual presence of Christ in the blessed bread and wine, but not a physical transformation. Calvin went much further: for him, the Communion service was merely a commemoration of the Last Supper, and the bread and wine remained merely bread and wine. They were what they were, nothing more than simple material entities; the rituals, words, and gestures performed by the priest could not affect them. Accordingly Protestants eschewed elaborate ceremony in their services, and also lavish decoration in their churches, rejecting, often violently, the statues and relics of saints that formed an important part of Catholic worship. Whereas for Catholics veneration of such objects was a means of access to God, for Protestants it constituted the worship of false idols in place of God. Such idolatry was forcefully condemned by Protestant preachers as spiritual adultery committed against God: one of the official homilies issued by the government to be preached in churches posed the rhetorical questions, 'Doth not the word of God call idolatry spiritual fornication? Doth it not call a gilt or painted idol or image, a strumpet with a painted face? Be not the spiritual wickedness of an idol's enticing, like the flatteries of a wanton harlot?'[21] There were various ferocious outbreaks of icon-oclasm in which images were angrily smashed and burned, both in the 1530s when Henry VIII broke from Rome, and in the staunchly Protestant reign of his son Edward VI (1547–53). Combined with the dissemination of vernacular Bibles and the emphasis on the Word of God, this meant that Protestantism marked a significant shift from a culture of objects and images to a culture of words.

This fierce controversy about what an image was and how images could be used naturally had significant consequences for the arts. The medieval church had been a major artistic patron, requiring statues, wall-paintings, and beautiful metalwork for chalices and reliquaries; all of this was now swept away, as wall-paintings were white-washed over and statues were destroyed or mutilated (as, for example, in the Lady Chapel at Ely Cathedral, which still presents the melancholy sight of numerous defaced figures). Many Protestants even regarded the crucifix as idolatrous. This assault on imagery had impact not only on the visual arts, but on poetry too. One of the most prolific genres of medieval literature had been religious lyric, often expressing devotion to the Virgin and other saints in passionate and highly sensual terms. This was no longer acceptable, and for several decades there was a hiatus in English religious verse as Protestant poets hesitated to find ways of expressing faith that would not give offence under the new dispensation. One answer lay in turning to Scripture, especially the Psalms, which offered an authorised sacred model for verse: hence Anne Locke in 1560 wrote a *Meditation of a Penitent Sinner*, a sequence of 26 sonnets based on Psalm 51; then Philip Sidney and his sister Mary, Countess of Pembroke, embarked on a translation of all the Psalms which Mary revised and completed after Philip's untimely death in battle in 1586, experimenting brilliantly with complex metres, intricate rhyme-schemes, and vivid imagery.[22] For Spenser the way forward lay in an unswerving devotion to Christ, 'Most glorious Lord of lyfe', which runs even through his love-sonnets, the *Amoretti* (1595), where Christ is asserted as the model for virtuous human love: 'So let us love, deare love, like as we ought, / love is the lesson which the Lord us taught'.[23] In *The Faerie Queene* Spenser also developed Protestant aesthetic principles whereby false, hollow imagery was to be rejected, but rich and engaging imagery was legitimised in the service of divine truth. The problem is that the two kinds of image can look very much like each other: in Book I of *The Faerie Queene* (1590) the allegorical character Una, personifying truth and the Protestant Church, is imitated by her beguiling arch-enemy Duessa, representing deceit and papistry. Duessa calls herself Fidessa (Faithfulness) and adopts public guises which resemble Una, concealing her secret depravity and deformity; both Spenser's questing knights and the reader must exercise constant vigilance and powers of interpretation to distinguish between them. Protestant poets thus came to embrace poetic imagery in the service of godly truth, but always in a context of active discernment and suspicion of surface appearances.

As England swung back and forth in its official religion – somewhat Protestant under Henry VIII, militantly Protestant under Edward VI, Catholic again under Mary I, then finally Protestant under Elizabeth I – both sides suffered persecution and acquired a pantheon of martyrs. For Protestants the English Bible was almost equalled as a totemic text by John Foxe's *Acts and Monuments* (first edition 1563),[24] also known as Foxe's *Book of Martyrs*, which depicted in graphic words and pictures the extreme physical sufferings of Protestant heroes and heroines under Henry VIII and Mary I. On the other side, from 1580 English Catholic missionaries who had trained on the continent of Europe began to arrive in England with the aim of reconversion of their home country. The Elizabethan authorities regarded them as traitors and subjected them to horrific fates; the priest and poet Robert Southwell (1561–95), for instance, endured two-and-a-half years of solitary confinement, torture on ten occasions, then public execution by hanging, drawing, and quartering. His chief tormentor was the notorious interrogator Richard Topcliffe (1531–1604), whose methods included the rack. The religious divisions of the age engendered extreme violence and hatred; and although Renaissance drama can often strike us as sadistic and sensationalist in its displays of mutilation and death, it is no more so than the spectacles of cruelty that were played out in real life in the name of religion. Yet in spite of these antipathies, artistic influences could cross the religious divide: Southwell's visionary lyrics were widely read by Protestants as well as Catholics, and their arresting imagery and deft play of paradoxes were important influences on Protestant devotional poets such as John Donne (1572–1631), himself a convert from Catholicism, and George Herbert (1593–1633).

Southwell's poetry is a product of the Catholic Church's response to the Reformation with its own Counter-Reformation, developing a new evangelism and rigour as exemplified by the Society of Jesus to which Southwell belonged, and cultivating a baroque exuberance and sensuality in the arts. It is important to recognise that English Catholicism did not cease with the creation of the Protestant Church of England in 1559, and that it continued to play an important role in English culture. This was a period not only of religious antagonisms, but also of conversions, including those of Donne from Catholicism to Protestantism, and of Ben Jonson from Protestantism to Catholicism and back again. Shakespeare's personal faith is a subject of continuing speculation and mystery.[25] Hamlet may seem typically Protestant in his introspection and soul-searching, and indeed is a student at Wittenberg, Luther's university (1.2.113, 119). Yet his father's ghost describes his own habitation after death in terms which resemble Purgatory, a place dismissed as a superstition and no longer deemed to exist according to Elizabethan Protestant doctrine: 'I am thy father's spirit, / Doomed for a certain term to walk the night, / And for the day confined to fast in fires / Till the foul crimes done in my days of nature / Are burnt and purged away' (1.5.9–13).[26] In this age of transition, the personal beliefs of many individuals who were not professional theologians may well have been a somewhat eclectic mixture of new Protestant ideas and residual Catholic ideas.

Clearly, just as it would be a mistake to equate Renaissance humanism in any simple way with secularism, so too the Reformation, although it began as a critique of the established church, was not a movement away from religion; in fact it was an attempt to reinvigorate and purify religion. Its effects for drama were complex. As we will explore further in chapter 1 below, much medieval drama took place in churches or in the form of mystery and morality plays with overt religious content. These did not die out overnight, but they encountered vigorous opposition from some Protestants who saw them as idolatrous, and by the middle decades of Elizabeth I's reign they had largely disappeared. In a counter-movement, in the early years of the English Reformation, drama was sometimes used to promote Protestant doctrine and anti-Catholic sentiment, as in the works of John Bale (1495–1563). To some extent this practice continued with the formation in 1583 of the Queen's Men, a government-sponsored playing company with a nationalistic and anti-Catholic repertory. On the whole, though, Elizabeth's regime preferred to keep explicit discussion of contentious religious matters off the stage, and exercised tight censorship. Consequently drama became more secular in its overt subject matter; yet even so, as we have seen, religion was the great ideological battlefield of the age, and this was inevitably reflected on the stage. Moreover, the shifts brought about by the Reformation in how individuals thought about themselves and their relations with others and with God were a major shaping force in Elizabethan and Jacobean drama.[27]

*

Introduction

The cultural turbulence and energy generated by the Renaissance and the Reformation created the conditions for a new drama.[28] They produced plays both rich in psychological depth and complex in their reflections upon destabilising forces of rapid social change. They produced writers able to wield the English language with subtlety and intensity, and determined to engage both the intellects and the emotions of their audiences. The result was a drama which explored corruption in the state and chasms in the spirit, the glamour of sexuality, and the horror of death. The task of this book is to trace the development and flowering of this remarkable art form, beginning with an exploration of the late medieval and early Tudor drama which provided both roots and points of departure for Renaissance drama.

Timeline

Dates given for plays are of first performance; often there is no firm evidence for this, so an approximate date or a span of possible dates is given.

1509	Accession of Henry VIII
c.1519	*Magnificence* by John Skelton
1528–33	*Play of the Weather* by John Heywood
1533	Coronation pageants for Anne Boleyn by Nicholas Udall and John Leland
1534	Act of Supremacy; England breaks away from the Roman Catholic Church
1536–38	*King John* by John Bale
1547	Death of Henry VIII; accession of Edward VI
1550–54?	Translation of Euripides' *Tragedy of Iphigenia* by Lady Jane Lumley
1550–60	*Gammer Gurton's Needle*, author unknown
1552	*Ralph Roister Doister* by Udall
1553	Death of Edward VI; accession of Mary I
1558	Death of Mary I; accession of Elizabeth I
1558–69	*Cambises* by Thomas Preston
1559	Establishment of the Protestant Church of England; coronation pageants for Elizabeth I
1562	*Gorboduc* by Thomas Norton and Thomas Sackville, the first English play in blank verse
1564	Birth of William Shakespeare; birth of Christopher Marlowe

1566	*Supposes* by George Gascoigne
1567	*Horestes* by John Pickering
1572	Birth of Ben Jonson
1575	Princely Pleasures at Kenilworth Castle
1576	The Theatre and the Curtain, the first purpose-built playhouses, open in Shoreditch
1576–84	Children of the Chapel Royal perform at Blackfriars
1577–80	Sir Francis Drake circumnavigates the globe
1577–83	Attacks on the playhouses by John Northbrooke, Stephen Gosson and Phillip Stubbes
*c.*1578–80	Birth of John Webster
1579	Last year of mystery play performances at Coventry; *The Lady of May* by Sir Philip Sidney
1580	Jesuit mission to England begins; birth of Thomas Middleton
1583	Formation of the Queen's Men
1584	*The Arraignment of Paris* by George Peele
1584–5	*Gallathea* by John Lyly
1587	Execution of Mary Queen of Scots; opening of the Rose playhouse on Bankside; *The Spanish Tragedy* by Thomas Kyd; *Tamburlaine parts 1 and 2* by Marlowe
1588	Armada victory; *Endymion* by Lyly
1588–9	*Doctor Faustus* by Marlowe
1590	Mary Sidney Herbert, Countess of Pembroke, translates *The Tragedy of Antony* by Robert Garnier
*c.*1590	*The Jew of Malta* by Marlowe
1591	*Henry VI parts 2 and 3* – perhaps Shakespeare's earliest plays
*c.*1592	*Edward II* by Marlowe
1592	First published notice of Shakespeare as a playwright, in a pamphlet attributed to Robert Greene; *Arden of Faversham*, author unknown
1592–3	Shakespeare writes *Venus and Adonis* and *The Rape of Lucrece* during playhouse closure for

	plague; *Richard III, The Comedy of Errors, Titus Andronicus, The Taming of the Shrew*
1593	Death of Marlowe
1594	Formation of the Lord Chamberlain's Men, with Shakespeare as resident playwright; *The Tragedy of Cleopatra* by Samuel Daniel
1594–6	*A Midsummer Night's Dream, Richard II, Romeo and Juliet*
1595	Swan playhouse opens on Bankside
1596	*The Merchant of Venice, Henry IV part 1*
1597	*The Merry Wives of Windsor; The Case is Altered,* Jonson's first known play
1598	*Henry IV part 2, Much Ado About Nothing; Every Man in his Humour* by Jonson
1599	Globe playhouse opens on Bankside; Will Kempe is replaced as leading comic actor with the Lord Chamberlain's Men by Robert Armin; *Henry V, Julius Caesar, As You Like It; Every Man out of his Humour* by Jonson; *The Shoemaker's Holiday* by Thomas Dekker
1599–1600	Boy-companies (St Paul's Children and Chapel Children) flourish
1600	*Hamlet;* opening of the Fortune playhouse in competition with the Globe
1601	Shakespeare's company perform a play about Richard II at the Globe on the eve of the Essex Rebellion; *Twelfth Night*
*c.*1602–4	*The Tragedy of Mariam* by Lady Elizabeth Cary, the first original English tragedy by a woman
1603	Death of Elizabeth I; accession of James I (already James VI of Scotland); Shakespeare's company become the King's Men; *A Woman Killed with Kindness* by Thomas Heywood
1603	*Sejanus* by Jonson
1604	*Measure for Measure, Othello; The Vision of the Twelve Goddesses* by Daniel, the first Jacobean court masque

1605	Gunpowder Plot; *All's Well That Ends Well*, *King Lear*; *The Masque of Blackness*, the first court masque by Jonson, designed by Inigo Jones; Red Bull playhouse is built
1606	*Macbeth*, *Antony and Cleopatra*; *Volpone* by Jonson; *The Revenger's Tragedy* by Middleton
1607	English colony established at Jamestown, Virginia; *The Knight of the Burning Pestle* by Francis Beaumont
1608	*Coriolanus*
*c.*1608–09	*The Faithful Shepherdess* by John Fletcher
1609	King's Men begin performing at indoor Blackfriars playhouse; publication of Shakespeare's Sonnets
1610	*The Winter's Tale*; *The Alchemist* by Jonson
1611	Publication of Authorised Version of the Bible; *The Tempest*; *The Roaring Girl* by Middleton and Dekker
*c.*1612	*The White Devil* by Webster
1612–13	Shakespeare collaborates with Fletcher on *Henry VIII* (*All is True*), *Cardenio* (now lost), and *The Two Noble Kinsmen*
1613	Globe playhouse burns down during a performance of *Henry VIII*, and is rebuilt; *A Chaste Maid in Cheapside* by Middleton
1614	*The Duchess of Malfi* by Webster; *Bartholomew Fair* by Jonson
1616	Death of Shakespeare; court scandal over the death of Sir Thomas Overbury in 1613; folio edition of Jonson's collected works; Jonson is awarded a royal pension and becomes in effect the first poet laureate
1618–19	Jonson walks from London to Scotland
*c.*1620–30	*Love's Victory* by Lady Mary Wroth, the first English comedy by a woman
*c.*1621	*Women Beware Women* by Middleton
1622	*The Changeling* by Middleton and William Rowley
1623	First Folio of Shakespeare's collected plays

1624	*A Game at Chess* by Middleton
1625	Death of James I; accession of Charles I
1626	Queen Henrietta Maria performs a pastoral drama with her ladies
1627	Death of Middleton
1629–33	*'Tis Pity She's a Whore* by John Ford
1633	Queen Henrietta Maria and her ladies perform in Walter Montagu's *The Shepherd's Paradise*; William Prynne attacks theatre in *Histrio-Mastix*
1634	*A Masque Presented at Ludlow Castle* (*Comus*) by John Milton
1637	Death of Jonson
*c.*1638	Death of Webster
1642	Civil War begins; Parliament orders the closure of the theatres
1644	Globe playhouse is demolished

1

ENGLISH DRAMA
BEFORE THE 1590s

William Shakespeare was born in 1564. As he grew up in Stratford-upon-Avon, where might he have experienced dramatic performance? How might his ideas of drama have been formed? Perhaps he made the 20-mile journey to Coventry, where the Corpus Christi pageants, a cycle of medieval Bible plays, continued to be performed annually until 1579.[1] Some scholars think he may have attended the Princely Pleasures at Kenilworth Castle, 12 miles from Stratford, a lavish 19–day festival of courtly masques and local drama laid on in 1575 to entertain Elizabeth I.[2] He could have read a variety of late medieval and early Tudor plays that were available in print (*Everyman*, for instance, a morality play which will be discussed below, survives in four early sixteenth-century editions).[3] He would certainly have seen performances by touring companies of professional players, who frequently visited Stratford: in 1569, for example, Shakespeare's father as the town's high bailiff presided over the payment of two such troupes, while in 1587 no fewer than five companies performed at Shakespeare's old school.[4]

Many different kinds of drama surrounded Shakespeare and his contemporaries in their childhoods. Long before the construction of the first purpose-built playhouses in the 1570s, England had a rich and thriving theatrical culture; indeed, two scholars of early drama have recently written, 'There was arguably more theatre, and were certainly more kinds of people involved in theatrical productions, before Shakespeare's time than after it'.[5] Much medieval drama was religious, and it used to be thought that much of this died out or was suppressed soon after the Reformation. Recent scholarship, however, has indicated that even liturgical drama in churches persisted in many places well into the seventeenth century.[6] Street performances of mystery plays continued well into Elizabeth's reign; while other forms of drama included morality plays, Robin Hood plays, and mumming plays (folk plays, often about St George, a fight, and a miraculous restoration of life). Entertainments of various kinds were staged in private houses, schools, universities, the Inns of Court (the centres of legal training in London), and the royal court. Around 100 plays survive from the first three quarters of the sixteenth century, more than 200 more are recorded but lost, and more still undoubtedly existed.[7] This chapter will briefly survey the fertile and diverse English dramatic traditions which preceded the drama of Shakespeare's adulthood.

MYSTERY OR CORPUS CHRISTI PLAYS

These plays were performed on the feast day of Corpus Christi, the first Thursday after Trinity Sunday. They are also known as mystery plays, not because of any enigmatic qualities, but because they were performed by the 'mysteries', meaning the craft-guilds or professions.[8] Corpus Christi might fall on any date between 23 May and 24 June, and so was an occasion for outdoor summer celebrations making the most of the long hours of daylight. The feast was introduced into the church calendar in 1311, and from the late fourteenth century onwards, at Coventry, York, Chester, and other towns, the central event was a cycle of plays telling Bible stories, performed on pageant wagons which processed around the town presenting each scene at a series of stations. The reasons why the cycles (apart from a very few local exceptions) died out by the late sixteenth century are many and complex; the banning of the feast of Corpus Christi in 1548 and the opposition of some Protestant churchmen undoubtedly contributed, but so too did economic problems in the towns that had staged them.[9]

The best preserved text is from York, where annual Corpus Christi performances continued into the late 1560s. The York cycle begins with the apocryphal story of the Fall of the Angels, presented by the guild of Barkers or Tanners, who prepared hides for use in leather goods. They performed this scene at the first pageant station at 4.30am, thus presenting at sunrise the story of the dawn of Creation; the play accordingly plays upon imagery of darkness and light. They then proceeded to perform the scene again at the other 11 stations through the town. They were followed at each station by wagon performances working through the Bible in sequence, sometimes assigned to appropriate guilds: the Shipwrights, for instance, presented the Building of the Ark, while the Bakers presented the Last Supper. By the time the Mercers presented the final play, the Last Judgement, at the twelfth and final station it would be after midnight, and once again the play-script makes use of the temporal setting, in this case of nocturnal darkness. Late fifteenth-century documents record some 50 pageants in total. Spectators could remain at one station all day to see the whole Old and New Testament narrative in sequence, or could move between stations at will to create a more flexible and individualised dramatic experience. It was a local and amateur performance, as audience-members watched their neighbours, relations, and colleagues on stage, but at the same time an epic spectacle, with over 300 speaking parts in the surviving York text.

We do not know any names of authors of the Corpus Christi plays, which were produced collectively and revised and expanded over a long period. Two modern editors of the York cycle liken it to 'the Gothic cathedrals of northern Europe, such as York Minster, built and decorated in a succession of styles by generations of craftsmen but unified by a single spiritual aim'.[10] Similarly each major role was shared between several actors, both across different years and in each single year in successive pageants in the procession: a day's performance of the cycle would involve more than a dozen different Virgin Marys and two dozen Christs.[11] Traditions of characterisation developed: Noah's wife, for instance, is a shrew who is sceptical of the prophesied Flood and vigorously resists boarding the Ark,[12] while King Herod is a tyrant whose pride and bombast anticipates Marlowe's Tamburlaine and Milton's Satan:

The prince of planets that proudly is pight
Shall brace forth his beams that our bield blithe,
The moon at my mint he musters his might,
And Caesars in castle great kindnes me kithe.
(The sun that is proudly adorned shall radiate his beams to gladden
our leisure, the moon at my gesture displays his might, and emperors
in castles show great kindness towards me.) (p. 66)

When he interrogates Christ, the latter's resolute silence drives Herod
to ever more violent ranting and raving:

How likes thou? Well lord? Say. What, devil, never a deal?
... Uta! Oy! Oy!
... Say, may thou not hear me? Hey, man, art thou wood?
(How does this suit you? Well lord? Speak. What, devil, not a word?
... Uta! Oy! Oy! ... Say, can't you hear me? Hey, man, are you
mad?') (p. 185)

The surviving texts of the Coventry mystery plays include the striking
stage direction 'Here Erode ragis in the pagond [pageant wagon]
and in the strete also.'[13] Clearly Shakespeare was recalling such roles,
either from his own experience or from the recollections of his
parents' generation, when Hamlet instructs the players not to 'tear
a passion to tatters ... it out Herods Herod' (*Hamlet* 3.2.7–13).

There was much comedy in such larger-than-life roles, and in the
mischief-making and profanity of the Devil, who begins the York
play of the Temptation of Christ by emerging from the crowd and
breaching the imaginary boundary between audience and performers:

Make room belive, and let me gang!
Who makes here all this throng?
Hie you hence, high might you hang
Right with a rope.
I dread me that I dwell too long
To do a jape.

(Make room quickly, and let me pass! Who is making all this commotion here? Get out of the way quickly, I hope you hang high from a rope. I am afraid I have delayed too long to do an evil deed.) (pp. 98–9)

His direct engagement with the audience, at once insulting them and saucily inviting them to collude in his villainy, anticipates later figures such as Shakespeare's Richard III and Iago.

At the same time the cycle includes moments of high tragedy and profound emotional depth; none more so, of course, than the crucifixion. This pageant begins with the soldiers nailing Christ to the cross. The audience can hardly see the prostrate Christ, and may be amused by the soldiers' workmanlike banter as they go about their gruesome task. Then suddenly, shockingly, the cross is erected, and Christ delivers a speech of heart-stopping beauty and pain:

> All men that walk by way or street,
> Take tent ye shall no travail tine.
> Behold mine head, mine hands, and my feet,
> And fully feel now, ere ye fine,
> If any mourning may be meet,
> Or mischief measured unto mine.

(All men that walk by way or street, take heed that you miss none of your suffering. Behold my head, my hands, and my feet, and fully feel now, before you pass, if any mourning may be equal, or misfortune measured unto mine.) (p. 220)

The speech draws upon both a well-known medieval lyric and the Good Friday liturgy, and it must have been startling to the audience to hear these familiar words delivered directly from the mouth of the crucified Christ. The grief and pathos is intensified as he prays to his Father to forgive his tormentors. Much medieval devotional writing is characterised by 'affective piety', a compelling appeal to the emotions, and we see this in action here. Theorists and historians of tragedy sometimes identify pity and terror as its defining characteristics; these are certainly present in abundance in this York play of Christ's passion.[14]

MORALITY PLAYS

Texts survive of five medieval morality plays: *The Pride of Life, The Castle of Perseverance, Wisdom, Mankind,* and *Everyman*. They are allegorical dramas presenting a journey through spiritual trials to salvation which often involves 'psychomachia', a battle for the human soul by representatives of good and evil. Some morality plays were performed outdoors, using 'place-and-scaffold' staging in which an open acting space (the place) was surrounded by individual symbolic structures (the scaffolds), representing such features as a palace, a mountain, or hell. A circular staging plan of this type exists for *The Castle of Perseverance*.[15] The audience may have sat around the outer circumference of the scaffolds, creating a kind of theatre-in-the-round, or they may have moved around the arena in promenade fashion. Some saints' plays and passion plays also used place-and-scaffold staging. *Mankind* and *Wisdom*, on the other hand, may have been performed indoors in a great hall. There is wide variation in the scale and manner of morality plays: *The Castle of Perseverance* has 35 speaking parts, requires the building of six scaffolds, and lasts for over four hours in performance, whereas *Mankind* and *Everyman* are much sparser in their staging.[16]

The protagonist of *Mankind* (*c*.1471–79) is a simple, well-meaning working man – a farmer – who explains that 'My name is Mankind. I have my composition / Of a body and soul, of condition contrary. / Betwixt them twain is a great division'.[17] He is caught between Mercy, a preacher who offers consolation and spiritual guidance, and Mischief, who seeks to lead him astray. In alliance with Mischief are three sinful revellers, Newguise, Nowadays, and Nought, and Titivillus, a devil traditionally associated with idle speech. These reprobate characters fill the play with scatological and slapstick humour, but it is far more than low farce; its most entertaining qualities involve the audience in the same temptations as Mankind. The play begins with a sermon addressed directly to the audience by Mercy. While its sentiments are admirable – 'O ye sovereigns that sit and ye brethren that stand right up, / Prick not your felicities in things transitory' (p. 91, lines 29–30) – we may be finding it just a little tedious when Mischief irreverently interrupts. As Mercy admonishes that '"The corn shall be saved, the chaff shall be brent"', Mischief retorts, 'Leave your chaff, leave your corn, leave your dalliation; / . . . / Driff-draff, mish-mash, / Some was corn and some was chaff' (pp. 92–3, lines 43–50). It is easy to imagine sighs of relief or even naughty giggles and cheers from the audience. Later, as Mankind sets about the worthy labour of digging the soil and sowing seed, Titivillus conceals a board in the earth which thwarts all his efforts, and the audience is divided between sympathising with Mankind's frustration and laughing at Titivillus's clever trick.

The play has little sense of a boundary between performers and spectators, repeatedly implicating the audience in its action. At one point Nowadays and Nought enter through the audience, irresistibly urging us to join in their merry-making: 'Make room sirs, for we have be long! / We will come to give you a Christmas song.' As Naught sings each line, Newguise and Nowadays make the audience repeat it after him. 'It is written with a coal, it is written with a coal', he sings, and the audience sings it back. Nought goes on, 'He that shitteth with his hole, he that shitteth with his hole . . .', and so on (p. 119, lines 331–43). Each audience-member is placed in an inescapable predicament: should they carry on singing? Would stopping make them a kill-joy? Which is more embarrassing, to sing the rude words, or to stand out from the crowd? Just like Mankind, the audience are beguiled into joining in with what seems at first to be just careless fun, but turns out to be something worse. In Mankind's case, he descends from weariness of his work to lechery and drunkenness and then to despair, in which he attempts to hang himself but is finally saved by Mercy and repents. The use of comedy and sophisticated play upon audience responses fully involve us in his difficult choices and his spiritual journey.

Everyman (first printed *c.*1518–19, based on a Dutch play) is a more sombre piece. The title character is touched by Death's dart, and reacts by trying to buy Death off, exposing himself as both worldly and unthinking: 'Yea, a thousand pound shalt thou have – / And defer this matter to another day.'[18] When Death is implacable, Everyman turns for help to Fellowship and Kindred, only to be abandoned by them. He repents of his sins, and finds that in his new virtuous life he is supported by Beauty, Strength, Discretion, and his Five Wits; but as he approaches the grave, they too desert him, leaving Knowledge and Good Deeds as his only companions.

As in *Mankind*, the protagonist is of necessity not a highly individualised character, but a figure with whom all spectators can identify. The allegorical names of the supporting characters demonstrate that these too are types rather than the distinctive and psychologically complex characters that we often associate with Renaissance drama. Yet such figures can be vividly drawn and well observed: Fellowship, for instance, is a convincing representation of a fairweather friend whose affection, despite gushing protestations to the contrary, does not run deep. He urges Everyman, his 'true friend', to tell him what is troubling him, and offers help no fewer than seven times, but when he understands that Everyman wants him to accompany him on his journey to death he quails; the best he can offer is that 'if thou wilt eat and drink, and make good cheer, / Or haunt to women the lusty company, / I would not forsake you' (pp. 196–9, lines 212, 272–4).

Everyman is based around two powerful metaphors. The first is life as a journey, or pilgrimage, during which features which appear to be stable, or at least predictable, such as family, friends, beauty, and strength, in fact come and go. It has been aptly described as 'a play about abandonment'.[19] The second metaphor is of life as a book in which accounts are kept. Everyman learns from Goods that 'because on me thou didst set thy mind, / Thy reckoning I have made blotted and blind' (p. 210, lines 418–20). From Good Deeds, who lies neglected, 'cold on the ground', he learns that the pages of his book of account are scattered and blank (p. 214, line 486; p. 501, lines 5–1–05). These accessible yet profound images compel both Everyman and the audience to confront inexorable truths: that the material world is transient, the soul must be nurtured, the grave gapes for us all, and death cannot be postponed, evaded or resisted. Both this tragic and symbolic force in *Everyman*, and the use in *Mankind* of comic techniques to serve a serious message, amply illustrate the power and sophistication of late medieval drama.[20]

EARLY TUDOR DRAMA

Many of the techniques and conventions of morality plays were used in early Tudor interludes, short dramas performed between the courses of a feast or between other entertainments in such venues as the court, aristocratic houses, university colleges, and the Inns of Court. At the court of Henry VIII identifiable dramatists emerged, taking as their subject reform of the state rather than the self, but continuing to deploy the allegorical methods of the morality play to comment upon topical political issues. Such plays include John Skelton's *Magnificence* (*c.*1519), John Heywood's *Play of the Weather* (1528–33), and John Bale's *King John* (1536–38).

By the mid sixteenth century, distinct genres of comedy and tragedy were also taking shape. Strong influences on the development of comedy came from the Latin authors Plautus (*c.*254–184 BC) and Terence (*c.*195–*c.*159 BC), whose plays were studied and performed at grammar schools and universities. Two original comedies of the mid sixteenth century adapted their conventions for use in English: these were *Gammer Gurton's Needle* (*c.*1550–60, author unknown) and *Ralph Roister Doister* (1552) by Nicholas Udall. The title page of *Gammer Gurton's Needle* tells us that it was performed at Christ's College, Cambridge, while Udall wrote *Ralph Roister Doister* for performance by the schoolboys of Eton. They adopt from their Latin models a five-act structure and a tight organisation of the action.

The subject of *Gammer Gurton's Needle* is exactly what it says in the title: an old lady (gammer) loses her needle. The characters hunt for it and become embroiled in mutual suspicion and false accusations – mostly instigated by Diccon, a mischief-maker – which rise to a comic crescendo. The play might equally well be called 'Much Ado About Nothing', and in its theme of over-inflation of a trivial incident also resembles Pope's *Rape of the Lock*, though it is much coarser in tone. It ends as Gammer Gurton's dim-witted servant Hodge realises that the needle was stuck in his buttock all the time (before she lost it, Gammer Gurton was mending his breeches). As this denouement indicates, the play is full of physical and scatological humour: as the characters scrabble around in the dark to find the needle, Tib the maid passes Hodge a cat's turd; when Diccon threatens to summon a devil to assist the search, the terrified Hodge fears that he will soil himself and runs away, with Diccon calling, 'What, devil, be thine arse-strings bursten?'[21] The play's comic climax is when Gammer Gurton and Dame Chat, a neighbour she suspects of stealing the needle, fall into a battle of words and then of blows:

DAME CHAT: Why, weenest thou thus to prevail?
I hold[22] thee a groat, I shall patch thy coat!
GAMMER GURTON: Thou wert as good kiss my tail!
Thou slut, thou cut, thou rakes, thou jakes,[23] will not shame make thee hide?
DAME CHAT: Thou scald,[24] thou bald, thou rotten, thou glutton, I will no longer chide,
But I will teach thee to keep home!
GAMMER GURTON: Wilt thou, drunken beast?
        [*They fight*]
HODGE: Stick to her, Gammer, take her by the head! Chill warrant you this feast![25]
Smite, I say, Gammer! Bite, I say, Gammer! I trow ye will be keen!
        (3.3.23–9)

A modern editor of the play has aptly described this as 'the first stage fight in English drama between two pantomime dames'.[26] In spite of its classical origins and academic setting, this comedy is earthy, vigorous, colloquial, and thoroughly English.

Ralph Roister Doister, being written for schoolboy performers, is more decorous than *Gammer Gurton's Needle* and indeed than its Roman sources. The bragging soldier of the title is egged on by the mischief-loving Matthew Merrygreek to woo a virtuous widow, Christian Custance, who is already betrothed to a merchant. Merrygreek, like Diccon in *Gammer Gurton's Needle*, is a Puckish prankster who delights in creating confusion and absurd situations. He knows from the outset that Roister Doister's courtship of Custance is hopeless, and incites his supposed 'friend' to increasingly ridiculous behaviour. Humour also lies in lively supporting characters such as Custance's old nurse Madge Mumblecrust and her two maids Tibet Talkapace and Annot Alyface. As in *Gammer*

Gurton's Needle, verbal conflict descends into fisticuffs, again with the energetic participation of women: Roister Doister advances on Custance's house with a kitchen pail for a helmet, and is stoutly repelled by Madge, Tibet, and Annot wielding a distaff, a broom, and a large spoon.[27] This play also deploys more intellectual humour, however; Roister Doister sends Custance a love letter which can be read in two ways, according to the punctuation. Custance reads that she is 'To be abhorred of every honest man; to be taken for a woman inclined to vice', whereas Roister Doister's version asserts that she is 'Of no living man to be abhorred, of every honest man to be taken for a woman inclined to vice nothing at all' (3.4.43–4, 3.5.55–8).[28] Such ambiguous punctuation would be used again in later drama, such as in Marlowe's *Edward II*, when the Machiavellian villain Mortimer sends a Latin letter to the gaolers of the deposed king which can be read as either ordering or prohibiting his murder;[29] and when the nervous Peter Quince in *A Midsummer Night's Dream* hilariously mangles the Prologue to *Pyramus and Thisbe* (5.1.108–17).

These innovative comedies were soon followed by the first English dramatic tragedy, *Gorboduc*. Composed by Thomas Norton and Thomas Sackville, it was performed at the Inner Temple on Twelfth Night 1562 and then soon afterwards at court. Its chief model was the classical tragedies of Seneca, an author much admired in the sixteenth century for his stoic moralism. It derived from him a five-act structure, a chorus which comments on events, and the use of a messenger to report off-stage violence. It also introduced the use of blank verse and of iambic pentameter, whereas English drama until now had mainly used longer, rhyming lines which to the modern reader can seem rather stylised and cumbersome.

Like the Henrician plays mentioned above *Gorboduc* had topical relevance, taking as its theme succession, a fraught issue in the early years of Elizabeth I's reign as her ministers and parliaments urged her to marry and produce an heir. The play relates how King Gorboduc surrenders his power and divides the realm between his two sons. This produces resentment and conflict: the elder son, Ferrex, thinks he should have gained the whole kingdom, while the younger son, Porrex, suspects Ferrex of plotting against him. Porrex invades Ferrex's land and kills his brother; Videna, Gorboduc's wife, then murders Porrex to avenge Ferrex's death. The people rise up and kill Gorboduc and Videna, and the country descends into chaos. It will be apparent from this synopsis that in many ways the play anticipates Shakespeare's *King Lear*, another drama of a 'great king, that doth divide his land / And change the course of his descending crown' with disastrous consequences (*Gorboduc* 1.2.388–93).[30] However, *Gorboduc* concludes with the topical message that monarch and parliament must work together to secure the succession.

Gorboduc was a forerunner of later Elizabethan history plays in using chronicle sources (Gorbodugo was an ancient king of Britain whose story had been recounted by chroniclers from Geoffrey of Monmouth onwards). In some ways it also perpetuated morality play conventions: we see the king and then each of his sons assailed by opposed and persuasive figures of good and evil counsel. Its chief model, however, was Seneca. Later Elizabethan tragedy would adapt Senecan practice by showing graphic violence on stage (in Seneca's plays it was simply reported), but *Gorboduc* resolutely excludes action, presenting a drama largely of talking. The play's long, sententious speeches can at their best convey noble resolution in the face of grim fate: 'The heart unbroken and the courage free / From feeble faintness of bootless despair / Doth either rise to safety or renown / By noble valour of unvanquished mind, / Or yet doth perish in more happy sort' (3.1.141–5). However, for the modern reader or spectator much of the play is overly didactic and static. Revenge, which would produce ingenious plot mechanisms and sensational murders in later Renaissance tragedy (see chapter 6 below), is here only briefly present in Videna's murder of Porrex, while other exciting Senecan features such as ghosts are absent.[31]

Other significant mid-sixteenth-century plays included George Gascoigne's comedy *Supposes* (1566), a translation from Italian of a play based on classical models, and the tragedies *Horestes* (1567) and *Cambises* (1558–69, by Thomas Preston). With developing generic conventions, increasingly secular subject matter, and the introduction of five-act structure, blank verse, and iambic pentameter, drama was evolving into the forms that we recognise as characteristic of the English Renaissance.[32]

ROYAL PAGEANTRY AND COURT DRAMA

Udall's other works besides *Ralph Roister Doister* included the coronation pageants for Anne Boleyn in 1533, which he co-authored with John Leland.[33] Such royal and civic ceremonies in London – for coronations, returning victors, visiting monarchs, and mayoral inaugurations – were another important kind of drama in the sixteenth century.[34] Their form was related to the Corpus Christi plays: a procession made its way along a set route through the streets, pausing at stations where symbolic tableaux, speeches and songs were presented by the City's trade companies. For coronation processions, the monarch would enter the City of London from the Tower, pass along Fenchurch Street, Gracechurch Street, Cornhill and Cheapside to St Paul's, then go on down Ludgate Hill and Fleet Street and past Temple Bar to Westminster. The pageant stations were at conduits and crosses along the way.[35] In Anne Boleyn's case, one tableau presented a white falcon (her personal crest), which descended from a cloud, alighted on a bush of roses (the Tudor crest), and was crowned by an angel.[36] Anne was six months pregnant, so several of the performances praised her fecundity and foretold the birth of a heroic prince.[37] At first sight such pageants can look like rather passive and obsequious acts of homage, but often, as here, they had much work to do in smoothing over political tensions and subduing potential dissent. Henry VIII had married his mistress Anne very recently and clandestinely; to do so he had not only repudiated his popular first wife, Catherine of Aragon, but had torn England away from the Roman Catholic Church. It was by no means certain that Anne would be well received. At the same time, many of Henry's subjects shared his anxiety that she should produce the long-awaited male heir to secure the succession. Such pageants were thus more than coerced expressions of allegiance: they were inwoven with a strong sense of the worries and hopes of the citizens of London, and of what they wanted from their rulers.

The child in Anne's womb famously turned out to be a girl, the future Elizabeth I. Twenty-six years later, in 1559, she undertook her own coronation procession through London. Richard Mulcaster, who published an account of the occasion, explicitly saw it as a dramatic performance: 'if a man should say well, he could not better term the city of London that time than a stage wherein was shown the wonderful spectacle of a noble-hearted princess toward her most loving people, and the people's exceeding comfort in beholding so worthy a sovereign'.[38] A centrepiece of the pageants, staged at the Little Conduit in Cheapside, presented Old Father Time leading forth his daughter Truth, who carried an English Bible. The performance included not only the speeches and gestures of the costumed actors, but the responses of the queen herself. According to Mulcaster, when she first caught sight of the figure of Time, she uttered, 'Time? . . . and Time hath brought me hither', succinctly identifying herself with Truth, implying that she had been brought to the throne by divine providence, and producing a memorable sound-bite to be repeated and treasured by her admirers (p. 27). It is impossible to judge whether her remark was spontaneous or rehearsed. When the English Bible was presented to her she 'kissed it, and with both her hands held up the same and so laid it upon her breast with great thanks to the city therefore', an eloquent sequence of gestures which decisively declared to the citizens of London, who were by now largely Protestant, that she would steer England away from the Catholicism of her unpopular sister and predecessor Mary (p. 29). These were the politics of theatricality. Elizabeth had an astute understanding of the staging of power: another of her aphorisms, which she used more than once, was that 'we princes, I tell you, are set on stages in the sight and view of all the world'.[39]

Masquing, mumming, disguising and tilting (ceremonial fighting) were all popular at court through the middle ages and continued under the Tudor monarchs.[40] In Elizabeth's reign royal entertainments developed a new sophistication as they were staged both at court and at the many country houses and towns that she visited on her summer progresses. They characteristically mythologised the queen's power and her covenant with her people, placed Elizabeth in a complex dual role of spectator and performer, and used myth and allegory to attempt to influence royal policy. *The Lady of May* by Sir Philip Sidney, performed at Wanstead in 1579, presents a May Lady who is torn between two suitors, Espilus the shepherd, who personifies the contemplative life, and Therion the forester, who personifies the active life. Wanstead, where it was staged, was the home of Robert Dudley, Earl of Leicester, Sidney's uncle and Elizabeth's chief favourite, who was at this time at odds with the queen over foreign policy; he favoured aggressive intervention in support of beleaguered Protestants in the Netherlands, whereas Elizabeth was more cautious. The May Lady speaks directly to Elizabeth in the audience, asking her to give judgement 'whether the many deserts and many faults of Therion, or the very small deserts and no faults of Espilus be to be preferred'.[41] Therion seems to stand for Leicester and his policy, and the playscript as published seems angled towards him. In the end, though, 'it pleased her Majesty to judge' in favour of Espilus (p. 43). In refusing to be steered by the drama she indicated her larger resistance to being steered in foreign policy.

By the 1570s and '80s court drama included professional performances, usually provided by companies of boy players from the choir schools of the Chapel Royal and St Paul's.[42] Their plays were mostly allegorical, exploring not only topical political issues but also more abstract philosophical and moral questions. They frequently drew on classical myth; in particular, association of the queen with literary goddesses such as Diana, the virgin huntress and moon-goddess, enabled her to be praised as 'divine' while evading controversial precision on the nature and extent of that divinity. Much court drama was also pastoral, that is, set in an idealised literary landscape peopled by eloquent and amorous shepherds. One example is *The Arraignment of Paris* (1584) by George Peele (1556–96) which relates the familiar story of how Paris was asked to award a golden apple to the fairest of three goddesses, Juno, Pallas, and Venus. After he awards it to Venus, in this version Juno and Pallas appeal to a council of the gods, who refer the matter to Diana. She awards the apple to 'a gratious Nymphe / That honour[s] Dian for her chastitie', a queen named Eliza who matches all the goddesses in her virtues. Diana 'delivereth the ball of golde to the Queenes owne hands', crossing the invisible line between performers and spectator.[43] While involving Elizabeth in the action, this also accentuates the fact that she is the primary spectator to whom the play is directed; she would have sat in her chair of state to watch, and the rest of the audience would in effect watch her watching the play. The gesture and theme of gift-giving also epitomised

Elizabeth I. Born 1533, Queen of England 1558–1603. Engraving by Crispin van der Passe after Isaac Oliver, after 1603.

the rituals of patronage and homage on which the structure of the Elizabethan court depended; the play itself is a gift which the author and players offer to the queen in hope of her favour.[44]

One of the leading playwrights for the court was John Lyly (?1554–1606). It seems likely that Shakespeare knew his *Gallathea* (1584–5), in which two young women are obliged to disguise themselves as boys, unleashing cross-currents of same-sex desire. *Endymion* (1588) relates how a shepherd falls hopelessly in love with the divine and unattainable Cynthia, clearly a persona for Elizabeth. It is a lyrical, elegiac, dreamlike play, in which Cynthia/Elizabeth is extolled by means of enigmas and paradoxes: she is 'she, whose figure of all is the perfectest and never to be measured, always one yet never the same, still inconstant yet never wavering'.[45] Endymion is cast under an enchantment by Elizabeth's rival, Tellus, which causes him to sleep for forty years, until released by a kiss from Cynthia. He wakes to find himself suddenly old: 'What, a grey beard? Hollow eyes? Withered body? Decayed limbs? And all in one night?' (5.1.53–4). The play is perhaps a dramatisation of how many courtiers – and authors – felt themselves wasting away over years and decades of service in hope of the queen's elusive favour.[46] Endymion is induced to confess his adoration of Cynthia, and she responds with a formula which decorously sums up the Virgin Queen's management of her male courtiers: 'Endymion, this honourable respect of thine shall be christened "love" in thee, and my reward for it "favour"' (5.4.177–8). The play has obvious affinities with *A Midsummer Night's Dream* (1594–96) in its themes of dreaming and of a mortal man's amorous encounter with a supernatural queen. Shakespeare may also have learned from Lyly the dramatic potential of several different pairs or groups of lovers. In *Endymion*, the protagonist's love for Cynthia is counterpointed by the love of his friend Eumenides for the hard-hearted Semele, by the bitter thwarted desire of Tellus for Endymion himself, and by the absurd desire of the comic braggart Sir Tophas for the old crone Dipsas. The parallel exploration of love on several different levels, and the use of a complex geometry of conflicting and seemingly impossible desires, were structures which Shakespeare would adopt and develop not only in *A Midsummer Night's Dream* but also in *As You Like It* (1599) and *Twelfth Night* (1601).

PLAYING COMPANIES AND THE FIRST PLAYHOUSES

Much medieval and early Tudor drama was performed by travelling entertainers – 'mummers' or 'tumblers'. As the sixteenth century progressed these performances developed into more formal and structured plays, and the companies increasingly focused their activities on London, where most money was to be made. Evidence of the erection of temporary playing spaces in and around London dates from as early as the 1520s, when John Rastell built a stage at Finsbury Fields.[47] The City authorities strongly disapproved of such idle pastimes: from 1549 there are items in the minutes of the Alderman's Court in London prohibiting plays, and by 1569 the City was forbidding innkeepers to sponsor 'any mannour of stage play, enterlude, or other disguising whatsoever' in houses, courtyards or gardens.[48] As this indicates, there were as yet no purpose-built playhouses; the players used adapted and improvised spaces, such as yards or rooms in the inns of London,[49] or, when on tour, the marketplaces and town halls of country towns, and the halls of great houses.

A further City document of 1574 deplored 'playes, enterludes, and shewes' as encouraging 'eavell practizes of incontinencye', 'unchaste uncomelye and unshamefaste speeches and doynges', absence from church, waste of the money of the poor and foolish, pickpocketing and purse-cutting, 'uttering of popular busy and sedycious matters', and 'manie other Corruptions of youthe and other enormities'.[50] The court, however, had a constant need for entertainments during festivals, progresses, and visits by foreign dignitaries, and so took a far more enthusiastic view of playing. An Act of 1572 decreed that players must be authorised by either a an aristocratic patron or two Justices of the Peace; this conferred respectability on the more professional performers and distinguished them from mere wandering jugglers, pedlars, tinkers and bear-keepers.[51] In 1574 the queen granted a royal patent to one of the leading companies, the Earl of Leicester's Men, commanding all civic authorities to allow them to perform, 'aswell for the recreacion of oure loving subiectes, as for oure solace and pleasure when we shall thincke good to see them'.[52] Three important lines of thought were developing in Elizabeth's regime: first, that public, commercial performances were necessary as a form of rehearsal for occasional court performance; secondly, that it was prudent to oversee and regulate drama, a task which fell to the Master of the Revels; and thirdly that drama could be a political medium. Consequently, in 1583 Sir Francis Walsingham, Elizabeth's principal secretary and spymaster, commanded the best actors from all the leading companies to be drawn together in the Queen's Men, who became the pre-eminent company in London until the late 1580s, and whose repertoire promoted nationalist, Protestant, and royalist sentiments.[53]

The playing companies continued to tour: as already mentioned, Stratford-upon-Avon was frequently visited by travelling players, and some biographers have speculated that Shakespeare may have joined one such company in the late 1580s to begin his dramatic career. In 1587, for instance, Stratford hosted no fewer than five troupes, including the Queen's, Sussex's, Essex's, and Leicester's Men.[54] However, the lucrative London market was increasingly important. Inns such as the Bel Savage on Ludgate Hill and the Bell and the Cross Keys in Gracechurch Street became regular venues for drama.[55]

The first purpose-built structure was the Red Lion, a large stage with a scaffold of galleries erected in Stepney in 1567, but for some reason this was not commercially successful. The story of the Elizabethan amphitheatre playhouses (of which the later Globe, built 1599, is the most famous example) really begins with the Theatre, erected by James Burbage of Leicester's Men in Shoreditch in 1576, and rapidly followed by another nearby, the Curtain.[56] The choice of location placed these playhouses outside the jurisdiction of the City Fathers, who mobilised Puritan preachers to fulminate against them. Tracts by John Northbrooke (1577), Stephen Gosson (1582), and Phillip Stubbes (1583) blamed the new playhouses for a host of social ills. For Northbrooke, the playhouses were no better than the brothels which shared their suburban location: 'I am persuaded that Satan hath not a more speedie way and fitter schoole to work and teach his desire, to bring men and women into his snare of concupiscence and filthie lusts of wicked whoredome, than those places and playes, and theaters are'.[57] For Gosson, drama was sinfully deceitful:

> Plays are no Images of trueth, because sometime they handle such thinges as never were, sometime they runne upon truethes, but make them seeme longer, or shorter, or greater, or lesse then they were, according as the Poet blowes them up with his quill, for aspiring heades, or minceth them smaller, for weaker stomakes.[58]

Their admonitions appeared to be justified when, on a Sunday in 1583, a scaffold collapsed at Paris Garden on Bankside, causing eight deaths and many injuries.[59] Paris Garden was a bear-baiting pit not a playhouse, but to the anti-theatricalists these were much the same thing, and this was a clear sign of God's wrath.[60]

Nevertheless, the public thirst for 'such thinges as never were' proved unquenchable. In 1587 the first playhouse on Bankside opened, the Rose, again outside City jurisdiction. Everything was in place: the playhouses and the audiences; court protection, but also the exciting frisson of controversy; a rich dramatic tradition combined with innovations in genre and dramatic form; and a generation of educated and gifted writers. Together they would produce one of the most remarkable explosions of dramatic creativity ever seen.

2

HOW PLAYS WERE MADE

Before we turn to look at the works of particular playwrights, we need to think a little about the circumstances in which they wrote, and how a Renaissance play was put together. When we go to the theatre today to see a play by Shakespeare or one of his contemporaries we may think that we are having an experience not dissimilar to that of Renaissance audiences. In fact the workings of the Renaissance playhouse not only departed significantly from the drama that came before, but also differed in major ways from the making of drama now. The processes by which plays were written, rehearsed, staged, and published were all fundamentally different from modern practice. Audiences were not like us either, but were citizens of a London that was very different from the city we know today. This chapter will explore how the conditions of Renaissance playing shaped the drama of the period, and how the means by which plays came to publication shaped the texts that have survived to be read and performed in modern times.

THE CITY AS STAGE

In order to understand the success of drama in Renaissance London, we have first to understand the city itself. London was in fact two cities: the City of London to the east, which, then as now, was the commercial centre; and Westminster to the west, the location of the court and the offices of royal government. Between them ran the Strand, where the leading noblemen had their grand houses, with grounds sloping down to the water's edge of the Thames where they each had personal landing stages. The river was the main thoroughfare of London, plied by some 3,000 watermen who ferried passengers up or down river; to hail a boat one called 'westward, ho!' to go upriver, or 'eastward, ho!' to go downriver, or simply 'oars'.[1] One might use a boat just to go from bank to bank: the only other means of crossing the river was by London Bridge, which was constantly congested with coaches, carts, riders, and herds of livestock coming to market. Nevertheless, Londoners were proud of their bridge, a magnificent medieval stone structure with 20 arches. *Londinopolis*, a description of London published in 1657, called it a 'stupendious site' that 'may be call'd, *The Bridge of the world*'.[2] It was lined with magnificent houses and shops, some as much as four storeys high; but it also supported the more grisly sight of traitors' heads, displayed on stakes above the great stone gateway on the Southwark side.[3]

Looming over the City of London was the vast bulk of old St Paul's, the medieval cathedral later destroyed in the Great Fire of 1666. Its churchyard and the surrounding area were of great importance to writers as the centre of the book trade, where stationers, printers and bookbinders had their shops. Also in its precinct was St Paul's Cross where open-air sermons were preached, drawing large crowds. London's preachers were highly theatrical performers,

Panorama of London by Claes van Visscher, 1616. Old St Paul's is to the left, London Bridge to the right.

and despite the animosity of some towards players, their oratory undoubtedly had an influence on playwrights and actors.[4] In any case God was cheek-by-jowl with Mammon, since running east from Paul's Cross was Cheapside, a broad thoroughfare lined with London's grandest shops and also hosting a market. The streets leading off Cheapside were also full of shops, and this whole merchandise district was in its way a theatrical space, with goods abundantly displayed and traders calling out their wares. We get a vivid idea of this from *The Roaring Girl* (1611) by Thomas Middleton and Thomas Dekker, where a row of shops is shown on stage, and the sempster's wife calls out: 'Gentlemen, what is't you lack? What is't you buy? See fine bands and ruffs, fine lawns, fine cambrics.'[5] Particular streets specialised in particular goods and trades. Isabella Whitney meticulously charted these in her 1573 poem 'The Manner of her Will, and What she Left to London' (1573), which reads almost like a shopping map of the city. Watling Street and Canwick Street are where to buy woollen goods, she tells us; Cheapside is where to get 'French Ruffes, high Purles,[6] Gorgets[7] and Sleeves'; while Birchin Lane is the place for hose, and St Martin's for boots and shoes.[8] Meanwhile for those seeking entertainment, taverns scattered throughout the city offered drink, food, music, and shows. Shakespeare's vivid evocation in the *Henry IV* plays of a tavern in East Cheap (a street towards the eastern end of the City), complete with Mistress Quickly the hostess and Francis the tapster, suggests that he was well acquainted with such establishments.

Cheapside was noted for its spaciousness, but most London streets were narrow and crowded. The population was expanding rapidly, from around 120,000 in the mid sixteenth century to some 200,000 by the century's end, doubling again to 400,000 by the 1640s; yet the whole of London, including Westminster and Southwark, was described in 1588 as only three miles long and two miles wide.[9] Around 7,000 inhabitants were foreigners, bringing exotic customs and costumes and unfamiliar tongues to the city's streets.[10] Everard Guilpin published a satire in 1598 which forcefully conveys the vitality of the urban scene, but also its oppressive noise and congestion. He implores, 'Entice me not into the Citties hell', which is a 'hotch-potch of so many noyses':

> There squeaks a cart-wheele, here a tumbrel[11] rumbles
> Heere scolds an old Bawd, there a Porter grumbles.
> Heere two tough Car-men[12] combat for the way,
> There two for looks begin a coward fray,
> Two swaggering knaves heere brable for a whore,
> There brauls an Ale-knight[13] for his fat-grown score.[14]

Pick-pockets and cutpurses took advantage of the crowds and confusion; beggars too, some with hideous injuries or deformities, were also numerous.

The city was hard to navigate: houses and businesses had no street numbers, but were identified by signs, such as the Rose, the Maidenhead, the Bull on the Hoop, the Angel and Bartholomew, or the Cow Face.[15] It was also dark for much of the time. From dusk till dawn the City gates were closed, businesses were shut, and the only lighting came from candles indoors and torches or lanterns in the streets.[16] The streets were dirty: only a few were paved or cobbled, and the rest turned to mud in wet weather.[17] Some parts of the city were appallingly squalid. Fleet Ditch, a river which today runs underground beneath Fleet Street, was used as an open sewer and refuse dump. Ben Jonson's poem 'On the Famous Voyage' is a mock-epic account of an occasion when two men took a boat along the Fleet for a wager. There they encounter not only the 'ghosts . . . of farts' and 'ample flakes' of excrement, but also the debris of pie shops: 'The sinks ran grease, and hair of measled hogs, / The heads, houghs, entrails, and the hides of dogs: / For, to say truth, what scullion is so nasty, / To put the skins, and offal in a pasty?'[18] Disease was rife, especially the plague, of which there were major outbreaks every few years. In 1593 there were 10,662 deaths from plague, accounting for two-thirds of all deaths in London that year.[19] Households affected by plague were highly visible: the residents were sealed inside for at least 20 days, and the inscription 'Lord have mercy upon us' was nailed to the door.[20]

In many ways we can think of this teeming city as a stage-set upon which various kinds of spectacle were performed. Parts of the Thames froze in 1565, 1595, 1608, 1621, and 1635,[21] and a 1621 poem by John Taylor paints a festive picture of activities on the 'Glassie face' of the 'conglutinated Frozen streame':

> There might be seene spic'd Cakes, and roasted Pigs,
> Beere, Ale, Tobacco, Apples, Nuts, and Figs,
> Fires made of Char-coles, Faggots, and Sea-coles,
> Playing and couz'ning at the Pidg'on-holes:[22]
> Some, for two Pots at Tables, Cards, or Dice:
> Some slipping in betwixt two Cakes of Ice.[23]

In balmier weather the river was the setting for water-pageants in which the Queen sometimes took centre stage. On St George's Day 1559, after supper, Elizabeth

> was rowed up and down in the River Thames; hundreds of boats and barges rowing about her; and thousands of people thronging at the waterside, to look upon her Majesty; rejoicing to see her, and partaking of the music and sights on the Thames; for the trumpets blew, drums beat, flutes played, guns were discharged, squibs hurled up into the air, as the Queen moved from place to place.[24]

Elizabeth's processions through London as she set off on progress, or returned, were equally spectacular; she was accompanied by a long and sumptuously arrayed retinue, and large crowds lined the streets.[25] Other stagings of power were more brutal. At Tyburn – site of the present Marble Arch – traitors were not merely hanged, but cut down while still alive, disembowelled, the heart burned, the head cut off, and the body cut into four quarters to be displayed on the city's gates. Again, large crowds gathered.

Such was Renaissance London: a city full of pageantry and performance, rich in visual symbolism, and offering an almost overwhelming variety of pleasures and dangers, splendour and filth, excitements and horrors. This was the city on whose borders the commercial playhouses grew up, and whose citizens furnished most of their audience. Following the success of the Theatre and the Curtain in Shoreditch in the 1570s, there was a burst of playhouse-building activity on the south bank of the Thames in Southwark, which was likewise beyond the jurisdiction of the City of London authorities. Here the Rose playhouse (1587) was joined by the Swan (1595) and the Globe (1599) to form a thriving theatre district. The Globe was

Detail of Visscher's panorama, showing the Bear Garden and the
Globe playhouse on Bankside. Archaeological evidence suggests
the Globe was in fact 20-sided.

in fact a relocation of the Theatre: the Lord Chamberlain's Men,
Shakespeare's playing company, who performed at the Theatre, fell
into dispute with the landlord, dismantled the playhouse, and trans-
ported its timbers across the river to Bankside to build the new
Globe. Dramatic activity also continued on the northern fringes of
London at the Fortune (built 1600), the Boar's Head (1602), and
the Red Bull (1604).[26]

The playhouses were outside the borders of the city, yet still
inextricably dependent upon and linked to the city. Playbills were
widely displayed on posts throughout the streets of London, along
with the title-pages of new books, including published plays, posted
as advertisements by booksellers.[27] Audiences had only to look
across the river to see the Bankside playhouses, with their flags raised
when plays were in progress. Yet audiences could only reach these
playhouses by boat or bridge, making a physical as well as psychological journey out of the workaday world before the play even
began.

The playhouses stood in entertainment districts alongside other
businesses excluded from the city, such as bear-baiting pits and
brothels. We may assume from evidence like the brothel scenes in
Measure for Measure that, despite their hectic rehearsal schedule,

players were not too busy to sample occasionally the services on offer from their neighbours. Meanwhile patrons might just as readily spend their money at the bear-pit or the brothel as on a play; indeed the Hope playhouse, opened in Southwark in 1614, was planned for dual use as a playhouse and bear-garden, though this proved to be unworkable.[28] Playgoing, then, was not a highbrow activity, and to some extent the players seem to have shared the disreputability of the traders in sex and violence with whom they co-existed. Yet they were also often invited to entertain at court, and had aristo-cratic patrons, making their social status rather indeterminate and mobile.

INSIDE THE PLAYHOUSE

The chief Elizabethan playhouses were all what is known as 'amphitheatres', because of their apparent indebtedness to classical theatre design. Evidence for their layout and appearance has been gathered from contemporary descriptions and pictures and from archaeological digs at the sites of the Rose and the Globe.[29] There is animated debate among scholars about the conclusions to be drawn from this evidence, and especially about how it has been interpreted in the Globe reconstruction in London's Bankside, where features including the wide diameter, half-timbered exterior, and interior decorations have been questioned.[30] Our understanding of the playhouses is also complicated by evidence that they varied in size and structure: the Rose, for instance, was significantly smaller than the Globe; and the Fortune was square, whereas most play-houses were round or polygonal.

Nevertheless, the available evidence enables some generalisations about the amphitheatres to be made. It cost only a penny (an afford-able price for most Londoners) to gain a standing-place in the yard, but those who paid more sat higher in the galleries in more comfort. The most expensive seats at sixpence were the lords' rooms, in the parts of the galleries nearest to the stage, where occupants could make ostentatious display of their wealth. The stage was large, around 40 feet across, and extended into the yard. Behind the stage was the tiring-house or dressing-room, from which players made their

Exterior of Shakespeare's Globe, the modern reconstruction
on Bankside. Photo by Schlaier.

entrances through two or more doors onto the stage. The tiring-
house might also contain a central alcove or 'discovery space' which
could be used to conceal a character behind a curtain (such as Polonius in the closet scene of *Hamlet*) or to represent an inset space
such as a shop or a scholar's study (such as Prospero's cell in *The
Tempest*). A trapdoor in the stage led down to an under-stage area
known as 'hell', from which characters could emerge or down into
which they could be dragged; the ghost of Hamlet's father ('this
fellow in the cellarage') would have been heard balefully commanding
'Swear' from this subterranean space (1.5.152–820). Complementing
this, a canopy over the stage from which characters could make
descents was known as the 'heavens', and was painted with celes-
tial bodies. A gallery in the tiring house facade above the stage
could be used for balcony scenes like the famous one in *Romeo
and Juliet*. Above the tiring-house and heavens was a 'hut', from
where machinery could be operated to raise or lower characters
and to create special effects. Alongside this, at the summit of the
playhouse, was a small platform from which a trumpeter announced

Interior of the Swan playhouse. Arnoldus Buchelius (Aernout van Buchel) (1565–1641), after a drawing by Johannes de Witt (1566–1622).

the beginning of a performance, and from which a flag flew while a play was in progress.

It has been estimated that the larger amphitheatre playhouses, including the Globe, could hold around 3,000 spectators.[31] They were probably only full for new plays and on public holidays, otherwise playing at around half capacity; but all the same, this means that in a city which grew from roughly 200,000 in the 1570s to 400,000 in the 1640s a significant proportion of the population were regular playgoers.[32] There has been debate as to the social composition of audiences, although many contemporaries represented them as socially diverse: John Davies, for instance, a law student, wrote that at the playhouses 'A thowsand townesmen, gentlemen, and whores, / Porters and serving-men together throng'.[33] It seems clear that the experience of attending a play was much noisier than it is today, with the audience loudly expressing either disdain or pleasure. The poet Michael Drayton wrote of how authors were tempted by the acclaim of the 'thronged Theaters', where the 'proud Round' might ring on every side with 'Showts and Claps at ev'ry little pawse'.[34] On the other hand, Edmund Gayton recalled in 1654 that if the audience were dissatisfied 'the Benches, the tiles, the laths, the stones, Oranges, Apples, Nuts, flew about most liberally'.[35] The playhouse experience could assault other senses too; the playwright John Marston, writing in 1600, described how audience-members risked being 'choakte / With the stenche of Garlicke' or 'pasted / To the barmy Jacket of a Beer-brewer'.[36]

We may think of the amphitheatre playhouse as a kind of apparatus for producing meanings and creating imaginary worlds. The theatres were magnificently decorated, creating a sense of occasion and of a transformative space. Visual spectacle was important, with much use of ceremonial processions and battle scenes. Special effects such as explosions and storm scenes could be created, and the many acts of bodily mutilation in the drama of the period were represented in graphic style: a playing text of *The Battle of Alcazar* (*c.*1589) by George Peele, a play which includes three executions and disembowellings, noted the need for '3 violls of blood & a sheeps gather [a bladder holding liver, heart and lungs]'.[37] Costumes were sumptuous – often the most valuable property of the playing companies – and their colours and styles spoke a visual language: black for a melancholic, scarlet gowns for doctors and cardinals, blue coats for serving men, and so on.[38] Props were also used: an inventory compiled by the theatre manager Philip Henslowe in 1598 began with 'i rocke,

Sketch of a performance of Shakespeare's *Titus Andronicus* by Henry Peacham, 1595. The costumes mix Elizabethan and Roman dress.

i cage, i tombe, i Hell mought', and went on to list numerous miscellaneous items including 'Cupedes bowe, & quiver', 'i tree of gowlden apelles', and 'ii lyone heades'.[39]

Yet at the same time there were no stage sets of the kind that are used in the modern theatre to evoke a particular place and time. The Renaissance playhouse stage was nowhere and anywhere. Although props were used in the playhouses, as Henslowe's inventory tells us, many of these were non-specific, and much of the work of bringing them to life and creating imaginary worlds was performed by the words of the playwrights. Indeed, it has been estimated that about 80 per cent of the scenes that Shakespeare wrote for the Globe could have been performed on a bare stage.[40] The prologue to *Henry V* famously urges the audience to exert their thoughts to create the 'vasty fields of France' within the 'wooden O' of the playhouse (lines 12–13), and this is how plays written for the public playhouses characteristically worked: the 'imaginary forces' (line 18) of the author and players combined with those of the audience to turn the non-specific stage into a temporarily specific time and place, whether Verona, the forest of Arden, a castle in Denmark, or ancient Rome; or, in the case of the city comedies of authors like Middleton, Dekker and Jonson, the streets and shops of the contemporary London in which their audiences lived. In *A Midsummer Night's Dream* the constant lyrical references to moonlight and night-time made the audience believe that they were in an enchanted nocturnal wood, even though both they and the players would have been bathed in daylight, since playhouse performances usually began at 2pm. The poetry of the play also evokes all the busy wildlife of the wood – the spotted snakes, thorny hedgehogs, and weaving spiders (2.2.9–20) – and makes Oberon's magic work when he declares 'I am invisible' (2.1.186). The fact that players and spectators shared the same daylight, and that the audience closely surrounded the stage on three sides, no doubt contributed to this collaboration between actors and viewers in creating the imaginary world of the play.

Many theatres in use today have a proscenium arch design, making the stage like a lighted box separated from the audience by an invisible screen or 'fourth wall' through which they watch from the hushed darkness of the auditorium. In the Renaissance play-

Interior of Shakespeare's Globe. Photo by Ester Inbar.

house, by contrast, everyone shared the same space, making audience-members more aware of one another's responses in a communal experience of the play, and also enabling actors, both in and out of character, to engage in various kinds of dialogue with the audience. Regardless of scholarly debates about the authenticity of its details, the Globe reconstruction on Bankside in London assists modern audiences to experience something of these forms of interaction, as do the various other reconstructions of Elizabethan playhouses around the world (there are more than ten, including at least five in the USA).[41] Continuing traditions from the medieval and early Tudor drama that we considered in chapter 1, Renaissance drama often played on the invisible and permeable borderline between performers and audience, in ways newly facilitated by the material form of the amphitheatre playhouses. In the epilogue to *As You Like It* (1599), the boy-actor who played the cross-dressing Rosalind steps half out of character to tease the audience: 'It is not the fashion to see the lady the epilogue ... If I were a woman I would kiss as many of you as had beards that pleased me' (lines

1–2, 14–16). In *The Roaring Girl* (1611) by Thomas Middleton and Thomas Dekker, Sir Alexander Wengrave, a wealthy gentleman, welcomes guests to his house, but when he invites them to 'look into my galleries' he seems in fact to be describing the Fortune play-house where the play was performed. His picture collection blurs into

> Stories of men and women, mixed together
> Fair ones with foul, like sunshine in wet weather.
> Within one square[42] a thousand heads are laid
> So close that all of heads the room seems made;
>   . . . Then sir, below,
> The very floor, as 'twere, waves to and fro,
> And like a floating island, seems to move,
> Upon a sea bound in with shores above.

These latter lines presumably refer to the undulating heads of the groundlings in the yard. There is even a cutpurse, with 'hanging villainous look . . . drawn so rarely' (1.2.14–32). Meanwhile Shake-speare's Prospero turns a masque within the play into a metaphor for the evanescence of human existence, and then looks outward with self-conscious irony to the Globe playhouse as a microcosm of the whole world in its mutability and mortality: 'like the baseless fabric of this vision, / The cloud-capped towers, the gorgeous palaces, / The solemn temples, the great globe itself, / Yea, all which it inherit, shall dissolve; /And, like this insubstantial pageant faded / Leave not a rack behind' (*The Tempest*, 1611, 4.1.151–56).[43]

The players were especially conscious of human mortality during the frequent outbreaks of plague: these enforced the closure of the public playhouses, where as officials noted audiences were 'close pestered together', and therefore vulnerable to 'great infeccion with the plague, or some other infeccious diseases'. The most prolonged closures were in 1581–82, 1592–93, 1603–04, 1608–09, 1625, 1630, 1636–37, 1640 and 1641, and caused major disruption to the playing companies.[44] Their authors turned to other kinds of writing; it was during the plague outbreak of 1592–93 that Shakespeare wrote his two long narrative poems, *Venus and Adonis* and *The Rape of Lucrece*, which brought him early fame and success. The playing companies often went on tour during plague-closures, and continued to tour at other times too. Touring troupes had fewer members and were more restricted in the kind of perform-ance they could offer; some plays, such as *King Lear*, exist in two versions of which the shorter may have been adapted for touring (of which more below).

As well as the plague, another challenge to the adult playing companies came from the boy-players who were organised in semi-professional acting companies attached to the choir schools of the Chapel Royal and St Paul's. From 1576 to 1584 the Chapel Chil-dren used an indoor playhouse at Blackfriars, in a monastic precinct or 'liberty' which was exempt from the jurisdiction of the city authorities. Paul's Children performed regularly at court in the 1580s, and had a playhouse near their cathedral which flourished from 1599, while the Chapel Children resumed playing at Black-friars from 1600.[45] Their popularity appears to be discussed in *Hamlet* (1600), where we hear of 'an eyrie [nest] of children, little eyases [young hawks]' who have deprived the adult players of audiences and driven them out on tour (2.2.326). London schoolboys were sometimes forcibly recruited by the boy-companies: this was the fate of Nathan Field, who was 'taken up' early one dark autumn morning in 1600, as he was walking from his home in Grub Street near Moorgate to St Paul's Grammar School, by an agent working under the authority of the choirmaster of the Children of the Chapel Royal.[46] Field went on to great success, not only as a boy-player but later as an adult actor and playwright. We can tell from the sophisticated parts written for them that many of the boy-players were highly gifted. Ben Jonson wrote an epitaph for Solomon (or Salathiel) Pavy, who died at 13, which grimly jested that he had played old men so well that the fates had mistaken him for one and taken him to heaven.[47]

The success of the boy-companies fluctuated, but the adult companies began to emulate their use of hall playhouses, also known as private playhouses. These were indoor theatres which accommo-dated fewer spectators than the amphitheatres and charged higher prices, thus catering to a somewhat more select and fashionable audience.[48] A hall playhouse at Whitefriars was built around 1608; from 1609 the King's Men, Shakespeare's company, began to perform at Blackfriars; and the Cockpit or Phoenix (1616) and Salisbury Court (1629) followed. Performance was by candlelight, with chandeliers suspended over the stage to light the acting space, and sparser lighting of the seating area. This created a darker and more mysterious space than the outdoor stages of the amphitheatre playhouses, one which could create spine-tingling effects and suggest perverse deeds or unseen dangers lurking in shadowy corners. It is understandable that revenge tragedy flourished in these settings (see chapter 6 below). The chandeliers could be raised or lowered to control the amount of light shed, while lanterns, candlesticks and torches held by characters could focus the audience's gaze on particular faces or props, and create startling moments. In John Webster's *Duchess of Malfi* (1614), for instance, the heroine is visited in her gloomy prison by her sadistic brother, Ferdinand, who insists that their interview take place in the dark. He pretends to extend his hand for the Duchess to kiss, which she does, only to realise, with sudden horror, that she is kissing the severed hand of a corpse. No wonder she calls out 'Ha! Lights!'.[49] The shock-value of the dead man's hand as a prop would have been considerably enhanced by its sudden glaring revelation in a pool of illumination.[50]

Candlelight also created more emphasis on sumptuously embellished costumes and glittering jewels that would catch the light. Moreover, the onstage visual feast consisted not just of the gorgeous costumes of the performers, but also of the silks and satins of wealthy spectators who paid for on-stage stools where they could watch the play while displaying their own status and fashionable taste. Since the stage was in any case significantly smaller than those of the amphitheatres, plays written for the indoor playhouses tend to present chamber-scenes rather than epic battles, and it is likely that this more intimate space fostered a less expansive performance style. Another significant innovation was that regular breaks in performance were needed to trim the candles, creating more pronounced division of the play into Acts.[51] Music was played in the breaks, and became a noted attraction of the indoor playhouses.

Performances at court, in private houses, in schools and universities, and in streets and civic buildings also continued throughout the period. However, the coming of the playhouses brought radical innovations in drama and transformed the life of London. Tourists came from abroad to marvel at them;[52] while in 1631 Edmund Howes, describing the recent construction of the Salisbury Court playhouse, declared with some amazement that 'this is the seventeenth Stage, or common Play-house, which hath beene new made within the space of threescore yeeres within London and the Suburbs'. He went on to list them (in fact amounting to 19 not 17), concluding that 'Before the space of threescore yeares above-sayd, I neither knew, heard, nor read, or any such Theaters, set Stages, or Playhouses, as have beene purposely built within mans memory'.[53] The playhouses were a wonder of Renaissance London, and a new technology for imagining the world.

THE PLAYERS

The fortunes of the various playing companies rose and fell over the late sixteenth and early seventeenth centuries; the landscape was a changing one as companies broke up and underwent various reconfigurations. From 1594, however, the leading London company was the Lord Chamberlain's Men, to which Shakespeare belonged. The Lord Chamberlain was the official responsible for organising entertainments at court and overseeing drama more generally. Now that the former Queen's Men had ceased to operate, his company was the nearest to the throne, and was summoned to court more than any other company;[54] their closest rivals were the Admiral's Men, who played at the Rose for Henslowe. The Chamberlain's Men were unusual in that rather than working for a landlord-manager like Henslowe, from the mid-1590s they became a sort of self-governing co-operative, with their leading members, including Shakespeare, all investing in the company and sharing in its profits, an arrangement that proved to be lucrative for them.[55] Another success was their adoption as the King's Men on James I's accession in 1603, officially recognising their status as the leading court players.

Strong friendships but also strong enmities were formed among the community of players. Shakespeare was attacked at the beginning

James I, born 1566, became King James VI of Scotland in 1567,
King of England 1603–1625. Adopted Shakespeare's company
as the King's Men on his accession in 1603. Artist unknown.

of his career as an upstart and a plagiarist, but seems to have become
well-liked; Ben Jonson described him as 'honest, and of an open,
and free nature', while two of Shakespeare's colleagues, the actors
John Heminges and Henry Condell, cared enough about him to
bring his collected plays to print after his death in the First Folio
of 1623.[56] Francis Beaumont and John Fletcher, who wrote a number
of plays together, were rumoured to be so close that they shared
clothes, a bed, and a wench. But violent animosity could also break
out among the playing fraternity, with fatal consequences. Christopher Marlowe, notoriously, died in a fight in 1593; Ben Jonson killed
the actor Gabriel Spencer in a duel in 1598; Spencer himself had
stabbed a man to death two years earlier; and in 1599 a quarrel
between two playwrights, Henry Porter and John Day, ended in
Porter's death.[57]

When not socialising or fighting, the players practised their art
with such skill that a number of star actors rose to great fame from
their ranks. Richard Tarlton of the Queen's Men was the most popular
comedian of the 1570s and '80s, but by the 1590s his mantle had

William Kempe's 'Nine Days' Wonder', a morris dance from London to Norwich (1600). Kempe was until 1599 the principal comic actor in Shakespeare's company.

passed to William Kempe of the Lord Chamberlain's Men. We know that Kempe played the illiterate servant Peter in *Romeo and Juliet* (1594–96) and the malapropising Dogberry in *Much Ado About Nothing* (1598),[58] and many of Shakespeare's earlier comic roles, as written for Kempe, are of this 'clown' type, amusing because of their simple-mindedness. Kempe left the company in 1599 and was replaced by Robert Armin, who was known for his singing and for a more intellectual kind of wit. Once Armin joined the company Shakespeare wrote a new kind of comic role for him, as seen in Feste in *Twelfth Night* (1601) and the Fool in *King Lear* (1605). These are witty fools who look at the world askance, from its margins, and tell sharp and uncomfortable truths in riddles.[59]

On the tragic side, the two leading actors were Edward Alleyn of the Admiral's Men and Richard Burbage of the Lord Chamberlain's Men, who were known for markedly different performance styles. Alleyn made his name in the early 1590s playing roles created for him by Marlowe: Tamburlaine, Doctor Faustus and Barabas. His acting style was characteristically described as 'strutting' and 'stalking';

Jonson called it 'scenical strutting, and furious vociferation' which impressed 'ignorant gapers'.[60] It may be Alleyn, or at least those who emulated him, that Bottom had in mind when he boasted of his ability to play 'a part to tear a cat in, to make all split' (*Midsummer Night's Dream* 1.2.22–3); it may also have been Alleyn's style that Hamlet was thinking of when he criticised players who 'strutted and bellowed' and 'tear a passion to tatters, to very rags, to split the ears of the groundlings' (*Hamlet*, 3.2.8–9, 29). Alleyn retired from the Admiral's Men in 1597 but returned to act again at the new Fortune playhouse for a few years from 1600, and his exaggerated manner created a tradition which successive actors perpetuated at the Fortune and also the Red Bull, playhouses described as 'mostly frequented by Citizens, and the meaner sort of People'.[61] Burbage, by contrast, was praised for the naturalism and truthfulness of his acting. John Webster, taking Burbage as an example of 'an excellent Actor', wrote that 'what we see him personate, we thinke truly done before us', while Thomas May praised his ability to 'paint griefe / In such a lively colour . . . / As had he truely bin the new man he seemd'.[62] When admiring Shakespeare's authorship of his great tragic roles, we should remember that he created them for Burbage, and could not have done so without this actor's particular and remarkable gifts.

The players had to cope with a turnover of changing repertory which seems astonishing by modern standards. The Admiral's Men at the Rose performed six days a week in the 1594–95 season, offering 38 plays in total, of which 21 were new. In January alone in the next season, they presented 14 different plays, of which six were never performed again.[63] Rehearsal time was minimal, and the demands upon the actors were compounded by the fact that none of them had a full copy of the script: each player was given only a 'cue-script' containing their own part, with very short cues of two or three words of the preceding speech each time they were to start speaking.[64] They had to listen very attentively in order not to miss their cues, and also to hear stage-directions and performance-notes embedded in the text. As Friar Laurence makes his last entrance in *Romeo and Juliet*, for instance, the Third Watchman instructs him how to act: 'Here is a friar that trembles, sighs, and weeps' (5.3.183).[65]

Performing in the Renaissance playhouse must have been an intense and sometimes rather improvised experience, requiring lots of thinking in the moment. At its best, it clearly produced performances of great power. In his description of 'an excellent Actor' (as mentioned above, probably based on Burbage), Webster created a striking image of his hold upon the audience: 'he charmes our attention: sit in a full Theater, and you will thinke you see so many lines drawne from the circumference of so many eares, whiles the *Actor* is the *Center*'.[66] If the Globe was a microcosm, Burbage, as he spoke Shakespeare's lines, was for a few moments the centre of the universe.

FROM PLAYHOUSE TO PRINT

We tend to identify Renaissance plays as the work of a single author: a play by Marlowe, or Shakespeare, or Jonson, and so on. The present book will not depart from this practice; it will contend that each of those authors made an important contribution to Renaissance drama, and so will devote a chapter to each of them. However, before those discussions begin we need to be aware that it is not always accurate to attribute a play to an individual writer, and that there are difficulties in determining exactly what each author wrote.

As the foregoing discussion suggests, actors as well as authors played an important role in the creation of Renaissance drama; roles were shaped to suit their particular talents, and might develop in performance. Clearly all drama involves acts of collaboration between author, actor, and stage managers, such that every play is produced by a team. Clearly also, every play exists in performance only as a transient moment, and will be different to some degree in each performance, so that its printed text can only ever be an imperfect record of a series of lost occasions. The difficulties of representing a Renaissance play in particular as a single fixed text by a single author are compounded by a number of features of playhouse and print-shop practice.

Ben Jonson published a grand folio (i.e. large format) edition of his collected works in 1616; the splendid title page declared it to be '*The Workes of Benjamin Jonson*', and was faced by a portrait of the author.[67] In emulation of this Shakespeare's colleagues published a folio edition of their late friend's works in 1623 (the 'First Folio'), again fronted by the author's name and portrait. Such volumes encourage us to think in terms of a clearly determined body of works flowing from the pen of a single inspired author. Yet very few Renaissance playwrights worked alone. The First Folio included one work which Shakespeare wrote towards the end of his career with John Fletcher, the up-and-coming playwright of the King's Men, *Henry VIII, or All is True*. Fletcher's co-authorship was not mentioned in the First Folio, and the play was presented as Shakespeare's alone. The First Folio also excluded two other plays written by Shakespeare with Fletcher, *Cardenio* (now lost)[68] and *The Two Noble Kinsmen*. The boundaries of the First Folio were not as impermeable as might at first appear; it included some more works in which other writers are thought to have had a hand (*Titus Andronicus, Henry VI part 1, Macbeth, Timon of Athens*), and excluded others which Shakespeare is thought to have co-authored (*Edward III, Pericles*).[69] The only dramatic manuscript we have in Shakespeare's

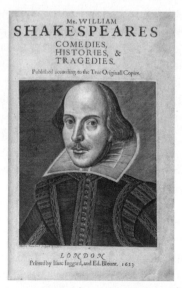

Title page of the First Folio edition of Shakespeare's plays, 1623. Portrait of Shakespeare by Martin Droeshout.

own hand gives clear evidence of his collaborative activity, and of collaboration as a habitual practice in the Renaissance playhouse: it is a fragment from the early 1590s of *Sir Thomas More*, a play to which not only Shakespeare but also Anthony Munday, Henry Chettle, Thomas Dekker, and Thomas Heywood all contributed.[70] Many writers collaborated even more than Shakespeare. Chettle was one of a stable of writers working for the impresario Philip Henslowe for £6 a play, and contributed to some 49 plays between 1598 and 1603, of which 36 were collaborations.[71] His colleague Heywood claimed to have had 'either an entire hand, or at the least a maine finger' in no fewer than 220 plays.[72]

Collaboration could work in various different ways, many of which make it difficult for the modern editor or reader to identify the work of different authors in different texts. In *Henry VIII* and *The Two Noble Kinsmen*, for instance, stylistic differences between Shakespeare and Fletcher can be identified in some passages,[73] but there are others where we simply cannot tell. In *The Two Noble Kinsmen* the Jailer's daughter runs mad for love, gathers flowers on the verge of a lake, and sings fragments of love-ballads including 'willow, willow, willow', strongly echoing Desdemona as well as Ophelia (4.1.52–95); yet the passage describing all of this seems on the basis of its stylistic characteristics to be by Fletcher, presumably writing in self-conscious imitation of or homage to his senior colleague.[74] We do not know whether collaborators worked on designated scenes separately, or discussed their scenes with each other, or read over and revised each other's work. All of this naturally creates difficulties for modern editors, some of whom think it important to seek to identify the contribution of each author, while others prefer to treat the play as an artistic whole jointly created.[75]

There was a specific professional role of 'play-fixer', employed to edit or update plays; much of Dekker's work for Henslowe was in this capacity. Revision of texts, by such fixers or by the main author or others, also complicates our sense of the unity of the text and creates difficult choices for modern editors. Marlowe's *Doctor Faustus* survives in two markedly different versions, now designated as the A-text (published 1604) and the B-text (published 1616). Both of these are significantly removed in time from the original composition and performances of the play, which may have been in 1588–89. The B-text is longer, adding 676 lines that are not in A; it also misses out 36 lines from A and makes numerous minor changes throughout. Scholars have debated the origins of the two texts and the relation between them. One theory is that A was set in type from an original authorial manuscript written by Marlowe with a collaborator who added the more slapstick scenes, whereas B represents an extensive revision of the play by someone else at least ten years after Marlowe's death in 1593. *Faustus* was a very popular play which no doubt continued to evolve in the playhouse over the years, a supposition supported by the fact that in 1602 Henslowe recorded a payment of £4 to William Birde and Samuel Rowley 'for ther adicyones in docter fostes'.[76] Modern editors may decide to print the A-text with passages from the B-text in an appendix, or vice versa, or to print both texts in full, on the grounds that they are different enough to constitute two different works, and that both versions of *Faustus* were read and performed in the early English theatre.[77]

A number of Shakespeare plays also present textual challenges arising from revision, either by Shakespeare himself or by others. The earliest published text of *Macbeth*, in the 1623 First Folio, includes two songs which were interpolated from *The Witch* (1616) by Thomas Middleton. The scenes in which these songs are performed, 3.5 and 4.1, introduce a new witch character, Hecate, and are different in style from the earlier witch-scenes, being more operatic, lighter, and less sinister; they seem likely to be by Middleton too. Gary Taylor believes that Middleton made cuts as well as additions to the play, and that around 11 per cent of the First Folio text is by him; consequently, Taylor and John Lavagnino included *Macbeth* in their Oxford edition of Middleton's *Collected Works*.[78]

In other cases issues arise from the differences between two or more early printed versions of a play. Many Shakespeare plays appeared not only in the First Folio (F), a large format, grand edition of the collected works, but also in quartos (Q), single play editions in a smaller, cheaper format. Differences between Q and F often originate in differences between the source materials on which they were based. The publication of plays was a recent phenomenon, and quarto playbooks were regarded as rather ephemeral items; playwrights did not take care to see their works into print, and indeed did not even own their scripts, which were the property of the playing company. Printers based play-texts on various kinds of material that reached them by a variety of routes, including 'foul papers' (authorial rough drafts), the playhouse promptbook, and memorial reconstruction, whereby an actor who had performed in a play would try to recall the script (this was usually the least reliable kind of source). In the case of *King Lear*, there is a quarto *(The History of King Lear)* published in 1608, probably from Shakespeare's foul papers, and the folio text *(The Tragedy of King Lear)* of 1623. The latter may derive from a marked-up copy of the second edition of the quarto, and perhaps from a lost manuscript of the play and from the promptbook. Both Q and F are thought to represent reasonably sound texts. Yet there are significant differences between them: Q has 300 lines that are not in F, but F has 100 lines that are not in Q; scenes are missing or abridged in F, including the mock-trial during the storm on the heath, which few modern directors would wish to omit; and the endings are significantly different. In F Lear famously dies on the words 'Do you see this? Look on her. Look, her lips. / Look there, look there' (5.3.285–6). He seems to think Cordelia is breathing, a crucial moment which creates conflicting and powerful emotions: should we be consoled that he dies happy, or is this deluded hope the cruellest joke of the play's harsh gods? Yet in Q all he says at this point is 'O, O, O, O!' (24.303).

Until the 1980s editors of *King Lear* worked on the assumption that Q and F represented two imperfect states of the text, and that therefore by combining the best bits of each they could approximately reconstruct the lost ideal play that Shakespeare wrote. However, Stanley Wells and Gary Taylor, the editors of the 1987 Oxford *Complete Works* of Shakespeare, argued that Q and F each represented distinct and valid versions of the play, the first written in 1605–06, and the second revised, probably by Shakespeare himself, in 1609–10. Consequently they printed *Lear* in their *Complete Works* as two separate texts, a decision seen as radical at the time, but now largely supported by scholarly consensus. Many editions continue to offer a conflated text of the play, for reading and studying convenience, but it is widely acknowledged that this is at several removes from any version of the play written by Shakespeare. Meanwhile, following similar lines of thinking to Wells and Taylor, the editors of the 2006 Arden *Hamlet* decided to print its two early quartos (Q1 and Q2) and its folio text (F) as three whole and discrete texts. This brings us the following rather disconcerting soliloquy from Q1 (possibly a memorial reconstruction):

> To be, or not to be – ay, there's the point.
> To die, to sleep – is that all? Ay, all.
> No, to sleep, to dream – ay, marry, there it goes,
> For in that dream of death, when we're awaked,
> And borne before an everlasting judge,
> From whence no passenger ever returned –
> The undiscovered country, at whose sight
> The happy smile and the accursed damned.[79]

Many of these editorial decisions have been controversial, but they highlight the fact that the authentic words of the Renaissance playwright are not as easily accessible to us as neatly produced modern texts may lead us to believe, and that an author might have produced more than one 'authentic' version of a play at different times. Moreover, in the sixteenth and seventeenth centuries the processes of turning play-texts, from whatever source, into printed texts introduced further vagaries. In the first place, the author's foul papers might well be messily written and in places hard to decipher; this is certainly the case with the example we have of Shakespeare's handwriting in the manuscript fragment of *Sir Thomas More*. Secondly, foul papers were often written out again as fair copy by either the playwright or a playhouse scribe, for use as the promptbook, and at this point errors of transcription might occur, or the scribe might make changes which he felt were improvements. The prompter would also make excisions and emendations, as would the Master of the Revels, whose approval of the text was required. Then, when the promptbook or some other manuscript source for a play passed to a printing house, the compositors (or typesetters) might introduce errors. In the folio text of *King Lear*, when Goneril and Regan are cutting down their father's retinue, he protests 'O reason not the need', but in the 1608 quarto he says 'O reason not the deed', no doubt because 'd' was just above 'n' in a compositor's compartmentalised tray of letters and the wrong one was picked up by accident.[80] Alternatively, a compositor might make deliberate changes to save space or to save on the use of frequently occurring letters of the alphabet. In short, on its journey from an author's writing desk to a printshop a play passed through many hands, and at every stage on this journey it was subject to alterations.[81] Some of these alterations, like the example of 'need' and 'deed' from *King Lear*, are noticeable and explicable errors, but there may have been many other non-authorial alterations which are not apparent to us. Before looking to the plays of Shakespeare, or those of his contemporaries, for insights into the mind of the author we must bear in mind that what we read is not necessarily what the author wrote.

Recent scholarship has drawn attention to the fact that Renaissance plays were made up of numerous different bits and pieces. The prologue and epilogue, songs, and various forms of plot summary for use by players and audience were frequently by different hands and circulated separately from each other and the main play-text. A prologue may be an ephemeral piece designed for the first night of the play only, or for a one-off court performance, whereas a song might become a hit and have a life beyond the play; different parts of the play, then, had differing levels of durability. A play might often arrive in the printing house with some of its bits missing, or with bits such as songs and epilogues inserted from other plays. It was not a unified or clearly bounded entity.[82]

Much recent work on Renaissance drama has emphasised such fluid and fragmentary aspects of play-texts. It could leave us feeling that plays were written on water, and that the words on the pages of modern editions are trickling through our fingers. More cheerfully, we may recognise that although a modern edition can only ever be an imperfect record of a play as written by the author and as originally performed, the editors, mindful of all the issues discussed in this chapter, have employed their scholarly expertise to provide as authoritative a text (or texts, where there are separate variant versions) as is reasonably possible. As we turn to the plays of Marlowe,

Shakespeare, and Jonson, we will be aware that they produced their works in collaboration with actors and sometimes co-authors, and that their texts may have been altered in transit by scribes and compositors. Nevertheless, there is a body of work attached to each of these three names which has a distinctive character, which repays discussion as a group, and in which we can be confident that each playwright had a leading hand. It is unlikely that even the most disintegrationist of textual scholars would deny that Marlowe, Shakespeare, and Jonson each made a particular and remarkable contribution to the history of English Renaissance drama. To these we now turn.

3

MARLOWE

In 1587 a bold new talent announced his arrival on the London stage:

> From jigging veins of rhyming mother-wits
> And such conceits as clownage keeps in pay
> We'll lead you to the stately tent of War,
> Where you shall hear the Scythian Tamburlaine
> Threat'ning the world with high astounding terms.[1]

This was the Prologue to part 1 of Christopher Marlowe's epic drama *Tamburlaine*, his first play to be performed in a public playhouse. Sweeping aside disdainfully the 'jigging' rhymes and 'clownage' of theatre hitherto, it proclaimed that audiences had never before seen or heard anything like this. They should prepare to be astonished; and astonished they duly were, by the spectacle, violence, and surging poetry of the play that ensued.

Born in 1564, the same year as Shakespeare, Marlowe was just 23 years old. Like Shakespeare, he was the son of a provincial tradesman: Shakespeare's father was a glover in Stratford, Marlowe's was a shoemaker in Canterbury. Like Shakespeare, too, Marlowe was the product of a grammar school (Marlowe attended the King's School in Canterbury), though unlike Shakespeare he proceeded to university, on a scholarship to Corpus Christi College in Cambridge.

Portrait of a 21-year-old man, possibly Christopher Marlowe, 1585.
Corpus Christi College, Cambridge.

Also unlike Shakespeare, he died young, a mere six years after those first sensational performances of *Tamburlaine*. Yet of the two of them it was Marlowe who usually took the lead in literary experiment and innovation, so that by his untimely death he had already produced some of the most thrilling and distinctive writing of the English Renaissance.[2] His literary legacy included *Tamburlaine parts 1 and 2*, *Doctor Faustus*, *The Jew of Malta*, *Edward II* (one of the first English history plays), the narrative poem *Hero and Leander*, and one of the most popular lyric poems of its age ('Come live with me, and be my love').

DEATH AND LIFE

Interpretation of Marlowe's death has been crucial to our understanding of his life and works. Hence, although it may seem perverse to start at the end, his death is a good place to begin an account of this particular author. The basic facts are well known – notorious, in fact. On 30 May 1593 Marlowe and three other men met at the rooming-house of Mistress Eleanor Bull in Deptford, then a village on the Thames three miles east of London. They spent the day together, then, after supper, a dispute arose between Marlowe and one of his companions, Ingram Frizer. According to the coroner's report, Marlowe 'suddenly and of malice aforethought towards the aforesaid Ingram, then and there maliciously unsheathed the dagger of the aforesaid Ingram . . . and with the same dagger then and there maliciously gave the aforesaid Ingram two wounds on his head'. Frizer retaliated 'in his own defence and to save his life', and with the same dagger 'gave the aforesaid Christopher then and there a mortal wound above his right eye to the depth of two inches and in breadth one inch, of which same mortal wound the aforesaid Christopher Morley then and there instantly died'.[3] Marlowe was 29 years old.

For some of Marlowe's contemporaries, including William Vaughan writing in 1600, his death was divine retribution for scurrilous writings and blasphemous opinions. Vaughan accentuated the gruesomeness of the poet's death – Frizer 'stabd this Marlow into the eye, in such sort, that his braines coming out at the daggers point, hee shortlie after dyed' – and concluded 'Thus did God, the true executioner of divine justice, worke the ende of impious Atheists'.[4] However, the coroner recorded that the dispute with Frizer was merely about 'the payment of the sum of pence, which is to say, *le recknynge*'[5] – in other words, the bill – and until quite recently the scene was thought of by modern commentators as a trivial tavern brawl, symptomatic of Marlowe's rowdy and dissolute way of life, and a bathetic end to a shortlived but glorious career. Yet as Charles Nicholl explored in his influential book *The Reckoning* (1992), several details of the coroner's report did not hang together. Frizer and the two other men present, Nicholas Skeres and Robert Poley, were shady characters involved in the Elizabethan underworld of crime and espionage, and there is suggestive evidence that Marlowe himself had served the government as a spy or double agent. In wielding the fatal dagger Frizer may have been backed less by God than by a faction or a powerful individual in the murky world of Elizabethan politics to whom Marlowe had become a nuisance or a risk.[6]

Thus we have at least three divergent versions of Marlowe's death: divine retribution, a trivial brawl, or a political conspiracy. The disparate retellings of and commentaries upon his untimely demise have coloured assessments of Marlowe's character, his life, and thereby of his works. Many have seen him as a man who was violent in life as well as death, yet this reputation has been questioned by rereadings of the evidence.[7] Others like Nicholl identify him as a spy, adept in cunning dissimulation and secret schemes. In 1587, when Marlowe was a student at Cambridge, the university was reluctant to confer his degree because he had been frequently absent. The Privy Council intervened to assure the university, somewhat mysteriously, that 'he had done Her Majesty good service . . . in matters touching the benefit of his country'.[8] Beyond this, though, there is only circumstantial evidence of his acquaintance with individuals involved in intelligence activities. Evidence for Marlowe's atheism, as asserted by William Vaughan, is similarly uncertain. At around the time of his death, Richard Baines attributed a number of highly provocative statements to Marlowe, including 'That Christ was a bastard and his mother dishonest', 'That St John the Evangelist was bedfellow to Christ and leaned alwaies in his bosome, that he used him as the sinners of Sodoma', and 'That all they that love not Tobacco & Boies were fooles'.[9] Baines paints Marlowe as a sodomite, then, as well as a blasphemer; and similar accusations were made by Thomas Kyd, a fellow dramatist with whom Marlowe had shared a writing chamber: 'He wold report St John to be our Savior Christes *Alexis* I cover it with reverence and trembling that is that Christ did love him with an extraordinary love'.[10] However, Kyd's evidence cannot be taken at face value, since it was given under torture in an attempt to exonerate himself from suspicion. Baines too was a highly unreliable witness, a double agent who lived by assuming false guises and telling people what they wanted to hear.

In fact, the more we look at the evidence, the more the real Marlowe seems to recede from view, or to splinter into diverse and contradictory personae. At one time critics tried to link Marlowe's works to his personality, and to interpret his protagonists as versions of himself. A persuasive and influential example of this was Harry Levin's *The Overreacher* in 1954, while ten years later A.L. Rowse simply asserted that 'Faustus *is* Marlowe'.[11] Recent scholars, however, have found it increasingly difficult to gain a fixed or stable view of the playwright's character, and also emphasise that literature is invention. This produces such views as this: 'It now appears rash in the extreme to assume that any of the characters in the plays actually voices Marlowe's opinion'.[12] Let us, then, turn to Marlowe's plays, the small but extraordinary body of work that he left at his early death, and attempt to let them speak for themselves.

'MOUNTING THOUGHTS'[13]

The 'high astounding terms' promised in the Prologue to *Tamburlaine* are most often used to express the protagonist's insatiable desire for power. Loosely based on a medieval Asian conqueror, Timur the Lame,[14] Marlowe's Tamburlaine is a Scythian shepherd who quashes the mighty potentates of Persia, Turkey, Damascus and beyond to amass a vast empire. Within the confines of the playhouse stage, Marlowe's poetry conjures exotic territories on an epic scale. Tamburlaine's generals report to him on their conquests:

> TECHELLES: And I have marched along the river Nile
> To Machda ...
> From thence unto Cazates did I march,
> Where Amazonians met me in the field,
> With whom, being women, I vouchsafed a league;
> And with my power did march to Zanzibar,
> The western part of Afric, where I viewed
> The Ethiopian sea, rivers, and lakes,
> But neither man nor child in all the land.
> Therefore I took my course to Manico ...
>   (*2 Tam*.1.3.186–98)

– and so on. Marlowe lived in an age of exploration, and he flaunts his modernity in drawing upon advances in the sciences of geography and cartography. His lists of place-names draw maps in the imagination and suggest an immense accumulation of power; they also, in their exoticism and musical sounds, create a kind of topographical lyricism.

Marlowe was enormously influential in establishing blank verse and iambic pentameter as the predominant verse-form of English Renaissance drama, and he did so by developing what Ben Jonson would later call his 'mighty line'.[15] His lines are usually end-stopped: that is, there is little enjambement or running-on from one line into the next, making each line a self-contained unit. Nevertheless, within each line there is immense energy, often driving towards an elaborate, evocative, aurally pleasing name at the end of the line which expresses the dream to which Tamburlaine aspires. 'Is it not passing brave to be a king', he asks, 'And ride in triumph through Persepolis?' (1 Tam.2.5.53–4). He also descants on his own name – 'For "will" and "shall" best fitteth Tamburlaine' (1 Tam.3.3.41) – and that of his prisoner-bride, Zenocrate, daughter of the Sultan of Egypt: 'My martial prizes, with five hundred men, / Won on the fifty-headed Volga's waves, / Shall all we offer to Zenocrate, / And then myself to fair Zenocrate' (1 Tam.1.2.102–5). Working in collaboration with the actor Edward Alleyn (see chapter 2 above), who brought a commanding stage presence to the role of Tamburlaine, Marlowe created a new and enthralling dramatic rhetoric.

Often Marlowe's mighty lines are piled upon one another in what Russ McDonald has called a 'rolling succession', creating exhilarating momentum.[16] In one extraordinary passage, they drive onward relentlessly to express Tamburlaine's dauntless and unstoppable will:

> Nature, that framed us of four elements
> Warring within our breasts for regiment,
> Doth teach us all to have aspiring minds.
> Our souls, whose faculties can comprehend
> The wondrous architecture of the world
> And measure every wand'ring planets course,
> Still climbing after knowledge infinite
> And always moving as the restless spheres,
> Wills us to wear ourselves and never rest
> Until we reach the ripest fruit of all,
> That perfect bliss and sole felicity,
> The sweet fruition of an earthly crown.
> (1 Tam.2.7.18–29)

At first Tamburlaine sounds here like an archetypal Renaissance man, as described by the fifteenth-century Florentine neo-Platonist Pico della Mirandola:

> A certain sacred striving should seize the soul so that, not content with the indifferent and middling, we may pant after the highest and so (for we can if we want to) force our way up to it with all our might. Let us despise the terrestrial, be unafraid of the heavenly, and then, neglecting the things of the world, fly towards that court beyond the world nearest to God the Most High.[17]

But after striving upwards through line after line, 'aspiring', 'climbing', and 'moving', Tamburlaine's speech ends by looking not to heaven, but to 'The sweet fruition of an earthly crown'. He does not 'despise the terrestrial' or 'neglect the things of the world'; on the contrary, his outrageous iconoclasm includes valuing worldly goods and power more highly than spiritual fulfilment.

Tamburlaine deals in the material and the physical, and he and his foes alike speak a poetry of violence. Even his feeble first opponent, Mycetes, the effete king of Persia, longs to 'view these milk-white steeds of mine / All loaden with the heads of killèd men / And from their knees ev'n to their hoofs below / Besmeared with blood, that makes a dainty show' (*1 Tam.*1.1.77–80). Marlowe's original *Tamburlaine* was so popular that it spawned a sequel, and both plays are packed not only with this poetry of violence, but also with spectacles of violence, from the humbled Bajazeth, Emperor of Turkey, braining himself on the bars of his cage (*1 Tam.*5.1), to Tamburlaine lashing the conquered kings of Trebizond and Soria as they pull his chariot like horses, with a memorable cry which later dramatists would parody: 'Holla, ye pampered jades of Asia!' (*2 Tam.*4.3.1).[18] Tamburlaine is a monster, and yet we find ourselves siding with him in spite of ourselves, partly because his adversaries are even worse, partly because of his heroic self-belief and force of will, and partly because of the complexities of his character. Marlowe tests to the limit an audience's propensity to find a dynamic protagonist attractive, especially in the final act of *Tamburlaine part 1*. Tamburlaine is besieging Damascus, and the virgins of the city are sent out to plead with him for mercy. Zenocrate, too, implores him to spare her native city, but Tamburlaine summarily orders his horsemen to charge the virgins 'and show my servant Death, / Sitting in scarlet on their armèd spears' (1 Tam.5.1.117–18). Within a few lines of this implacable brutality, startlingly, he embarks upon a philosophical disquisition upon beauty and its effects on the soul: 'What is beauty, saith my sufferings, then?' (1 Tam.5.1.160). He may be a monster, but he is a sensitive, questioning, meditative monster, reducing the audience's moral sense to a state of confusion. As Mark Thornton Burnett has aptly written, 'an audience, like Tamburlaine's captives, often finds itself in a stunned, perplexed, or ambiguous state'.[19]

Most shockingly of all, *Tamburlaine part 1* does not end, as we might expect, with punishment for the conqueror's crimes. This first play was evidently conceived as a self-contained whole; the prologue to *Tamburlaine part 2* (also 1587) is explicit that this sequel is an afterthought, written in response to the popular success of part 1. The first play, then, was originally intended to be performed alone, but it does not follow the expected rise-and-fall arc of a tragedy; Tamburlaine does not incur divine retribution for his hubris (complacent pride and self-belief, of which he arguably has more than any other Renaissance protagonist), but ends the play at the height of success, celebrating his accumulated victories with marriage to Zenocrate. Even at the end of part 2, when the more conventional rise-and-fall structure is observed by means of his death, he expires in a state of heroic insatiability and unquenched aspiration. He calls for a map and traces his many campaigns and conquests, but instead of rejoicing in his achievements he looks beyond them to lament, 'And shall I die, and this unconquerèd?' (2 Tam.5.3.150, 158).

None of Marlowe's other protagonists quite matches Tamburlaine's breathtaking will to power, and they do not escape justice as does the Tamburlaine of part 1. However, they all in their different ways have 'mounting thoughts' and, despite meeting tragic fates, their ambitions, desires, and defiant acts linger to create deeply ambiguous and unsettling dramas. Barabas, the eponymous *Jew of Malta* (c.1590), is a Machiavellian villain who ends by being boiled in the pot he had set as a trap for his enemies. However, the play strongly conveys the gleeful vitality and ingenious revenge with which he encounters persecution and hypocrisy: rather than despair when stripped of all he has, he declares, with Tamburlaine-like self-conviction, 'No, Barabas is born to better chance / And framed of finer mould than common men / That measure naught but by the present time … No, I will live, nor loathe I this my life' (1.2.219–21, 267). *Edward II* (*c.*1592) has a complex structure which offers several aspirants to power, especially Gaveston, the king's favourite, who coins the phrase 'mounting thoughts' (2.2.77), and Mortimer Junior, who usurps the throne. Though both ultimately fall and are punished with death for their transgressions, it is their energies that animate the play, especially Gaveston's poetry of sensual indulgence (of which more below), and Mortimer's virile force and assertion, declaring that he 'now makes Fortune's wheel turn as he please' (5.2.52–3). Even in death, Mortimer displays an indomitability and appetite for adventure that once again recall Tamburlaine: 'Weep not for Mortimer, / That scorns the world, and as a traveller / Goes to discover countries yet unknown' (5.6.64–6). Gaveston and Mortimer are adversaries, diametrically opposed in their values and characters, yet we are never sure which is the hero and which is the villain.

After *Tamburlaine*, then, Marlowe's plays conform more closely to conventional tragic structure, but place ingredients within that structure which are profoundly challenging and unsettling. This is perhaps especially true of *Doctor Faustus* (1588–9), another play whose protagonist has 'mounting thoughts'. He turns to magic because, having run through logic, medicine, law, and theology, he finds that no other field of scholarship satisfies him. He rises from 'parents base of stock'[20] to taunt the Pope, entertain the Holy Roman Emperor, and embrace Helen of Troy. Yet he ends in hell; and many other ingredients of the play might lead us to question whether his pact with the Devil brought him everything that he hoped for. This then leads us to the complex question of the treatment of religion in Marlowe's plays.

RELIGION

It is possible to read *Doctor Faustus* as an orthodox late medieval morality play. The dramatic conventions of the moralities are solidly in place, such as the allegorical figures of psychomachia: Faustus is torn between a Good Angel who admonishes him and a Bad Angel who leads him on. The personifications of the Seven Deadly Sins, the good Old Man who urges Faustus to repent, and the hell-mouth prop with which the play ends would all be at home in a morality play. Alongside these somewhat backward-looking dramatic devices, much of the content of the play may also be read as in line with Christian theology. In simple terms, Faustus wilfully errs, and therefore receives the expected punishment. At the play's opening he mounts a subversive intellectual critique of Christian dogma, but this is unlikely to convert the audience to atheism since it is patently based on selective and distorting quotations from Scripture (1.1.38–41). It is true that the Bible says 'The reward of sin is death', but the same verse goes on to say, 'but the gifte of God is eternal life through Jesus Christ our Lord'.[21] Many members of Marlowe's original audience would no doubt have known their Bible well enough to know that Faustus was misrepresenting it, rather than making a convincing case for the cruelty of God and the point-lessness of virtue as he purports to do. Moreover, the powers that Faustus gains from the Devil are delusory and derisory: they amount to little more than cheap conjuring tricks, and often descend into farce, as in the scene with the horse-courser who buys a horse from Faustus which turns out to be merely a bundle of hay (4.1). Even the figure of Helen of Troy that Faustus embraces is not the real Helen, but a devilish simulation; as Faustus admits when he conjures Alexander the Great and his paramour for the Emperor, 'it is not in my ability to present before your eyes the true substantial bodies of those two deceased princes, which long since are consumed to dust' (4.1.43–5).

Above all, the presentation of Faustus's fate is entirely in line with Christian understanding of the sin of despair. The possibility for repen-tance and divine mercy is always open to Faustus, as the Good Angel, the Old Man, and others repeatedly remind him: 'SECOND SCHOLAR: Yet, Faustus, look up to heaven. Remember God's mercies are infinite' (5.2.11–12). Faustus refuses God's mercy because he commits the sin of despair, which is closely related to the sin of pride.[22] He believes that his sins are too great for God's forgiveness – 'Faustus' offence can ne'er be pardoned. The serpent that tempted Eve may be saved, but not Faustus' (5.2.14–15) – whereas Christianity teaches that God's mercy is in fact boundless.

Yet even though a framework of orthodox dogma is present in the play, it is foregrounded and tested in ways that must have caused extreme disquiet to Renaissance audiences. Marlowe makes the actor playing Faustus actually speak the words and perform the gestures to conjure devils (1.3). To a Renaissance audience of believers, it would have been by no means apparent that this was mere play-acting and therefore safe; part of the power of the play was the risk that a real devil might actually be summoned. A superstitious mythology grew up around the play, as attested to by several anecdotes about devils actually appearing on stage. Here is one example:

> Certaine Players at Exeter, acting upon the stage the tragical storie of Dr. Faustus the Conjurer; as certain nomber of Devels kept everie one his circle there, and as Faustus was busie in his magicall invocations, on a sudden they were all dasht, every one harkening other in the eare, for they were all perswaded, there was one devil too many amongst them; and so after a little pause desired the people to pardon them, they could go no further with this matter; the people also understanding the thing as it was, every man hastened to be first out of dores. The players (as I heard it) contrarye to their custome spending the night in reading and in prayer got them out of the town the next morning.[23]

William Prynne in 1633 similarly recalled 'the visible apparition of the Devill on the stage at the Belsavage Play-house ... the truth of which I have heard from many now alive, who well remember it'.[24] The play, then, daringly exploits the fears of believers – although Marlowe's audiences clearly did not believe quite strongly enough in the devil to keep them away, for the play was a huge success, playing many times in the 1590s and early 1600s and making handsome profits.[25] What made the play dangerous also made it irresistibly exciting. By pressing on a sensitive point where reality and performance, belief and scepticism met, Marlowe created a hit.

Beyond merely testing belief, the play may also be read as entertaining the possibility of unbelief, and as anticipating a modern sense
of God's distance or even absence. Is it indeed the case that Faustus
is damned because he commits the sin of despair and refuses to turn
to God? Or is there no God there to hear his impassioned cries of
'See, see, where Christ's blood streams in the firmament!' (5.2.70)?
Perhaps, the play may suggest, Lucifer is more powerful than God
– 'O, I'll leap up to my God! Who pulls me down?' (5.2.69) – and
Lucifer is the true ruler of a malign universe. Or perhaps humanity
is utterly isolated and alone. The Good and Bad Angel may be understood simply as dramatic representations of Faustus's inner
psychological divisions, especially when set against the eloquent and
anguished soliloquies with which he begins and ends the play. Perhaps,
the play can be read as suggesting, even the God and Lucifer on
whom he calls exist only in his mind.

In Faustus's soliloquies, Marlowe takes a huge leap forward in
the representation of interiority on the English stage, and at the
same time creates a presciently modern sense of self, one which is
alienated, conflicted, and fractured. Faustus is cursed by his own
intelligence and pained by his highly developed sensibility: 'Why
wert thou not a creature wanting soul? / Or why is this immortal
that thou hast?' (5.2.97–8). Mephistopheles, the devil-companion
who serves (or perhaps controls) Faustus, also contributes to this
proto-modern and deeply psychological exploration of subjectivity,
especially in his assertions that hell is not a place but a state of
mind: 'FAUSTUS: How comes it then that thou art out of hell?
MEPHISTOPHELES: Why, this is hell, nor am I out of it' (1.3.76–
77). Once again this position can be seen as entirely in accord with
orthodox theology: as Mephistopheles goes on to explain, hell is
defined as eternal banishment from the sight of God. However, the
effect of his words is a potentially secular sense of hell as inward
and self-created. This could be the writing of a committed Christian,
or of a committed atheist, or of a brilliant mind dancing in the
flicker between these two opposed yet mutually dependent positions.

Marlowe's other plays are equally ambiguous in their treatment of
religion. *The Jew of Malta* deploys anti-semitic stereotypes and depicts
Barabas as a scheming and amoral villain, but he is more attractive

than the Christians, who cynically invoke religion in order to justify their seizure of the Jew's wealth. As Barabas pretends to conspire with both the Turks and the Christians, he explains: 'Thus, loving neither, will I live with both, / Making a profit of my policy; / And he from whom my most advantage comes / Shall be my friend. / This is the life we Jews are used to lead, / And reason, too, for Christians do the like' (5.2.111–16). The play thus cunningly incites anti-semitic sentiment in its audience only to throw it back against them. In *Tamburlaine* too the Christians deploy religious rhetoric to serve their slippery morality, breaking an alliance with the Natolians on the grounds that 'with such infidels, / In whom no faith nor true religion rests, / We are not bound to those accomplishments / The holy laws of Christendom enjoin' (*2 Tam*.2.1.33–6). The consequence is their bloody defeat by the Natolians, which Christians and Muslim Natolians alike understand as the revenge of the Christian God (*2 Tam*.2.3.2–3, 33). Is this anti-Christian? The play is highly critical of Christians, but the criticism is for their deviation from the true tenets of Christianity, and the power of the Christian God is arguably affirmed.

Tamburlaine repeatedly calls himself the scourge of God, a resonantly ambiguous title. Much of the time it implies that he is acting on behalf of divine powers – often non-committally named as 'Jove' – to punish injustice and tyranny. He explains that he is enjoined

> To scourge the pride of such as heaven abhors;
> Nor am I made arch-monarch of the world,
> Crowned and invested by the hand of Jove,
> For deeds of bounty or nobility.
> But since I exercise a greater name,
> The scourge of God and terror of the world,
> I must apply myself to fit those terms,
> In war, in blood, in death, in cruelty,
> And plague such peasants as resist in me
> The power of heaven's eternal majesty.
> (*2 Tam*.4.2.148–57)

It seems, then, that Tamburlaine is merely an instrument of divine justice; yet at other times, it is the gods themselves that he threatens.

Indeed, in his very first scene, when he woos the Persian commander Theridamas to join him with visions of future glory, he promises not only that 'we will triumph over all the world', but that 'by those steps that [Jove] hath scaled the heavens / May we become immortal like the gods' (*1 Tam*.1.2.173, 200–01). Much later, at the end of his career, he declares, 'Come let us march against the powers of heaven / And set black streamers in the firmament / To signify the slaughter of the gods' (*2 Tam*.5.3.48–50) – yet this most hyperbolic of threats comes as Tamburlaine mourns the death of Zenocrate and himself succumbs to illness, and is arguably a mark of newly-felt weakness rather than of strength.

Most ambiguously and thought-provokingly of all, Tamburlaine's illness follows immediately upon his act of publicly burning the Quran and other Muslim holy books. Would an Elizabethan audience have applauded this destruction of 'infidel' books? Or would they have regarded Tamburlaine's act as blasphemous? Tamburlaine says that he burns the Quran in the name of 'a God full of revenging wrath, / From whom the thunder and the lightning breaks, / Whose scourge I am, and him will I obey' (*2 Tam*.5.1.181–3), but does not specifiy whether this is the Christian God, Jove, or some other deity imagined by himself. If the God of Islam inflicts illness and death on Tamburlaine to avenge the burning of the Quran, this may suggest that He is more powerful than the Christian God – or is perhaps identical with the Christian God. All these questions, intensely topical and contentious in Marlowe's time, are left provocatively open by the play.

SEXUALITY

As we saw earlier, Marlowe had a reputation among his contemporaries not only as an atheist, but also as a lover of boys. As we have seen by looking at his works, the evidence they offer of his religious views is far from conclusive, though they certainly suggest a desire to engage in controversy. What might they tell us about Marlowe's attitudes to sexuality, about Renaissance understandings of sexuality, and about the representation of sexuality on the Renaissance stage?

The term 'homosexual' did not exist in the sixteenth century; it is a late nineteenth-century invention. Since the latter period, varieties of sexuality have been defined by scientific and medical investigation. Sexuality has also come to be regarded as a source of identity: a person may define themselves as 'a homosexual', or as 'gay'. None of this was the case in Marlowe's period. The words which most closely corresponded to what we now understand as homosexual acts were 'buggery' and 'sodomy', though buggery could also include bestiality, and sodomy could include a range of sexual acts deemed to be unnatural, especially those which were not procreative. Both were associated with a wide range of crimes, including heresy, witchcraft, and treason, and sodomy was a capital offence.[26] Yet at the same time, classical philosophy, art, and literature offered many celebrated examples of love between men. In Plato's *Symposium*, male-male love was valued more highly than any other form of love, and was extolled as a route to spiritual transcendence; in myth, Jove not only seduced numerous women, but also loved his boy cupbearer, Ganymede. Paintings and sculpture both of the classical world and of the Renaissance dwelt upon the beauties of the naked male form.[27] Marlowe's narrative poem *Hero and Leander* (1593) strongly suggests that he appreciated those beauties. It offers a luscious description of its young hero:

> Even as delicious meat is to the tast,
> So was his necke in touching, and surpast
> The white of *Pelops* shoulder,[28] I could tell ye,
> How smooth his brest was, and how white his bellie,
> And whose immortall fingers did imprint,
> That heavenly path, with many a curious dint,
> That runs along his backe.[29]

This is so closely observed and tactile that it is hard to doubt that the author has himself playfully bitten the shoulder of a white-skinned boy and run his fingers down each perfectly formed vertebra of his spine, or at the least has fantasised intensely about these pleasures. Marlowe's plays also include several homoerotic moments. In *Tamburlaine*, the protagonist woos his bride Zenocrate with far less eloquence and force than he directs to the Persian general Theridamas, who is ravished by his words: 'What strong enchantments 'tice my yielding soul? . . . Won with thy words and conquered with thy looks, / I yield myself' (1 Tam.1.2.224, 228–9).

On this issue as others, however, what we get from Marlowe is by no means a straightforward endorsement of a single point of view. The lubricious description of Leander in a poem about a famous pair of heterosexual lovers – much fuller and richer than the description of the heroine, Hero – is on one level a joke about literary convention, since it is the lady whose beauties would usually be attentively catalogued in Elizabethan poetry. Marlowe also finds much comedy in older men who lust after young boys. As Leander swims the Hellespont, Neptune finds his physical charms irresistible, and is reduced to folly and indignity: 'He clapt his plumpe cheekes, with his tresses playd, / And smiling wantonly, his love bewrayd' (p. 286, lines 665–6). *Dido, Queen of Carthage*, probably Marlowe's earliest play, written around 1586 while he was still a Cambridge student, opens with a besotted Jupiter 'dandling Ganimed upon his knee'. The god invites his boy-lover to ask for anything he desires; the petulant Ganymede replies, 'I would have a jewell for mine eare, / And a fine brouch to put in my hat, / And then Ile hugge with you an hundred times'.[30] Here, again, a frank recognition that men may have sexual feelings for other men is combined with a sense that this may be demeaning. These examples suggest that in authority figures, Marlowe regarded dalliances with boys as a form of weakness and therefore a source of satire.

Marlowe's fullest and most intriguing depiction of male-male love is in *Edward II*. Like *Tamburlaine part 2*, *Doctor Faustus* and *The Jew of Malta*, this play can be read as deploying a conventional rise-and-fall tragic structure to present a cautionary tale of a protagonist whose transgression incurs divine retribution. King Edward abandons his kingly responsibilities in order to indulge in private pleasures with his favourite, Gaveston; consequently, he falls from power and meets a gruesomely fitting death. In fact the published play-text refers only to a table as the instrument of Edward's death; the murderers lay it on his body and stamp on it (5.5.110–13). However, audiences would have been aware of the account given in Holinshed's *Chronicles*:

They came suddenlie one night into the chamber where he laie in bed fast asleepe, and with heavie featherbeds or a table (as some write) being cast upon him, they kept him down and withall put into his fundament an horne, and through the same they thrust up into his bodie an hot spit, or (as other have) through the pipe of a trumpet a plumbers instrument of iron made verie hot, the which passing up into his intrailes, and being rolled to and fro, burnt the same, but so as no appearance of any wound or hurt outwardlie might be once perceived.[31]

In the same way that sinners in traditional depictions of hell were subjected to apt penalties – gluttons forced to eat rats, toads, and snakes, and so on – Edward's punishment may be seen as a grotesque parody of his crime, inflicted on him by a stern God. Several aspects of the scene suggest this providential aptness and divine sanction. The dungeon where Edward is housed is 'the sink / Wherein the filth of all the castle falls' (5.5.56–7), the metaphorical anus of the castle. His sinister murderer is called Lightborn, a translation of the name Lucifer. Such ingredients point towards symbolism and allegory. Yet we also feel intensely the monstrous brutality of Edward's death, and his pain and humiliation that precede it. Indeed, in his patient suffering he becomes a saintly and martyr-like figure. His gaolers and tormenters observe that 'He hath a body able to endure / More than we can inflict, and therefore now / Let us assail his mind another while' (5.5.10–12). Any aptness to his death, and any sense that he has brought it on himself, are exceeded by a sense of the horror and pitifulness of his fate.

If we look back over the events of the play that led to Edward's death, the lines between right and wrong become even less easy to draw. Edward's love for Gaveston clearly makes him a bad king: in the play's first scene, Edward greets Gaveston, who has returned from exile, with the words, 'I have my wish, in that I joy thy sight, / And sooner shall the sea o'erwhelm my land / Than bear the ship that shall transport thee hence' (1.1.150–52). Meanwhile Gaveston's own dramatic poetry is likely to engender divided feelings in modern readers and spectators which help us to guess at the conflicting responses that he may have provoked in Marlowe's first audiences.

Some may feel that there is something queasily decadent about the pleasures that he offers the king:

> I must have wanton poets, pleasant wits,
> Musicians that with touching of a string
> May draw the pliant king which way I please.
> Music and poetry is his delight;
> Therefore I'll have Italian masques by night ...
> Sometime a lovely boy in Dian's shape,
> With hair that gilds the water as it glides,
> Crownets of pearl about his naked arms,
> And in his sportful hands an olive tree
> To hide those parts which men delight to see,
> Shall bathe him in a spring.
>   (1.1.50–54, 60–65)

Yet others may feel that this is gloriously camp, and it is certainly true that Gaveston offers Edward a world of pleasure, wit, and imagination which in many ways is more appealing than the martial feudalism of the lords. The word most often used for what Edward does with Gaveston is 'frolic' (1.2.67, 1.4.73, 2.2.62), and it particularly irks the lords that the king and his favourite have fun, dress up, and are style-conscious. Mortimer complains that 'Whiles other walk below, the king and he / From out a window laugh at such as we, / And flout our train, and jest at our attire' (1.4.416–18). He confronts Edward: 'When wert thou in the field with banner spread? / But once, and then thy soldiers marched like players, / With garish robes, not armour; and thyself, / Bedaubed with gold, rode laughing at the rest, / Nodding and shaking of thy spangled crest' (2.2.181–5). It is hard to argue against the rebellious lords when they say that Gaveston is a bad influence on the king, yet at the same time Gaveston perfectly sums up their dullness: 'Base leaden earls, that glory in your birth, / Go sit at home and eat your tenants' beef' (2.2.74–5).

Apparently transcending all of these debates, Gaveston offers Edward not only escapism and pleasure, but also love. When Mortimer asks Edward scornfully, 'Why should you love him whom the world hates so?' Edward replies, heart-stoppingly, 'Because he loves me more than all the world' (1.4.76–7). Yet even this is undermined by a persistent sense that Edward may be deluded, and that Gaveston's true motivation may be not love but self-interest; after all, he opens the play by declaring, 'What greater bliss can hap to Gaveston / Than live and be the favourite of a king?' (1.1.4–5). There are topical political issues here around Elizabeth I's predilection for dashing young favourites, her advancement of commoners like Walter Raleigh, and the consequent factional divisions of the Elizabethan court. In the play, the lords' objections to Gaveston often seem to be grounded less in sexuality than in issues of class and power. Mortimer Senior points out that 'The mightiest kings have had their minions', listing Alexander and Hephaestion, Hercules and Hylas, and more (1.4.387–401). At points like this Edward's relationship with Gaveston appears to be understood not as shockingly sodomitical, but as a harmless youthful infatuation. The problem with Gaveston, then, is not what a modern audience understands as his sexuality, but the fact that he is a 'night-grown mushroom', and, as we have seen, plans to 'draw the pliant king which way I please' (1.4.284, 1.1.52). Yet these political ambitions once more take us back to his hold over the king's affections, and the way he inflames and caters to the king's desires and fantasies, so that conflicts of politics, class, sexuality, and aesthetics are all inextricably intertwined. Once again, a Marlowe play opens up fiercely provocative issues in such a way as to cast conservative and subversive positions into a dynamic and unresolved debate.

As we explored in chapter 2, Renaissance drama was largely produced by means of different kinds of collaboration. Marlowe sold several of his plays to Philip Henslowe for performance by the Admiral's Men at the Rose playhouse, though he was never tied to any particular playing company and maintained his independence as a kind of freelance. What he gained from working with the Admiral's Men was the invaluable opportunity to work with Edward Alleyn, who gave voice and body to the roles of Tamburlaine, Faustus, and Barabas, and whose passionate performances undoubtedly played a significant part in their success. Marlowe may also have collaborated with other authors, too: perhaps Thomas Nashe on *Dido, Queen of*

Carthage and *Tamburlaine*; perhaps Kyd on *The Jew of Malta*.[32] Yet a distinctive, flamboyant voice speaks through all his works and makes them characteristically Marlovian. His plays were widely imitated and parodied; and, in a period when many plays disappeared after only one or a few performances, they brought audiences flocking throughout the 1590s and early 1600s. There were an unmatched 36 performances of *The Jew of Malta* at the Rose from 1592 to 1596 alone, and 24 performances of *Faustus* in 1594–97.[33] Every playwright who came after Marlowe was very much aware of his work. We do not know whether Shakespeare liked him or loathed him as man, but he certainly paid tribute to him as a writer in *As You Like It*, where he quotes Marlowe's *Hero and Leander*: 'Dead shepherd, now I find thy saw of might: / "Who ever loved that loved not at first sight?"' (3.5.82–3).

Clearly it would be inadequate to represent Marlowe as merely a forerunner, yet it is true that his many significant innovations showed the way for other Renaissance dramatists and enabled them to build on his achievements. He showed that iambic pentameter and blank verse could create muscular and inspiring dramatic poetry. He showed that through such poetry the playhouse stage could evoke vast and exotic territories; yet at the same time he also developed the soliloquy as a means of delving into the depths of individual subjectivity. Perhaps above all, he showed that drama was an ideal medium for addressing contentious issues, challenging moral assumptions, setting opposed value-systems in conflict with each other, and leaving the audience with no easy answers.

A scholar recently surveying the state of Marlowe studies has written: 'there is no recognised fixed or established perspective from which to view Marlowe's plays and poems. This assertion applies to biographies of Marlowe as well'.[34] If we find it impossible to make up our minds about Marlowe, after generations of study of his life and works, we can perhaps gain a small sense of how startling, perplexing, and exhilarating his plays must have seemed to his contemporaries.

4

SHAKESPEARE

Shakespeare began to write plays at around the same time as Marlowe, in the late 1580s and early 1590s. By 1592 he was being attacked in a pamphlet as an upstart and plagiarist, suggesting that he had already achieved enough success to make enemies.[1] By his death in 1616, at the age of 52, he had achieved acclaim and wealth, and had contributed to around 40 plays. He had been instrumental in the development of the history play, he had taken both comedy and tragedy to new heights, and he had experimented extensively in the mixing and stretching of genres. He had also written highly successful narrative poems (*Venus and Adonis* and *The Rape of Lucrece*), while his Sonnets were to become some of the most influential poems in English.[2] This chapter will briefly describe his place in the history of English Renaissance drama, and explore some of his major contributions to the genre.

REFLECTING ON THE ART OF THEATRE

A good way of understanding Shakespeare's dramatic achievement is to look at his own thinking about it, which comes to the fore in various places in his works. In *A Midsummer Night's Dream* (1594–96), the crazy, dream-like events of the night in the wood outside Athens provoke Duke Theseus to deliver a speech which purports to be scornful of imagination, but ends up as a celebration

Shakespeare monument, Holy Trinity Church, Stratford-upon-Avon, photo by Tom Reedy. This and the Droeshout portrait (p. 66 above) are the images with the strongest claim to be authentic likenesses of Shakespeare.

of imagination in spite of itself. He dismisses the 'seething brains' and 'shaping fantasies' of lunatics, lovers, and poets, but ascends from this to an eloquent description of the creative powers of the mind: 'The poet's eye, in a fine frenzy rolling, / Doth glance from heaven to earth, from earth to heaven, / And as imagination bodies forth / The form of things unknown, the poet's pen / Turns them to shapes, and gives to airy nothing / A local habitation and a name' (5.1.4–5, 12–17). It is surely justifiable to read this as an account of Shakespeare's own sense of the powers of his art; especially at this point, in the mid-1590s, as he moved into the middle years of his career and found himself composing a masterpiece in the very play in which Theseus appears. The framing irony of course is that, in dismissing the 'shaping fantasies' of poets, Theseus – a figure of myth and now a character in a play – is cancelling out his own existence.

Theseus delivers his speech just before the play-within-a-play performed for him by the 'mechanicals' (Bottom and his friends). The purpose of this group of characters is of course to make us laugh, but also to make us think about what happens in the theatre.

They are foolish to think that everything in a play must be literalistically represented on stage: 'Some man or other must present Wall; and let him have some plaster, or some loam, or some rough-cast about him, to signify "wall"' (3.1.57–9). It is equally absurd to think that the audience will believe everything on stage to be real. The mechanicals, fearing that the lion in their performance of *Pyramus and Thisbe* will terrify the ladies, decide that the actor must speak through a hole in his costume to explain that he is not a lion: 'No, I am no such thing. I am a men as other men are' (3.1.37–8). By simultaneously placing too little and too much faith in theatre, the mechanicals tell us a great deal about how it works. An audience can believe in the presence of a wall, even on an empty stage, if the poetry of the play creates it in their imaginations, and if the performers have a strong enough hold on their spectators to carry them along with them and command their assent. When Oberon declares 'I am invisible' (2.1.186), clearly he is not so, in any literal sense, but we consent to believe that he is for the purposes of the play. Likewise, although Snug the joiner in a costume is obviously not really a lion, an audience will allow him to be one in their imaginations – but this is a delicate compromise, which will collapse if he punctures the illusion by announcing that he is only a man after all.

The mechanicals serve as a negative example to outline, by contrast, the kind of naturalistic drama that Shakespeare and the Lord Chamberlain's Men were developing in the years following Marlowe's death (see chapter 2 above). Bottom is still addicted to the kinds of rhyming, jogging lines that predated Marlowe's iambic pentameter, and to the kind of bombastic rant that imitators of *Tamburlaine* produced:

> my chief humour is for a tyrant. I could play 'erc'les rarely, or a part to tear a cat in, to make all split:
>
> > The raging rocks
> > And shivering shocks
> > Shall break the locks
> > > Of prison gates,
> > And Phibus' car

> Shall shine from far
> And make and mar
> The foolish Fates.
This was lofty.
  (1.2.21–32)

Similarly in *Hamlet* (1600) Shakespeare distinguishes between the weighty neo-classical rhetoric of the Players and the surrounding dialogue among the 'real' members of the Danish court. At Hamlet's request, the First Player performs an oration on the fall of Troy and the grief of Hecuba:

> FIRST PLAYER: 'But who, O who had seen the mobbled queen' –
> HAMLET: 'The mobbled queen'?
> POLONIUS: That's good; 'mobbled queen' is good.
> FIRST PLAYER: 'Run barefoot up and down, threat'ning the flames
> With bisson rheum; a clout upon that head
> Where late the diadem stood, and for a robe,
> About her lank and all o'er-teemèd loins,
> A blanket in th'alarm of fear caught up –
> Who this had seen, with tongue in venom steeped,
> 'Gainst Fortune's state would treason have pronounced.'
>   (2.2.482–91)

This is highly artificial rhetoric, and it is to some extent ridiculed in order to make the speeches of Hamlet and his companions appear more realistic by contrast. Yet Shakespeare's attitude to artifice does not stop at mockery, but is far more complex than this. The performance of *Pyramus and Thisbe* by Bottom and the mechanicals is clearly the opposite of naturalistic, absurdly so; yet in performance it is often a highlight of *A Midsummer Night's Dream*, turning into a kind of triumph as we root for the mechanicals in the face of the scornful asides of the Athenian courtiers, and even in the end becoming unexpectedly moving. Equally, Hamlet requests the Trojan speech from the First Player because he remembers a previous performance with such pleasure and admiration. He recalls the beginning of the speech word for word, and after the First Player completes it with tears in his eyes, Hamlet castigates himself for bringing less passion to life than the Player does to drama: 'O, what a rogue and peasant slave am I! . . . What's Hecuba to him, or he to Hecuba, / That he should weep for her? What would he do / Had he the motive and the cue for passion / That I have?' (2.2.527, 536–9). Shakespeare sets up complex layers of 'reality' and 'artifice', but if we examine them closely they shade into one another. Hamlet, after all, is no less a player, merely 'in a fiction, in a dream of passion', than is the First Player (2.2.529). His soliloquies may not use the ponderous rhetoric of the Player's speech, but they are far from naturalistic.

Shakespeare's interest in the complex relationship between reality and art is present throughout his body of work, but becomes especially marked in his late plays. In the final scene of *The Winter's Tale* (1610), Leontes is invited to view a statue of his wife, Hermione, who died 16 years earlier because of his harsh treatment. Leontes marvels at the accuracy and lifelike qualities of the statue: it shows Hermione's wrinkles as if she had aged 16 years, and he asks his companions, 'Would you not deem it breathed, and that those veins / Did verily bear blood?' (5.3.28–9, 64–5). Together they all admire the skill of the sculptor; Polixenes acclaims the statue as 'Masterly done' (5.3.65). Yet as music sounds, the statue stirs and embraces Leontes, for it is the real Hermione after all, preserved in secret for 16 years by her friend Paulina.

There are many kinds of art involved in this scene: the supposed art of the sculptor, whose skill was evident in so closely imitating nature; the art of Hermione, and of the actor playing Hermione, in imitating a statue; and the art of Paulina, who cunningly concealed Hermione, who stage-manages this scene, and who presents the vivification of the statue as an act of magical art. Indeed art here shades not only into magic but also into religion: before she commands the statue to move, Paulina tells the onlookers 'It is required / You do awake your faith', highlighting how theatre and sacred ritual alike depend upon faith (5.3.94–5). At the same time, art and reality merge, with Leontes exclaiming 'O, she's warm! / If this be magic, let it be an art / Lawful as eating' (5.3.109–11). The scene creates a sense of wonder in which art and reality can barely be distinguished:

is Hermione really a work of art, or is the work of art real? Have we seen a statue really, miraculously, coming to life, or a real living woman performing the astonishing feat of impersonating a statue? While we grapple with these paradoxes, the scene invokes the deepest and strongest of emotions, calling up the grief of anyone who has ever been bereaved or otherwise separated from a loved one, and offering a fantasy of return and restoration. And at the same time, Shakespeare frankly reminds us that the whole thing is, after all, only a play, only a foolish story: 'PAULINA: 'That she is living, / Were it but told you, should be hooted at / Like an old tale' (5.3.116–8). With the audacity of a seasoned playwright, Shakespeare pushes to the limit his audience's willingness to believe in unbelievable events, while at the same time adeptly demonstrating that a highly artificial scene can also be deeply moving. While entirely untrue in the actions it presents, it is profoundly true in the emotions that it expresses and evokes.

Shakespeare's self-consciousness about his art made him particularly fascinated by the metaphors of the world as a stage, and the stage as a world, that were so popular in his period (see Introduction above). A notable example is Prospero's interruption of the masque in *The Tempest* (1611):

> Our revels now are ended. These our actors,
> As I foretold you, were all spirits, and
> Are melted into air, into thin air;
> And like the baseless fabric of this vision,
> The cloud-capped towers, the gorgeous palaces,
> The solemn temples, the great globe itself,
> Yea, all which it inherit, shall dissolve;
> And, like this insubstantial pageant faded,
> Leave not a rack behind. We are such stuff
> As dreams are made on, and our little life
> Is rounded with a sleep.
>   (4.1.148–58)

The metaphor developed here seems fairly straightforward: roles and scenes on the stage are evanescent and illusory; human life, likewise, quickly fades away. On closer examination, however, it becomes more complex. Prospero's actors were merely spirits, conjured up by him. The speech distinguishes between these spirits within the masque and, outside the masque, Prospero and the other main characters of *The Tempest*, who are implied to have a greater materiality and reality – but do they? Moving outward to another frame again, do we? Different layers of illusion and reality are at once delineated in opposition to each other and collapsed into one another. When Prospero speaks of 'cloud-capped towers' and 'gorgeous palaces', he appears to be gesturing beyond the stage to the real world – yet his descriptions closely resemble the sets of recorded Jacobean court masques, which were highly artificial productions (see chapter 5 below).[3] When he refers to 'the great globe itself', he invokes both the world and the Globe playhouse where *The Tempest* may have had its first performances. The world and the stage are even more closely intertwined in the speech than we first realised, constantly blurring and merging into one another to underline their shared ephemerality. And if reality is as evanescent as the stage, then this of course makes the stage profoundly real.

SIMULATING REAL PEOPLE

In spite of – or perhaps because of – the way that Shakespeare constantly and self-consciously draws attention to the artificiality of theatre, it is for his naturalism that he has been most often praised. As early as 1623, in his prefatory verses for the First Folio volume of Shakespeare's collected plays, his friend Ben Jonson wrote: 'Nature herself was proud of his designs, / And joyed to wear the dressing of his lines! / Which were so richly spun, and woven so fit, / As, since, she will vouchsafe no other wit'.[4] This idea took hold, and was repeated and developed to represent Shakespeare as pre-eminent in his depictions of human nature. Alexander Pope, for instance, wrote in 1725 that 'Homer himself drew not his art so immediately from the fountains of Nature . . . His Characters are so much Nature her self that 'tis a sort of injury to call them by so distant a name as Copies of her . . . every single character in Shakespeare is as much an Individual as those in Life itself'.[5] Samuel Johnson forty years later similarly averred that 'Shakespeare is above all writers, at least above all modern writers; the poet of nature; the poet that holds up to his readers a faithful mirrour of manners and of life'. He felt that Shakespeare's characters are not bound by a particular place or time, but 'are the genuine progeny of common humanity, such as the world will always supply, and observation will always find'.[6] In recent decades, academics have tended to challenge this idea of Shakespeare as distilling essential and timeless truths about human nature, emphasising instead how Shakespeare reflects the specific contexts of his time, and stressing the fact that his plays are artistic constructions. Nevertheless, theatre audiences and general readers continue to praise Shakespeare for representing universal truths, and often discuss his characters almost as if they were real people.

Given that Shakespeare's plays are indeed, obviously, manufactured works of art, how is it that he has brought so many spectators and readers over the centuries to feel that his characters are as close to being real people as an artistic simulacrum can be? One answer is that he gives them lines which gesture towards a fuller life outside the immediate events of the play. In *Henry IV part 2* (1598), Justice Shallow and Justice Silence share news of their growing children, whom we never meet, and this leads them into reminiscences of their own youth:

> SHALLOW: And how doth my cousin your bedfellow? And your fairest
>   daughter and mine, my god-daughter Ellen?
> SILENCE: Alas, a black ouzel,[7] cousin Shallow.
> SHALLOW: By yea and no, sir, I dare say my cousin William is become
>   a good scholar. He is at Oxford still, is he not?
> SILENCE: Indeed, sir, to my cost.
> SHALLOW: A must then to the Inns o'Court shortly. I was once of
>   Clement's Inn,[8] where I think they will talk of mad Shallow yet.
> SILENCE: You were called 'lusty Shallow' then, cousin.
>   (3.2.5–14)

Our response to them is a complex mixture of enjoying the particularities of their characterisation and personal details, and perhaps recognising them as a type of middle-aged man (garrulous, slightly self-satisfied, clinging on to vestiges of youth) that we feel we have encountered in life.

Yet Shakespeare sometimes uses this device – reference to events and people beyond the play – almost casually, creating confusion even as he fleshes out character. In *Twelfth Night* (1601), the reunited Viola and Sebastian confirm that they are indeed brother and sister by means of shared reminiscence:

> VIOLA: My father had a mole upon his brow.
> SEBASTIAN: And so had mine.
> VIOLA: And died that day when Viola from her birth
>   Had numbered thirteen years.
> SEBASTIAN: O, that record is lively in my soul.
>   He finishèd indeed his mortal act
>   That day that made my sister thirteen years.
>   (5.1.235–41)

This is a curious thing for Sebastian to say, since he told us earlier that he and Viola were 'both born in an hour' (2.1.16): they are twins, so Viola's thirteenth birthday would have been his own too. Perhaps at this point in the play we are not too inclined to worry about this; events are rushing towards a satisfying comic conclusion, and it is enough that Viola and Sebastian should 'match up' in some sense without the details necessarily being logical. Similarly, and notoriously, Lady Macbeth speaks of a child of which there is no other evidence in the play:[9] 'I have given suck, and know / How tender 'tis to love the babe that milks me. / I would, while it was smiling in my face, / Have plucked my nipple from his boneless gums / And dashed the brains out, had I so sworn / As you have done to this' (*Macbeth*, 1.7.54–9). We can choose to respond to this in several divergent ways. We may wish to fill in a whole personal history in which the Macbeths have lost a child – indeed a son and heir, as implied by the reference to '*his* boneless gums' – explaining much about their marriage and their characters. Or, we may see this child as not having any literal existence, simply forming part of the train of imagery that runs through the play of desecrations of childbirth and parenthood – the 'Finger of birth-strangled babe' in the witches' cauldron (4.1.30), the apparition of a bloody child (4.1.92 s.d.), the murder of Macduff's children (4.2), and so on – developing the atmosphere of the unnatural and the theme of fair made foul. Or, we may take a middle way, seeing the speech as symptomatic of Lady Macbeth's psychology while recognising that this is a dramatic fiction, and she has no larger life beyond the play.

Indicating experiences and relationships for the characters beyond the confines of the play, then, can work to deepen our sense of their reality, but can in some cases create inconsistencies or puzzles which return us to the knowledge that this is only a play. A more significant means by which Shakespeare endows his characters with reality is by presenting layers to their being: a public self which conceals a more private self, or selves, to which the audience is given privileged access. There are three principal means of doing this: disguise, asides, and the soliloquy. None of these were techniques invented by or exclusive to Shakespeare, but he uses each of them with particular sophistication to simulate emotional and psychological depth. In the case of Viola, for instance, we know that she is a girl disguised as a boy, so that when she speaks to Orsino in coded terms of her 'sister' who 'sat like patience on a monument, / Smiling at grief' (*Twelfth Night*, 2.4.113–14), we understand her more fully than Orsino and therefore feel that we have special insight into her 'true' feelings and 'true' being.[10] Hamlet adopts the disguise of an 'antic disposition' (1.5.173) to assert a difference between the persona he shows the court and the 'true self' that he shows to us in his soliloquies. Even before this, he has drawn attention to his clothes, his outer self, in order to claim an inner, deeper self: 'I have that within which passeth show – / These but the trappings and the suits of woe' (1.2.85–6).

A character's hidden depths could also be suggested by the use of asides, a device with a long history which reached back to the medieval Vice figure, and had been developed by Marlowe in *The Jew of Malta*. Such witty asides often function to draw the audience into complicity with a villainous character, an effect compounded by confessional – or apparently confessional – soliloquies. Shakespeare's Richard III is of course a notable example, telling us from the outset of his play that 'since I cannot prove a lover / To entertain these fair well-spoken days, / I am determinèd to prove a villain / And hate the idle pleasures of these days' (*Othello*, 1.1.28–31). We are thus drawn into uncomfortable pleasure in his ingenuity and audacity as he deceives and destroys everyone around him. Similarly 'honest' Iago frankly tells us that 'I hate the Moor' (1.3.368) and makes us privy to all his plots. The effect of access to the workings of his mind is compounded by versification which suggests thinking aloud and ideas in process: 'Cassio's a proper man. Let me see now, / To get his place, and to plume up my will / In double knavery – how, how? Let's see. / After some time to abuse Othello's ears / That he is too familiar with his wife' (1.3.374–8).

This effect, of a character as having an outside and inside, is more complex than it may at first sight appear. One of Iago's first statements is 'I am not what I am' (1.1.65). What is he then? Since he is so obviously untrustworthy – indeed the main thing he keeps telling us is that he is not to be trusted – can we believe him when he apparently reveals himself to us? Might not his apparent honesty with us be just another manipulative performance, just as he deceives Othello into regarding him as 'honest Iago'? Might he not be drawing back the curtain to show simply another curtain? This effect is not confined to villainous characters. Early in *Henry IV part 1* (1596) we see Prince Harry, the future King Henry V, idling and joking with Falstaff at the tavern, our first encounter with both of them. At the end of the scene the Prince moves into soliloquy to tell us that he is not a juvenile delinquent after all; his messing about with Falstaff and his friends is just a temporary playtime which is planned to make his reformation appear all the more glorious when he casts off these 'base contagious clouds' (1.2.176). Suddenly the Prince looks less like an amusingly irresponsible companion and more like a Machiavellian schemer, and for every subsequent scene in which he appears we are uncertain whether we are seeing his true character or a calculated performance. Indeed, it is precisely because all these layered roles depend upon performance that they work so well on stage. The supposedly 'private' self is as much a performance as the 'public' self; yet even this perception doubles back to give the characters a kind of realism. We will never fully know the 'real' Prince Harry, the 'real' Iago, or the 'real' Hamlet, and this is just like our experience of life, where even the people we get to know most intimately are never fully knowable to us.

Soliloquies are of course one of Shakespeare's most powerful tools in appearing to reveal to us the inner thoughts of his characters. A close look at his most famous soliloquy, 'To be or not not be' (*Hamlet*, 3.1.58–90) can reveal much about how this device works. It is poised on a knife-edge between public and private utterance: Hamlet appears to be talking to himself, perhaps even speaking aloud thoughts which only exist in his mind, yet a packed theatre of auditors is hanging on his every word. The situation which provokes the soliloquy is specific and even bizarre: Hamlet's father's ghost has told him that he was murdered by Hamlet's uncle, who has now married Hamlet's mother; Hamlet feels duty-bound to murder his uncle. Few of us (thankfully) are likely to have found ourselves in such circumstances, yet, as with the surreal statue scene in *The Winter's Tale*, they evoke emotions which many of us will have felt: grief, betrayal, tension between children and parents, procrastination and guilt. Correspondingly, Hamlet speaks in the soliloquy not of 'I' and 'me' but of 'we' and 'us' – 'When we have shuffled off this mortal coil', 'Thus conscience does make cowards of us all' (3.1.69, 85) – drawing us in to share his predicament and state of mind, and turning this moment of intense subjectivity and inwardness into an exposition of universal truths. His subject is life and death, and the possibility of self-extinction, perhaps the most essential of human questions which has relevance to everybody.

The speech is written in verse – iambic pentameter, like most of Shakespeare's plays – giving an effect of heightened, crafted language which commands our attention. This is obviously non-naturalistic – nobody speaks in iambic pentameter – yet its stresses (on every second syllable) and ten-syllable lines are closer to the rhythms of colloquial English speech than are many other metres, which have cumbersome longer lines or jogging shorter lines and often use more insistent stress-patterns. The lack of rhyme also makes the speech more like that of a real talking voice. Furthermore, Shakespeare makes many of the lines irregular in both stress-patterns and length. While built on an underlying framework of iambic pentameter, not one of the opening lines of the soliloquy is regular; they all exceed ten syllables, and disrupt the iambic rhythm: 'To be, or not to be; that is the question: / Whether 'tis nobler in the mind to suffer / The slings and arrows of outrageous fortune, / Or to take arms against a sea of troubles . . .' (3.1.58–61). These extended, over-flowing lines give an effect of urgency of thought and speech, and of Hamlet's ideas and feelings spilling over uncontainably.

The speech twists and turns:

> To die, to sleep –
> No more, and by a sleep to say we end
> The heartache and the thousand natural shocks
> That flesh is heir to – 'tis a consummation
> Devoutly to be wished. To die, to sleep.
> To sleep, perchance to dream. Ay, there's the rub.
> (3.1.62–7)

We find much enjambement (running over of one line into the next) and many mid-line breaks and half-lines as Hamlet interrupts himself, questions, jumps from one position to another, and doubles back to earlier points. We gain a strong sense of inner debate and a mind in turmoil. All of this helps us to feel that Hamlet is like us, that we are like Hamlet, and that we are being drawn deeply into his mind and character. Yet there is no real Hamlet; there are only words written on a page and spoken by an actor. The 'real' Hamlet will inevitably always remain elusive; and this paradoxically adds to our sense of his depth of character and reality.

DRAMATIC POETRY

A further pleasure of 'To be or not to be' is its rich imagery: 'The slings and arrows of outragous fortune', 'the whips and scorns of time', death as 'The undiscovered country from whose bourn / No traveller returns' (3.1.60, 72, 81–2). The last metaphor echoes Marlowe's Mortimer, who faced death 'as a traveller' who 'Goes to discover countries yet unknown' (*Edward II*, 5.6.64–6); but where Mortimer confronted his fate with impressive Tamburlaine-like bravado, Hamlet's feelings of uncertainty and his anxiety to cling

on to life are easier to identify with. Again, nobody talks quite like
this, and it is unlikely that they did so even in Shakespeare's time,
but Shakespeare's imagery precisely captures a universally recognisable state of mind.

In his early career Shakespeare was more famous as a poet than
as a playwright. His narrative poem *Venus and Adonis* (1592–93)
was a huge hit: it went through nine editions in Shakespeare's life-
time, and was more frequently quoted by his contemporaries than
any of his other works. His poetic gifts were unquestionably among
the most significant contributions that he made to Renaissance drama.
In *A Midsummer Night's Dream* he uses them to evoke the wood
outside Athens:

> OBERON: I know a bank where the wild thyme blows,
> Where oxlips and the nodding violet grows,
> Quite overcanopied with luscious woodbine,
> With sweet musk-roses, and with eglantine.
> There sleeps Titania sometime of the night,
> Lulled in these flowers with dances and delight;
> And there the snake throws her enamelled skin,
> Weed wide enough to wrap a fairy in.
>   (2.1.249–56)

Here the lines have a more regular rhythm than in 'To be, or not
to be', creating the effect of an incantation, and almost lulling us
into a trance, just as Oberon intends for Titania. The complex,
multiple nature of the wood is succinctly called into being. It has
the small, pretty, familiar wild flowers of an English wood; yet at
the same time these are heavily scented, entwining, and sensually
overpowering ('luscious woodbine', 'sweet musk-roses'). We gain a
sense of the tininess of the fairies – they dress themselves in cast
snakes' skins – and of how they bring supernatural animation to
the natural world of the wood through their 'dances and delight'.

The word 'enamelled' brilliantly evokes the hard, shiny beauty of
a snake's skin, and the presence of a snake, while not impossible in
an English wood, reminds us that we are supposed to be near Athens.
The snake also contributes to a train of imagery running through

the play which suggests the lurking presence of sinister threats in the nocturnal wood, and in the emotions of the characters. In their lullaby for Titania, the fairies fend off 'You spotted snakes with double tongue' (2.2.9); and when Hermia wakes, before she realises that she has been abandoned by Lysander she has a startlingly vivid dream of a serpent:

> Help me, Lysander, help me! Do thy best
> To pluck this crawling serpent from my breast!
> Ay me, for pity. What a dream was here?
> Lysander, look how I do quake with fear.
> Methought a serpent ate my heart away,
> And you sat smiling at his cruel prey.
> Lysander – what, removed?
> (2.2.151–7)

Like all troubling dreams, this one resists precise interpretation, but the serpent is evidently connected with both betrayal and desire. Its resonance is increased by the incidental mentions of snakes that have preceded it, illustrating how Shakespeare, as a poet, deploys arresting images not only at single places, but also as part of a larger network of imagery running through each play and giving it artistic unity.

Just as the poetry of *A Midsummer Night's Dream* creates the beautiful yet potentially hazardous wood in our imaginations, so in *Macbeth* (1606) many passages conjure a world of darkness and horror.

> MACBETH: Come, seeling night,
> Scarf up the tender eye of pitiful day,
> And with thy bloody and invisible hand
> Cancel and tear to pieces that great bond
> Which keeps me pale. Light thickens, and the crow
> Makes wing to th'rooky wood.
> Good things of day begin to droop and drowse,
> Whiles night's black agents to their preys do rouse.
> (3.2.47–54)

The 'bond / Which keeps me pale' is Banquo's hold on life and posterity; Macbeth has just sent the murderers after Banquo and his son Fleance to try to avert the witches' prophecy that they will inherit the throne. The early language of the speech is all about blindness: 'seeling' was the sewing shut of falcons' eyelids in training, while to 'scarf up' is to blindfold. On one level, this simply refers to the way in which night conceals actions in darkness, but it also implies that acts will be committed too horrible to be seen, and that Macbeth is wilfully blinding himself to their wickedness. 'Light thickens' is a wonderfully succinct and unexpected way of describing the coming of dusk; while the rooks in the wood recall the hoarse raven that Lady Macbeth invoked to 'croak the fatal entrance of Duncan / Under my battlements' (1.5.36–8). It is an intensely foreboding, unsettling passage, which in its creation of an atmosphere of evil sets a model for many later Gothic novels and horror films.

The 'rooky wood' ominously surrounding the castle anticipates the later fateful coming of Birnam Wood to Dunsinane that will fulfil the witches' prophecy and bring about Macbeth's death. Key images such as this serve to draw the action of the play together into a providential pattern of cause and effect, action and consequence. At the same time, as in *A Midsummer Night's Dream*, they make the play work like an extended poem, where recurring images, which we may barely notice with our conscious minds, accumulate, reverberate, and bind the play together. In the passage just discussed, we may pass rapidly over the mention of the 'bloody and invisible hand' of night; yet 'blood', and related terms such as 'bloody' and 'bleed', occur over 40 times in the play, most famously, of course, in the sleepwalking Lady Macbeth's futile efforts to wash imaginary blood from her hands (5.1.). Blood connotes not just murder, violence, and guilt, but also the blood-line of inheritance which Macbeth is so desperate to secure; it also casts a horrific pall of red across the whole play. Hands, too, recur many times, from the visionary dagger with its 'handle toward my hand' (2.1.34) to Macbeth's appalled cry 'What hands are here! Ha, they pluck out mine eyes' (2.2.57). Hands represent agency and responsibility, and are repeatedly spoken of in the play as if they simultaneously belong to, yet are oddly separate from, their owners. Again such recurrent images, varying subtly on each appearance, create effects which resonate atmospherically and thematically through the play and give it artistic unity.

BREAKING RULES

In the early 1580s, before Shakespeare had left Stratford for London to become a playwright, Sir Philip Sidney wrote a *Defence of Poesy*, one of the earliest English works of literary theory. By 'poesy' Sidney means all creative writing, including drama. He was roundly critical of contemporary plays, firstly because

> you shall have Asia of the one side, and Afric of the other, and so many other under-kingdoms, that the player, when he cometh in, must ever begin with telling where he is . . . Now you shall have three ladies walk to gather flowers: and then we must believe the stage to be a garden. By and by we hear news of shipwreck in the same place: and then we are to blame if we accept it not for a rock.

He went on to object that in a typical play a couple fall in love, and 'after many traverses, she is got with child, delivered of a fair boy; he is lost, groweth a man, falls in love, and is ready to get another child; and all this in two hours' space'. Even worse, 'all their plays be neither right tragedies, nor right comedies, mingling kings and clowns' and 'hornpipes and funerals'.[11]

Sidney was judging plays by dramatic rules developed by sixteenth-century commentators on Aristotle.[12] These asserted that a play should observe 'unity' of time and place, presenting a story which takes place in one setting and within one day; and that it should conform to a genre, either comedy (amusing, ending happily) or tragedy (doleful and ending in deaths). We shall never know what Sidney would have made of Shakespeare's plays, since he died in 1586, before Shakespeare had begun his career. However, based on his statements in the *Defence of Poesy*, he may have been appalled, especially by plays like *Antony and Cleopatra* (1606), which switches between Egypt and Rome and then wanders around the Mediterranean (Act 4 has no fewer than 16 scenes, scattered among various far-flung locations); or *The Winter's Tale*, which moves between

Sicilia and Bohemia and back again, gives land-locked Bohemia a sea coast, and employs a personification of Time to tell us that 16 years have passed between Acts 3 and 4. Although in a few plays Shakespeare did observe the unities of time and place (such as in *The Comedy of Errors* and *The Tempest*), on the whole he evidently had little interest in the classical rules that Sidney valued so highly.

Some of Shakespeare's greatest dramatic innovations were in mixing genres and testing their limits. It is clear from Sidney's *Defence* that already in the 1580s English playwrights were heedlessly mingling kings and clowns, tragedy and comedy, but Shakespeare took this to a new level. He seems acutely aware, even when writing plays which we might think of as 'pure' comedies or tragedies, that these genres are interdependent. *A Midsummer Night's Dream*, for instance, which we might think of as one of Shakespeare's lightest and brightest plays, is always shadowed by the possibility of turning into a tragedy. Hippolyta has been conquered in war; Hermia is threatened with death or the nunnery if she does not marry her father's choice; Demetrius plans to murder Lysander, and warns Helena that he could rape her (1.1.16–17, 1.1.65–73, 2.1.190, 2.1.214–19). Our pleasure in the happy ending is accentuated – indeed, reliant upon – our awareness that at several points events could very easily have taken an opposite direction. Hermia and Lysander may laugh at the closing performance of *Pyramus and Thisbe*, but their story came alarmingly near to that of the doomed lovers.

Some Shakespeare plays lurch so disorientatingly from tragic opening to comic ending that critics have had to invent special classifications for them. The 'problem plays' are a group from the middle years of Shakespeare's career, usually considered to include *Troilus and Cressida* (1602), *Measure for Measure* (1604), and *All's Well That Ends Well* (1605). Each of these plays is problematic in relation to genre, and may also address a thematic problem. In the case of *Measure for Measure*, this is the nature of justice, as strict laws are revived in Vienna after a period of laxity. Isabella's brother will be executed for fornication unless she sleeps with the corrupt deputy, Angelo. The problem seems utterly intractable: Isabella aspires to be a nun, and states flatly, 'More than our brother is our chastity' (2.4.185). Yet in Act 4 a discarded fiancée of Angelo's is produced to sleep with him in Isabella's place, and the plot is resolved. All of this is arranged by the Duke, disguised as a friar, who concludes the play by proposing to Isabella. Shakespeare has not scripted any words of response for her, and by this point we have passed through such a gamut of emotions that we cannot feel any certainty as to how she will respond. Should we and the characters simply be swept along by the tide of dramatic convention, so that Isabella accepts the Duke, we accept this ending, and comic closure is achieved? Or should this troubling, discordant play end on a disharmonious note, with Isabella making a gesture of rejection, as she does in some modern productions? Moreover, is this open question at the end of the play evidence of hasty and careless construction by Shakespeare, or is it an intentionally and appropriately problematic ending to a problematic play? The work as a whole appears to be an example of Shakespeare testing out just how far he can take a play in a tragic direction before he can pull it back to a comic ending. He continued to experiment with the mingling of tragic problems and comic endings in his late plays or 'romances' (that is, fantastical, fairytale-like stories), a term usually applied to *Pericles* (1607), *Cymbeline* (1609), *The Winter's Tale* 1610), and *The Tempest* (1611).[13]

A little before that group of late romances, Shakespeare specifically mixed kings and clowns by including a Fool in *King Lear* (1605). Working with the actor Robert Armin, Shakespeare had done much to develop the figure of the Fool in his middle comedies. Feste in *Twelfth Night* (1601) is a witty wordsmith whose marginal position – not quite part of civil society, perhaps not quite sane – gives him insight and the ability to tell truth in jest. Humanist writers such as Erasmus and Thomas More had highly valued 'serious play' as a means of advancing uncomfortable truths, and had sought to practise this in their own works like *The Praise of Folly* (1511) and *Utopia* (1516). Feste is their heir. As Viola observes, 'This fellow is wise enough to play the fool, / And to do that well craves a kind of wit' (3.1.53–4). It is entirely apt that Feste ends the play with a song which is foolish yet melancholy, meaningless yet deeply evocative: its refrain is 'the rain it raineth every day'.[14]

In *King Lear* we meet a cousin or brother of Feste who by rights is completely out of place and out of genre. Yet what we quickly see is that this bleakest of tragedies is exactly the right place for a truth-telling fool. His word-play of inversions and paradoxes is the indigenous language of a world turned upside-down by unnatural events: he sings of Lear's daughters, 'Then they for sudden joy did weep, / And I for sorrow sung, / That such a king should play bo-peep, / And go the fools among' (1.4.152–5).[15] It also enables him to say to Lear what no-one else can say: 'LEAR: Who is it that can tell me who I am? / FOOL: Lear's shadow' (1.4.205–6). He plays an essential part in the tableau on the storm-lashed heath of the Fool, the feigned madman (Poor Tom), and the real madman (Lear), which takes on the force of an allegory of the human condition. And it is Lear's bond with the Fool that lead him to feel compassion in the storm, and thereby to move towards a softening of his heart, repentance, and self-reformation, albeit at the price of his sanity: 'LEAR: My wits begin to turn. / Come on, my boy. How dost, my boy? Art cold? . . . Poor fool and knave, I have one part in my heart / That's sorry yet for thee' (3.2.65–6, 70–71). The Fool does not appear again after the scenes on the heath, arguably because after this point Lear has internalised his riddling way of truth-telling, and in his madness speaks for himself the Fool's nonsensical yet insightful language of 'handy-dandy': 'LEAR: A man may see how this world goes with no eyes. Look with thine ears' (4.6.149, 146–7).

Examples like this make the classical rules of drama seem irrelevant. The presence of the Fool in *Lear* only adds to the tragedy's intensity and pathos, and to a sense of the drama as symbolising something bigger than its immediate events. When Lear grieves, in his final words, that 'my poor fool is hanged', it is unclear whether he is referring to the Fool or to the dead Cordelia who lies in his arms (5.3.304). Either way, the statement compounds the sense of general waste and devastation. Lear's companions ask: 'KENT: Is this the promised end? / EDGAR: Or image of that horror?' (5.3.237–8). The scene does indeed feel apocalyptic. By following his own artistic instincts and breaking rules, Shakespeare created one of the most excoriating tragedies in world literature.

There are of course numerous other ways in which Shakespeare contributed to English Renaissance drama. One might point to his development of the genres of English history play and Roman play; his exploration of English and British national identity; his interest in marginalised 'others' such as Shylock the Jew and Othello the Moor; his creation of complex female characters; and much, much more. Although there is not space to discuss all of these here, Shakespeare will continue to feature in later chapters of this book, including the discussions of tragicomedy in chapter 7, of cross-dressing heroines in chapter 8, and of the afterlives of Renaissance drama in the epilogue. For the time being, this chapter has tried to indicate a few of the reasons why, in an age of great dramatists, Shakespeare stands out as exceptional.

5

JONSON

In 1638 Richard West wrote in tribute to a recently dead author: 'Strangers,[1] who cannot reach thy sense, will throng / To heare us speake the Accents of thy Tongue ... Thou shalt be read as Classick Authors; and / As Greeke and Latine taught in every Land'.[2] These are the kinds of praises that we usually associate with Shakespeare: exemplary use of English, admiration beyond England's shores, and timeless, classic status. However, this was an elegy for Ben Jonson (1572–1637), who for much of the seventeenth century was regarded as England's greatest author. In the year of Shakespeare's demise, 1616, Jonson was granted a royal pension of 100 marks (around £70) per annum, making him in effect England's first poet laureate.[3] In the same year he published a handsome folio edition of his collected Works, asserting the prestige of the profession of author.[4] As well as writing for the public playhouses, he was also the chief writer of masques for the court. Yet Jonson had grown up as the stepson and apprentice of a bricklayer, and had been imprisoned in 1597 for contributing to *The Isle of Dogs*, a play deemed offensive and seditious. In 1598 he had killed a fellow actor, Gabriel Spencer, in a duel, and had narrowly escaped hanging, though not prison (again) and a brand on his thumb.

Jonson, then, was a man of contradictions, and these extended to his thinking about drama. Jonson's decision to include plays – widely regarded as ephemeral and lowbrow compositions – in his grand edition of his Works was a radical assertion of the high literary worth of drama. Yet at other times he expressed disdain for the commercial stage: 'Make not thyself a page, / To that strumpet the stage, / But sing high and aloof'.[5] He was revered as the most learned writer of his age, and prized his role as the chief author of the Jacobean court; yet much of his writing depicts the scurrilous and grubby reality of the London of his time, and relishes the demotic vitality of its language. He often expressed deference to the classical rules of drama (see chapter 4 above), as in the Prologue to *Volpone* (1606): 'The laws of time, place, persons he observeth, / From no needful rule he swerveth'.[6] He also declared his purpose to be the representation of nature with proportion and realism, being 'loath to make Nature afraid in his plays, like those that beget Tales, Tempests, and such like drolleries', implicitly setting up Shakespeare as the kind of fantastical and undisciplined writer that he did not want to be.[7] Yet all this enthusiasm for order, regulation, and naturalism was frequently contradicted in Jonson's works by a persistent pleasure in the excessive, the grotesque, the crazed and bizarre. Let us trace these contradictions, then, as they run through the course of his dramatic career.

EARLY PLAYS

Jonson's early career is a story of turbulence and uncertain success. His first known play is *The Case is Altered*, performed in 1597. In the same year his controversial collaboration with Thomas Nashe, *The Isle of Dogs*, landed him in prison, and provoked the temporary closure of all the London playhouses. There is evidence that he wrote a number of other plays in the 1590s, either alone or with others, but these have been lost; Jonson himself did not consider them worthy of inclusion in his folio collected Works.

His first significant success was the satirical comedy *Every Man in his Humour* (1598), with Shakespeare and Burbage in leading roles. 'Humour' was a term from Renaissance medicine: an imbalance in the body of the four humours, blood, phlegm, choler, and melancholy, was believed to produce illness or aberrant behaviour. Jonson used it as a metaphor, explaining it in a sequel, *Every Man out of his Humour* (1599): 'As when some one peculiar quality / Doth so possesse a man, that it doth draw / All his affects, his spirits, and his powers, / In their confluctions, all to runne one way, / This may be truly said to be a Humour'.[8] A Jonsonian humour, then, is an obsession or affectation which renders a person ridiculous, out of line with society, and in need of comic reformation. His humours plays were at the cutting-edge of literary fashion, drawing on the Characters of Theophrastus (published in Latin in 1592), a set of pithy descriptions of urban stock types which inspired various English imitations.

Despite these successes, the next few years of Jonson's career were marked by frustration and irascibility. Between *Every Man In* and *Every Man Out*, in late 1598, he killed a fellow actor, Gabriel Spencer, in a duel. He escaped hanging by means of the ancient legal device of 'benefit of clergy' (originally, a convicted criminal who could read a Latin psalm was deemed to be a priest, and sentenced more leniently; by Elizabethan times this had become a procedure for mitigating sentences for first-time offenders). However, Jonson emerged from the experience not only with a felon's brand on his thumb, but also as a convert to Catholicism.

His next play, *Cynthia's Revels* (1600), was a somewhat strained attempt at rehabilitation, an allegory of the Elizabethan court in the manner of Lyly. The Prologue declared Jonson's ambitions to be an innovative artist and a moralist: his Muse 'shunnes the print of any beaten path; / And proves new wayes to come to learned eares'. She does not seek 'popular applause', but the acclaim of those 'Who can both censure, understand, define / What merit is'.[9] The court perform-ance of the play in January 1601 was not well received, perhaps partly because it could be seen as supportive of the disgraced Earl of Essex, but maybe also because Jonson rather self-promotingly made the moral centre of the play a humbly born scholar, Crites, who becomes the confidant and adviser of Cynthia (a conventional dramatic persona for Elizabeth I).[10] A similar figure, this time named Horace, appeared in *Poetaster* (1601) to castigate some of Jonson's fellow playwrights, particularly John Marston and Thomas Dekker, who avenged themselves with an attack on Jonson in *Satiromastix* (also 1601), an exchange known as the 'war of the theatres'.

Jonson then tried his hand at tragedy with *Sejanus* (1603); as in *Every Man In*, Shakespeare again took a leading role. It was not a popular success: Jonson ruefully observed in a dedicatory epistle that it 'suffered no less violence from our people here than the subject of it did from the rage of the people of Rome', referring to the tearing to pieces of Sejanus, disgraced favourite of the Emperor Tiberius, which forms the climax of the play.[11] It made enemies in high places too: Jonson was summoned before the privy council on charges of popery and treason. In 1605 he was in prison again for perceived satire against the Scottish followers of King James I in *Eastward Ho!*, a collaboration with George Chapman and Jonson's erstwhile enemy Marston. Once free again, in early October 1605, Jonson attended a dinner with most of the conspirators who were about to attempt to blow up the king and parliament on the fifth of November. This time Jonson turned events to his advantage by offering some assistance to the investigation of the plot. Nevertheless, on several occasions in 1606 he was summoned with his wife to appear in court on charges of recusancy (refusal by Catholics to attend services of the Church of England). Yet by this date this seeming trouble-maker and anti-establishment figure was on his way to becoming the leading author of the Jacobean court.

COURT MASQUES

From the moment of James I's accession in March 1603 Jonson devoted himself to seeking his favour, busily composing pageants, entertainments, and poems of praise for the new monarch and his queen, Anne of Denmark. A crucial turning point was *The Masque of Blackness*, devised in collaboration with the architect and designer Inigo Jones for performance by Queen Anne and her ladies at the Banqueting House in Whitehall on 6 January 1605. We explored in chapter 1 the rich tradition of court drama in sixteenth-century England, including civic pageants, progress entertainments, and the plays of Lyly and Peele. We saw how such productions frequently deployed sophisticated allegory, and how the line between performance and audience was often crossed as the royal spectator was invited to respond or intervene. Now Queen Anne decided that she herself wanted to be at

Inigo Jones, costume design for a Daughter of Niger,
The Masque of Blackness, 1605.

the centre of performance. According to Jonson in his published preface
to *The Masque of Blackness*, she also devised its leading concept: the
presentation of herself and her ladies as 'blackamoors'.[12]

The experience of a Stuart court masque is inevitably difficult to
reconstruct, because it relied heavily not only on text but also music,
dance, and visual effects. Nevertheless, it is evident from Jonson's
description and surviving drawings by Jones that *The Masque of
Blackness* was spectacular. The masquers 'were placed in a great
concave shell, like mother of pearl', which appeared to move on the
billows of an artificial wave. 'A chevron of lights . . . struck a glorious
beam upon them', and arranged around them were huge sea-monsters
and fish-tailed tritons with blue hair (pp. 1–2). Most sensational of
all, though, was the appearance of Queen Anne and her ladies, as
described by the courtier Sir Dudley Carleton:

> Their Apparell was rich but too light and Curtizan-like for such great
> ones. Instead of Vizzards, their Faces, and Arms, up to the Elbows,
> were painted black, which was Disguise sufficient, for they were hard

to be known; but it became them nothing so well as their red and white, and you cannot imagine a more ugly sight than a Troop of lean-cheek'd Moors.[13]

For observers like this, the performers were too naked and too black. There was also something profoundly transgressive about performance by women, especially when those on stage included a queen. Queen Anne and her ladies had already performed in one masque, Samuel Daniel's *Vision of the Twelve Goddesses* (January 1604), but to persist in doing so was to contradict both the conventional exclusion of women from the public stage in this period, and the conventions of the Elizabethan court, whereby the queen might momentarily intervene in a performance to receive a gift or make a judgement, but never took a central performing role.[14]

The plot of *The Masque of Blackness* concerns the quest of the daughters of Niger for a land whose name ends in the sound '–tania', where their dark complexions will be made pale. They learn that this land is 'Britannia', which is 'Ruled by a sun ... / Whose beams shine day and night, and are of force / To blanch an Ethiop and revive a cor'se ... / Their beauties shall be scorched no more; / This sun is temperate, and refines / All things on which his radiance shines' (pp. 6–7). The masque was self-evidently a compliment to King James on his sun-like power, his moderation, and his union of the thrones of Scotland and England to create 'Britannia'. Yet it was also an assertion by Queen Anne of an independent public presence, artistic sensibility, and desire to perform, foreshadowing an increasing distance between the royal couple and their courts that would develop over the coming years. At the same time, while the conclusion of the *Masque* affirms the superiority of white complexions, earlier passages subversively celebrate the dark beauty of the daughters of Niger: 'in their black the perfect'st beauty grows, / ... Their beauties conquer in great beauty's war; / ... how near divinity they be, / That stand from passion or decay so free' (p. 4). Both these passages, and Queen Anne's desire to appear as a black woman, were in their period highly unusual assertions of the beauty of dark complexions.

Jonson composed three more masques for Queen Anne, including *The Masque of Queens* in 1609. This introduced the 'antimasque', which was a 'spectacle of strangeness', in this case performed by twelve 'hags or witches', played by male actors, whose dancing was 'full of preposterous change and gesticulation . . . with strange fantastic motions of their heads and bodies'.[15] They were dispelled by the figures of Heroic Virtue and Fame, who presented an orderly procession of the queen and her ladies dressed as renowned queens from history and myth. Once again Jonson attributed this device to Queen Anne,[16] but the antimasque became an established feature of his masques, setting up an antithetical structure whereby forces of chaos were conquered and dispersed by the forces of virtue, personified by the principal masquers.

Although other authors also composed masques for the Stuart court, Jonson was foremost among them. He created many others beyond those for Queen Anne, and continued into the reign of Charles I, with his final masques as late as 1631. Most were collaborations with Inigo Jones, who devised not only ingenious stage machinery and exotic costumes, but also perspectival scenery, a crucial innovation in the history of theatre. Yet relations between these two brilliant men were frequently tense, because of Jonson's view that

Inigo Jones, costume design for a masquer representing a star.

his texts for the masques were of more value and importance than Jones's visual spectacles. In a preface to *Hymenaei* (1606), Jonson described Jones's shows as merely the transitory body of the masque, whereas his own words were the immortal soul: 'the one sorte are but momentarie, and meerely taking; the other impressing, and lasting: Else the Glory of all these Solemnities had perish'd like a Blaze, and gone out, in the Beholders eyes'.[17]

Masques were indeed usually performed for one night only, despite their extravagant and costly stagings: for example, *The Masque of Blackness* alone was rumoured to have cost nearly £3,000. This ephemeral magnificence lent itself to be invoked as an image of worldly transience; but at the same time it was a bold statement of the wealth and largesse of the crown. Masques were self-evidently affirmations of monarchical authority. This was true not only of their plots, in which peace and order were dispensed from the throne, but even of the arrangement of the performance space, since only the king had a perfect view of the perspectival set. The king himself was also part of the spectacle, watching the performance from a raised chair of state where he was on public display.[18]

We might, then, view Jonson's masques as deeply conservative and authoritarian, or even dismiss them as merely fawning exercises in flattery. It is certainly true that Jonson placed high value on order, and that his assertions of his own moral and artistic authority were linked to his belief in the need for a controlling authority in the state.[19] His masques celebrated a beautiful philosophical ideal of order and harmony; the dancing which made up much of their action became a symbol of cosmic as well as political pattern and symmetry:

> as all actions of mankind
> Are but a labyrinth or maze,
> So let your dances be entwined,
> Yet not perplex men unto gaze;
> But measured, and so numerous too,
> As men may read each act you do;
> And when they see the graces meet,
> Admire the wisdom of your feet.[20]

Jonson's poems in praise of various aristocratic patrons also identified them with an abstract ideal of order and harmony. Yet Jonson
did not necessarily believe that his monarchs and patrons always
lived up to this ideal. Panegyric (literature written in praise of a
ruler or patron) can in fact be strongly admonitory and corrective,
holding up an ideal model for the addressee to aspire to, but implying
that he or she is not as yet fulfilling that ideal. Jonson explained
this in a somewhat rueful poem: 'Though I confess (as every muse
hath erred, / And mine not least) I have too oft preferred / Men past
their terms, and praised some names too much, / But 'twas with
purpose to have made them such'.[21] The difficulty of reconciling
morality with art, and the duty of the author nevertheless to attempt
this, are themes running through his career.

THE MIDDLE COMEDIES: *VOLPONE, EPICENE, THE ALCHEMIST, BARTHOLOMEW FAIR*

While Jonson's court entertainments repeatedly presented the triumph
of order over chaos, the great comedies that he wrote from 1606
to 1614 for the public playhouses create a dynamic interplay between
these forces. Indeed, despite Jonson's repeated assertions of order as
his guiding ideal, these plays often leave us feeling that he takes
greater pleasure in the disorderly, extravagant, and out-of-control.

Volpone (1606) is set in Venice, and relates how the title character, by pretending to be a wealthy and childless dying man, tricks
various avaricious suitors. They compete to present him with ever
more lavish gifts in hopes of becoming his sole heir. The characters
are given Italian names of beasts and animals, invoking allegory and
beast-fable: the cunning Volpone is the Fox, his nimble-witted servant
and 'parasite' is Mosca the Fly, and the suitors who cluster to prey
on his decaying flesh like carrion birds are Voltore (the Vulture),
Corbaccio (the Raven) and Corvino (the Crow). Jonson dwells with
perverse relish on the hideousness of Volpone's supposedly rotting
body: 'Those filthy eyes . . . that flow with slime, / Like two frog-
pits; and those same hanging cheeks, / Covered with hide instead
of skin . . . / That look like frozen dish-clouts'.[22] His decaying flesh
may be a pretence, but is a true sign of his inner moral corruption,

and on one level he is the villain of the play; yet when we see him out of disguise we cannot help enjoying and even admiring his energy and ingenuity. The play opens with Volpone's glorious celebration of his gains: 'Good morning to the day; and next, my gold! / Open the shrine that I may see my saint' (1.1.1–2). In the soaring rapture of the verse we may at least half forget that such worship of wealth is morally wrong. He woos a young woman, Celia, with enticements that are at once queasily decadent and exhilaratingly exotic: 'The heads of parrots, tongues of nightingales, / The brains of peacocks, and of ostriches / Shall be our food . . ./ Thy baths shall be the juice of Jùly-flowers, / Spirit of roses, and of violets, / The milk of unicorns, and panther's breath / Gathered in bags' (3.7.202–4, 213–16). We sense that Jonson is hugely enjoying the opportunity that Volpone gives him to let rip, and to explore all the bizarre corners of his own imagination.

The deftness and wit of Mosca the Fly is also hard to resist: 'I could skip / Out of my skin, now, like a subtle snake, / I am so limber' (3.1.5–7). Rather than Volpone and Mosca, the worst villains of the piece are the preying suitors who hypocritically feign affection and concern for Volpone while in fact thirsting for every scrap of news of his deterioration. They are gulls, fools whose greed blinds them to the truth and makes them easy victims of clever manipulation. Indeed, one comes to feel that Jonson is constructing an alternative moral scale based not on virtue, but on intelligence. The play does contain two apparent representatives of goodness, Celia and Bonario, but they are entirely wooden and uninteresting. When Volpone tries to rape Celia, Bonario leaps out of hiding to defend her with a distinctly unimpressive cry of 'Forbear, foul ravisher, libidinous swine!' (3.7.267). By contrast, Volpone's pleasure in his own ingenuity is far more appealing: 'I glory / More in the cunning purchase of my wealth / Than in the glad possession' (1.1.30–32).

Indeed, in the end, as the forces of virtue seem entirely ineffectual, it is this very enjoyment of his own wit that is Volpone's downfall. For a fresh joke against the suitors he pretends to die, making Mosca his sole heir; but Mosca seizes the opportunity to confirm his master's death, repudiate the living Volpone, and claim his wealth. 'To make a snare for mine own neck!' laments Volpone, 'And run / My head into it wilfully! With laughter! / When I had newly 'scaped, was free and clear! / Out of mere wantonness!' (5.11.1–4). It seems that the only person who can beat Volpone is Volpone – and the accomplice that he himself trained up. At the end of the play, firmly retributive sentences are finally applied by a court of law, which condemns the lively, mobile Mosca to be chained down as a galley slave, and the feigned invalid Volpone 'to lie in prison cramped with irons, / Till thou be'st sick and lame indeed' (5.12.123–4). Even here, though, order and authority are subverted as the lawyers are shown to be hypocritical and self-interested, and Volpone returns to seek the approval of the audience: 'though the Fox be punished by the laws, / He yet doth hope there is no suffering due / For any fact which he hath done 'gainst you; / ... fare jovially, and clap your hands' (5.12.153–7).

For his next play, *Epicene* (1609), Jonson moved to a London setting. Morose finds all noise intolerable, making city life comically unbearable for him. He is introduced to Epicene, an attractive young gentlewoman who speaks only to express deference and compliance in almost inaudible tones. Delighted, Morose marries her, only to find that she immediately becomes domineering, opinionated, and flirtatious with other men. In fact the marriage was a trick set up by Morose's nephew and his friends, and it has another level too: at the end of the play, Epicene is revealed to be a boy in disguise. In a playhouse culture in which women were invariably played by boys anyway, this was obviously a moment charged with self-referential irony. The play was popular and influential on the Restoration stage, and has also attracted attention in recent times because of its sophisticated gender-politics, particularly its implication that gender-identity may be a matter of social performance.

In 1610, as legal restrictions upon Catholics became increasingly punitive, Jonson re-converted to the Church of England, though traces of affinity with Catholicism persisted in his conduct and writings until his death. In the same year he wrote *The Alchemist*, for which he again used a London setting, explaining in the Prologue that 'No clime breeds better matter for your whore, / Bawd, squire, impostor, many persons more'.[23] It was also set in a time of plague, which did indeed affect London in 1610; and in the Blackfriars district, where the play was probably performed at the Blackfriars playhouse, creating precise symmetries between the stage action and its immediate surroundings.[24] The premise of the play returns to and expands upon that of *Volpone*, with a team of cunning tricksters – here, Face the housekeeper, Subtle the alchemist, and Doll Common, a prostitute – preying upon gulls whose folly and self-interest make them easy targets. The play opens arrestingly with a violent quarrel between the three conspirators, demonstrating from the outset that they too are fundamentally self-interested and have as little loyalty to one another as Volpone and Mosca. These lines also show Jonson skilfully mimicing in dramatic verse the explosive and earthy qualities of demotic speech:

> FACE: Believe't, I will.
> SUBTLE: Thy worst. I fart at thee.
> DOLL: Ha' you your wits? Why, gentlemen! For love –
> FACE: Sirrah, I'll strip you –
> SUBTLE: What to do? Lick figs
>   Out at my –
> FACE: Rogue, rogue, out of all your sleights.
>   (1.1.1–4)

The gulls enter one by one to be worked upon by Face in a succession of disguises, each of them hoping that Subtle will produce for them the philosopher's stone which turns base metal into gold. The action speeds up as gulls arrive in rapid succession or even simultaneously, compelling Face to switch roles with dizzying speed and producing the frenetic 'revolving doors' effect typical of later farces.

The personalities and ambitions of the various gulls create deliciously absurd situations. Dapper, a clerk, is induced to believe that the Fairy Queen, impersonated by Doll, is his aunt and holds him in high favour. Face and Subtle blindfold him and pick his pockets while making elf-noises: '*Ti, ti ti, ti ti ti /* . . . She now is set / At dinner in her bed, and she has sent you / From her own private trencher, a dead mouse / And a piece of gingerbread, to be merry withal' (3.5.58, 65–8). Two Puritan brethren, Tribulation Wholesome and Ananias, rant in pseudo-Biblical language: 'Thou look'st like Antichrist in that lewd hat' (4.7.55). Most gloriously of all, the voluptuary Sir Epicure Mammon rhapsodises extravagantly, and sometimes nauseatingly, on the pleasures that the philosopher's stone will bring him:

> I will have all my beds blown up, not stuffed;
> Down is too hard ...
>   ... Then, my glasses
> Cut in more subtle angles, to disperse
> And multiply the figures as I walk
> Naked between my *succubae*[25]...
>   ... I myself will have
> The beards of barbels,[26] served instead of salads;
> Oiled mushrooms; and the swelling unctuous paps
> Of a fat pregnant sow, newly cut off,
> Dressed with an exquisite and poignant sauce.
>   (2.3.41–2, 45–8; 81–5)

By association, inflatedness, oiliness, and fatness become properties of Mammon himself, while combined with the kind of weird refinement and debauched delicacy that we saw earlier in the decadent pleasures offered to Celia by Volpone.

The central theme of alchemy also inspires Jonson's linguistic inventiveness, as Subtle impresses and beguiles the gulls with his pseudo-scientific, pseudo-magical, pseudo-mystical jargon:

> The work is done; bright Sol is in his robe
>   ... Infuse vinegar,
> To draw his volatile substance and his tincture,
> And let the water in glass E be filtered,
> And put into the gripe's egg. Lute him well;
> And leave him closed *in balneo*.
>   (2.3.29, 37–41).

As the play proceeds he and his colleagues juggle no fewer than seven different plots, which overlap and intertwine and become ever more frantic, culminating in 'A great crack and noise within'

(4.5.63 s.d.). The laboratory explodes, the plots collapse, and Face's master, who had left town to avoid the plague, returns. All he finds is 'The empty walls, worse than I left 'em, smoked, / A few cracked pots, and glasses, and a furnace, / The ceiling filled with poesies of the candle, / And madam with a dildo writ o' the walls' (5.5.39–42). Like the playwright in whose play they appear, Face, Subtle and Doll have conjured an elaborate fiction out of a few crude ingredients, linguistic inventiveness, and the imaginations of their audience.

We saw that in *Volpone* the dispensation of justice at the end of the play is undercut by several counter-forces. The Prologue to *The Alchemist* promises 'wholesome remedies' and 'fair còrrectives' to 'cure' the 'vices' of the age (lines 14, 15, 18), and we might expect Face's homecoming master to be the agent of such justice. However, his name is Lovewit, and his first response on hearing reports of Face's misdemeanours is 'What device should he bring forth now? / I love a teeming wit, as I love my nourishment' (5.1.15–16). Far from punishing Face, he scoops up from one of his servant's unfinished plots a wealthy young widow, Dame Pliant, as his bride. The gulls come off worse than the tricksters, and once again we see how highly intelligence – including appreciation of a good joke – ranks in Jonson's scale of values.

In 1611 Jonson again turned his hand to Roman tragedy with *Catiline his Conspiracy*, but this play enjoyed no more success than his earlier *Sejanus*. He returned to comedy with the boldly experimental *Bartholomew Fair* (1614), which extends the contemporaneity of *Alchemist* to turn the busy, noisy streetlife of London into a sprawling structure of interlocking plots and a teeming dramatic spectacle. The fair which gives the play its title and is both the scene and the engine of all its action was an annual event based at Smithfield on 24 August, St Bartholomew's Day. The fair had medieval origins, and by the seventeenth century was a two-week event, increasingly notorious for its rowdiness, covering a vast area with diverse stalls and entertainments. It thus enables Jonson to bring together a multitudinous cast of colourful and socially mixed characters – a gambler, a cutpurse, a ballad-singer, a Puritan, a gullible young heir, a Justice of the Peace, a prostitute, a madman, and more – in encounters which facilitate trickery and create comic confusion.

The play is full of authentic voices of London. Lantern Leather-head the hobby-horse seller, Joan Trash the gingerbread woman, and other stallholders cry their wares:

> LEATHERHEAD: What do you lack? What is't you buy? What do you
> lack? Rattles, drums, halberts,[27] horses, babies[28] o'the best? Fiddles
> o'the finest?
> COSTERMONGER: Buy any pears, pears, fine, very fine pears!
> TRASH: Buy any gingerbread, gilt gingerbread![29]

At the centre of this seething panorama of human life, and in many ways its personification, is Ursula the pig-woman, a vastly corpu-lent presence who roasts hogs and sells their meat, and also sells flesh as a bawd. Her stall is the focal point of the play, where char-acters cross paths and converge to create unlikely acquaintances, absurd misprisions, and unexpected consequences. Ursula is an emblem of humanity in its most essential and grotesque form as she sweats over her roasting pork like a gigantic lump of lard: 'I am all fire and fat ... I shall e'en melt away to the first woman, a rib again, I am afraid. I do water the ground in knots as I go, like a great garden-pot;[30] you may follow me by the S's I make' (2.2.49–52). A figure of abundance, she inspires abundant linguistic invention in others: she is a 'walking sow of tallow', 'an inspired vessel of kitchen-stuff', a 'quagmire'; a man who attempted to have sex with her 'might sink into her and be drowned a week ere any friend he had could find where he were ... 'Twere like falling into a whole shire of butter' (2.5.70–71, 85–9). Quarlous sums her up in the oath he utters when he first catches sight of her: 'Body o' the Fair!' (2.5.67).

As in *Volpone* and *The Alchemist* the force of law, this time person-ified by Justice Adam Overdo, is shown to be limited in its ability to detect crime and its authority to punish it. Once again, also, Puri-tans are mocked, this time specifically for their opposition to theatre. Zeal-of-the-Land Busy interrupts and denounces a puppet-show as an idolatrous work of the devil, and Jonson has much fun with his prophetic and apocalyptic manner of speech:

Thy profession is damnable, and in pleading for it, thou dost plead
for Baal. I have long opened my mouth wide and gaped, I have gaped
as the oyster for the tide, after thy destruction, but cannot compass
it by suit or dispute; so that I look for a bickering ere long, and then
a battle.

 (5.5.18–22)

This leads him into an absurd pantomime-style spat with one of
the puppets:

BUSY: I say, his calling, his profession is profane, it is profane, idol.
PUPPET DIONYSIUS: *It is not profane!*
LEATHERHEAD: It is not profane, he says.
BUSY: It is profane.
PUPPET DIONYSIUS: *It is not profane.*
BUSY: It is profane.
PUPPET DIONYSIUS: *It is not profane.*
 (5.5.59–65).

Finally Busy invokes one of the Puritans' chief arguments against
theatre: 'you are an abomination; for the male among you putteth
on the apparel of the female, and the female of the male' (5.5.86–8).
In response, the puppet simply 'takes up his garment' (5.5.94 s.d.),
showing that he is merely a piece of wood, with no genitals. Busy
is confounded and converted, and sits down with everyone else to
enjoy the show.

 Thus although in his prologues and elsewhere Jonson often declares
a purpose of moral reform, his comedies frequently end on a note
of tolerant good humour, with a recognition of shared humanity. At
the end of *Bartholomew Fair*, Justice Overdo is forced to acknowledge that he has misjudged nearly everyone at the fair, and that he
is 'but Adam, flesh and blood!' (5.6.93–4). He invites the whole
crowd back to his house for supper, explaining – with sentiments
that his author, despite sterner pronouncements elsewhere, seems to
have shared – that 'my intents are *ad correctionem, non ad destruc-
tionem; as aedificandum, non ad diruendum*' (for improvement, not
destruction; for building up, not tearing down; 5.6.107–8).

LATER YEARS

Jonson's publication of a folio edition of his Works in 1616 laid claim to a new dignity for the profession of authorship. This was not the first such enterprise: the poet Samuel Daniel had published his collected Works in folio in 1601. However, Jonson took the radical step of including nine of his plays in his Works volume. The rapid turnover of plays in the playhouses, the disappearance of most of them after one performance or one season, and the fact that those plays that made it to print often did so in cheap, shoddy editions, all meant that they were regarded as ephemeral and inconsequential entertainments, not proper literature. When founding his library in Oxford Sir Thomas Bodley specifically excluded playbooks, dismissing them in a letter of 1611 as 'idle bookes, & riffe raffes'.[31] Jonson's inclusion of them in the Works provoked some mockery: 'Pray tell me Ben, where does the mystery lurk, / What others call a play you call a work'.[32]

However, Jonson seems throughout his career to have had a heightened consciousness of the material differences between a play in performance and a play in print, and of the opportunities that these offered to an author. The 1600 quarto edition of *Every Man in his Humour* asserted that it presented the play 'As It Was First Composed by the Author', not as modified on stage, and 'Containing more than hath been publicly spoken or Acted'.[33] A printed edition offered an author an opportunity to reclaim his original artistic conception, to address learned and discerning readers over the heads of the playhouse crowds, and to promote the literary value of dramatic writing. Jonson's groundbreaking inclusion of plays in his folio Works thus declared their worth and status, and paved the way for the publication of Shakespeare's collected plays in the First Folio of 1623. Through this enterprise and by means of the assertion of his public voice throughout his career, Jonson made a highly significant contribution to the emerging role of the professional author. We consistently find in him an unprecedentedly self-aware and sophisticated understanding of the role and place of an early modern author, as one who arbitrated between the demands of patrons and the wider public, and as one who sought to safeguard morality and art while depending on commercial success and fame.

For the folio Works Jonson extensively revised *Every Man in his Humour*, changing the setting from Italy to London. There was perhaps a recognition here that much of his greatest dramatic success had been achieved in holding up a satiric mirror to his native city; indeed, even when he had used Italian settings, such as the Venice of *Volpone*, these were arguably in many respects merely depictions of contemporary London in another guise. In the distinctively urban and topical qualities of his writing, in his use of type-characters as a means of categorising and classifying the innumerable inhabitants of the seething metropolis, and in his intricate and fast-paced plots Jonson was a leading contributor to the genre of city comedy, which will be discussed in more detail in chapter 7.

Jonson was a leading member of social and intellectual circles in London, participating in early 'clubs' at the Mermaid tavern and later the Apollo Room, and gathering around himself a band of friends and younger admirers known as the 'tribe of Ben'. These tavern societies must have created convivial scenes: Jonson, surrounded by congenial companions, enjoying literary discussion but also food, drink and banter. However, after writing *The Devil is an Ass* (1616), and now in his mid-forties, Jonson left London in 1618 on an extraordinary expedition: to walk, by stages, to Edinburgh. The journey was undertaken perhaps partly to explore his Scottish roots (Jonson's father was of Scottish ancestry), perhaps partly to fulfil a wager. In Scotland he stayed with William Drummond of Hawthornden, who made notes of Jonson's opinions which were published in the eighteenth century. Drummond left us a vivid portrait of his guest:

> He is a great lover and praiser of himself, a contemner and scorner of others, given rather to lose a friend than a jest, jealous of every word and action of those about him (especially after drink, which is one of the elements in which he liveth) ... passionately kind and angry ... Oppressed with fantasy, which hath over-mastered his reason, a general disease in many poets.[34]

Jonson's appetites had also made him into a large man. We have seen that he was fascinated by characters like Sir Epicure Mammon and Ursula the pig-woman who were expansive in both their speech and their physiques. He now ruefully and endearingly referred to his own girth in several self-portraits, writing of 'My mountain belly, and my rocky face', and of 'rowling [my]selfe up and downe, like a tun'.[35]

Although he returned to London in 1619, Jonson did not write another play for the public stage until *The Staple of News* in 1626, which was followed by *The New Inn* (1629), *The Magnetic Lady* (1632), and *A Tale of a Tub* (1633). To put these in perspective, although Jonson was only eight years younger than Shakespeare, and has frequently been characterised as Shakespeare's contemporary, friend, and rival, Jonson was still writing plays 20 years after the last works of Shakespeare (who died in 1616), in the quite different cultural milieu of the 1630s. Some modern critics have seen Jonson's late plays as expressing nostalgia for the literature and culture of the Elizabethan court;[36] others have seen them as acutely attuned to contemporary events and issues, and as fresh departures in their movement away from city comedy and their experimentation with romance conventions (that is, fairytale-like qualities, as found in Shakespeare's late plays).[37] Nevertheless, they were not commercial successes, and in his later years Jonson often complained of financial hardship (though this might also have been caused by his liberal style of living). Some time in 1628 he was 'strucken with the palsy', probably a stroke.[38] He died in 1637, and was buried in Westminster Abbey. For reasons that remain somewhat mysterious, he was buried in a vertical (not horizontal) position, and not upright, but with his head pointing downwards.

We saw in chapter 4 that Shakespeare often reflected on his own art within his plays. Jonson was no less self-conscious about his art, but often set out his thinking more didactically, in prologues, inductions, and other kinds of ancillary texts. A Prologue for the revised 1616 folio edition of *Every Man in his Humour* stated his aspirations as a writer. He valued the reformation of his audiences above easy popularity: he 'hath not so lov'd the stage, / As he dare serve th'ill customes of the age'. He also aimed to write a model form of comedy that would set the standard for others: 'He rather prayes you will be pleas'd to see / One such, to day, as other playes should be'.[39] In statements such as these, Jonson's self-appointed role as arbiter of taste and morals can seem high-handed; but it is frequently endearingly offset by his crazed flights of linguistic invention, his fascination with the grotesque, and his resistance of neat retributive endings.

Since the eighteenth century Jonson has sometimes been un-favourably compared with Shakespeare. To some extent this is justified by the fact that Jonson himself knew Shakespeare well as a friend and rival, and clearly harboured complicated and contradictory feel-ings towards him. He declared that he 'loved the man, and do honour his memory – on this side idolatry – as much as any'; but also complained that Shakespeare wrote too easily, without sufficiently editing or controlling himself: 'he flowed with that facility, that sometime it was necessary he should be stopped'.[40] Jonson clearly measured himself against Shakespeare, and found Shakespeare's art wanting. In the 1616 Prologue to *Every Man In*, Jonson expresses contempt for special effects and blatant devices, in terms which put us in mind of Shakespeare: 'neither *Chorus* wafts you ore the seas; / Nor creaking throne comes downe, the boyes to please' (lines 15–16). His own aim was to depict 'deedes, and language, such as men doe use', and to 'shew an Image of the times' (lines 21, 23). Again he writes in *Every Man out of his Humour*:

> The argument of his *Comoedie* might have beene of some other nature, as of a duke to be in love with a countesse, and that countesse to bee in love with the dukes sonne, and the sonne to love the ladies waiting maid: some such crosse wooing, with a clowne to their servingman, better then to be thus neere, and familiarly allied to the time.[41]

Ultimately, statements like this reveal that evaluation of Jonson against Shakespeare is futile, since Jonson himself sets out a funda-mentally different conception of comedy: satirical, not romantic; holding up a mirror to show society its reality and its flaws. Judged by his own standards, he was undoubtedly a resounding success. His technical skill is unsurpassed, and all his plays, including his masques, engage incisively with their contemporary world. Moreover, in his assiduousness in overseeing the publication of his Works and fashioning his public voice, he did more than any other Renaissance dramatist to forge the modern idea of the professional author.

6

SEX AND DEATH: REVENGE TRAGEDY

A young woman is raped and mutilated by two brothers; in revenge, her father kills the two perpetrators, cooks them, and serves them in a pie to their mother (this is Shakespeare's *Titus Andronicus*, 1592–93). In another play, a decade later, a young man addresses the skull of his mistress, Gloriana, who was poisoned by a lecherous Duke because she resisted his advances. He in turn poisons the skull, dresses it up as a courtesan, and tricks the Duke into kissing it. The poison eats away the Duke's teeth and tongue as he dies in agony, while forced to overhear his illegitimate son and his wife profess their lust for one another and their hatred of him (this is Thomas Middleton's *Revenger's Tragedy* of 1606).[1] Elsewhere, another adulterous Italian duke cries out in torment after putting on a poisoned helmet; or, a Cardinal's discarded mistress kisses a poisoned Bible and dies (John Webster's *White Devil*, c.1612, and *Duchess of Malfi*, 1614).[2] Another young man, 'trimmed in reeking blood', bursts into a banquet with a human heart on the point of his dagger; it is the heart of his sister, who was pregnant with his child (John Ford, *'Tis Pity She's a Whore*, 1629–33).[3]

Such are the horrific and perverse spectacles presented by a prolific genre of Elizabethan and Jacobean tragedy which since the early twentieth century has been identified by critics as 'revenge tragedy' or 'the tragedy of blood'.[4] The first work in the genre was *The Spanish Tragedy* (c.1587) by Thomas Kyd, the dramatist whom

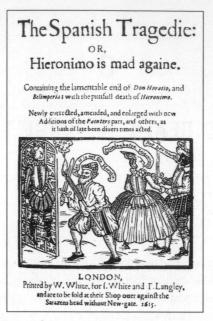

The Spanish Tragedie:
OR,
Hieronimo is mad againe.

Containing the lamentable end of *Don Horatio*, and
Belimperia ; with the pittifull death of *Hieronimo*.

Newly corrected, amended, and enlarged with new
Additions of the *Painters* part, and others, as
it hath of late been diuers times acted.

LONDON,
Printed by W. White, for I. White and T. Langley,
and are to be sold at their Shop ouer against the
Sarazens head without New-gate. 1615.

Title page of Thomas Kyd's *Spanish Tragedy*, showing Hieronimo's
discovery of his murdered son.

we encountered in chapter 3 sharing a writing-chamber with Marlowe
and giving evidence against him at around the time of his death.
After Kyd's groundbreaking play revenge tragedy was a prominent
feature of the Renaissance repertoire for more than four decades
until Ford's works of around 1630, and produced such masterpieces
as Shakespeare's *Hamlet* (1600) and Webster's *Duchess of Malfi*.
This chapter will seek to identify the defining characteristics of this
distinctive genre, and to account for its appeal.

GENERIC CONVENTIONS

To some extent revenge tragedy looked back to classical sources:
revenge had been a central theme and structuring principle in ancient
Greek tragedy, and came to sixteenth-century readers mainly via the
Roman tragedies of Seneca. Thomas Newton in 1581 edited a collected
volume of English translations of Seneca (some of which had also

been published earlier). However, Seneca's plays merely described gruesome acts of violence, rather than showing them on stage. One of the most arresting and characteristic features of English Renaissance revenge tragedy is the graphic depiction of mutilation and death.

In spite of their cruelty and gore, the varied and original forms in which death is inflicted in Elizabethan and Jacobean revenge tragedy are typified by a weird kind of satisfaction and even beauty in their ingenuity and stylisation. This is particularly so in the works of John Webster (*c*.1578–80–*c*.1638). As the eponymous heroine of his greatest play, *The Duchess of Malfi*, prepares to be murdered, she self-consciously muses on the aesthetics of death that are typical of the revenge-tragedy world: 'What would it pleasure me to have my throat cut / With diamonds? Or to be smothered / With cassia? Or to be shot to death with pearls? / I know death hath ten thousand several doors / For men to take their exits' (4.2.208–12). To some extent these torturous deaths, designed to prolong and display agony, reflect the real-life theatre of cruelty of the Elizabethan and Jacobean regimes. Traitors had their bodies broken on the rack, or were suspended from prison walls by manacles; at their public executions they were cut down from the gallows while not quite dead to be disembowelled and castrated. By such means the government staged its power, and it may be that such real-world practices desensitised sixteenth- and seventeenth-century audiences to violence on stage; or perhaps it was in some way therapeutic to see cruelties acted out in the relatively safe space of drama. Certainly the lurid violence of revenge tragedy is often separated from reality and framed by self-consciousness of its own artificiality.

Part of this self-conscious artifice is created by the prominence in the genre of plays-within-plays. These serve not merely to prick consciences, as in *Hamlet*, but often as the very means of fatal retribution: death by art, if you like, or death by performance. Ritualistic death-by-masque appears first in *The Spanish Tragedy* and recurs in various plays thereafter, including Thomas Middleton's *Women Beware Women* (*c*.1621). Middleton (1580–1627) was one of the most prolific and wide-ranging of Renaissance playwrights, particularly notable for his satirical sensibility, his dark and cynical vision of human nature, and his skill in expressing this in biting imagery and arresting dramatic spectacles (see chapter 7 below for discussion of his city comedies). *Women Beware Women*, one of his later plays and a relatively late revenge tragedy, seems sometimes like a knowing commentary on the genre. In its concluding masque, characters playing gods and goddesses enact their vendettas against each other with poisoned incense, flaming gold, trapdoors, Cupids firing arrows, and the relatively run-of-the-mill method of a poisoned cup. Needless to say their plots go awry, and several characters are unintentionally killed by their own devices. The ensuing confusion is as comical as it is tragical, and the spectating Duke speaks for the off-stage audience when he confesses 'I have lost myself in this quite' (5.1.180). The whole scene at once complies with and satirises the convention that death in revenge tragedy is a highly stylised and aestheticised affair.

Revenge tragedy litters the stage not only with corpses, but also with body-parts. In Webster's *Duchess of Malfi*, Duke Ferdinand comes to visit his sister, the Duchess of the title, in her prison. In the darkness he seems to offer her his hand, which she kisses, only to find as the light comes up that she is holding the severed hand of a corpse.[5] 'O horrible!' she understandably exclaims (4.1.53). Some have seen Webster as dealing in gratuitous horrors, but this dead hand is meaningful on several levels. Ferdinand claims, falsely, that it was taken from the body of the Duchess's husband, Antonio; in an attempt to drive her to despair, he shows her effigies which appear to be the corpses of Antonio and her children (4.1.56–60). In fact Antonio is still alive, but the dead hand and the false corpses foreshadow his imminent death, and the even more imminent death of the Duchess herself. At the same time Ferdinand's gesture with the dead hand embodies his own emotional coldness towards his sister, and the metaphorical dead hand of ancestral honour and patriarchal control with which he and his brother, the Cardinal, are attempting to oppress the Duchess and stifle the warmth and humanity of her love for her low-born husband and her children. Other body-parts in revenge tragedy include Gloriana's skull in *The Revenger's Tragedy* and the severed finger of her murdered fiancé presented to Beatrice-Joanna in *The Changeling* (1622); they are totemic objects, at once reminders of the departed dead and portents of deaths to come.

Ghosts, too, bring the past into the present, and connect memory with action. *Hamlet* is of course a revenge play, with just such a ghost coming back from the dead to incite his living heir to remember, to act, to deal out retributive death, and to embrace his own death.[6] Shakespeare is thought to have been partly inspired by an older *Hamlet* play, now lost, probably by Kyd; certainly in Kyd's surviving play, *The Spanish Tragedy*, the whole drama is framed by an avenging ghost who spectates and provides an embittered commentary on the action, complaining when retribution against his enemies seems to be proceeding too circuitously and slowly. *The Duchess of Malfi* has a different kind of ghost: after the Duchess's death in Act 4, she returns as a spectral echo in Act 5 scene 3 to intimate, riddlingly, to her husband that she is dead and his own death will soon follow. All these ghosts, though, share an overall role in revenge tragedy of the *memento mori*: a reminder to characters and audience alike of their essential and inevitable mortality.

Ferdinand's cruel trick with the dead hand is typical of a partic- ular stock character in revenge tragedy, the Machiavel. These scheming, ruthless villains were related less to the actual substance of Machiavelli's pragmatic political writings than to his reputation in England as an advocate of immorality and deviousness in affairs of state. Early examples included Kyd's Lorenzo (in *The Spanish Tragedy*) and Marlowe's Barabas and Mortimer Junior (in *The Jew of Malta*, c.1590, and *Edward II*, c.1592). Barabas is overtly presented as a disciple of Machiavelli, who speaks the prologue to the play, claims Barabas as his follower, and declares that 'I count religion but a childish toy / And hold there is no sin but ignorance'.[7] The Machiavel character commonly works in uneasy alliance with a tool- villain or malcontent, who puts into practice his master's ingenious plots to destroy his enemies; thus Lightborn, the sinister figure hired by Mortimer to murder Edward II, boasts:

> I learned in Naples how to poison flowers,
> To strangle with a lawn thrust through the throat,
> To pierce the windpipe with a needle's point,

> Or, whilst one is asleep, to take a quill
> And blow a little powder in his ears,
> Or open his mouth and pour quicksilver down.
> (5.4.31–6)

Edward II is not entirely classifiable as a revenge tragedy, but such characters clearly had a natural home in this genre. As they developed they became choric figures, disaffected and impoverished scholars struggling to find patronage and employment – much like many of the authors who created them – who cast a jaundiced eye over the sordid events around them. Vindice in *The Revenger's Tragedy* opens the play with an excoriating analysis of each member of the corrupt court as they process across the stage. He becomes their servant and pander, but will use the intimate access which this gains him in order to become their nemesis. As this implies, however, he becomes a somewhat compromised participant in the corrupt world that he is seeking to purge. This is even more true of Bosola in *The Duchess of Malfi*, who is at once the hired tormentor and murderer of the Duchess and the character with the deepest appreciation of her virtues. He aspires to the moral probity of a satirist, castigating the decadent creatures of the court that surround him, but his social insecurity forces him to abandon all integrity and commit the crimes of others. This makes him a conflicted and fascinating dramatic character, a cynic with a heart.

Characters under pressure are the main concern of revenge tragedy, and are central to its continuing appeal. Revenge is essentially a moral dilemma: should a wronged victim become an avenger, serving ancient honour codes to seek an eye for an eye and a tooth for a tooth? Or should he or she leave divine justice and the forces of human law to do their work? To seek vengeance may set in motion a chain of retribution and violence, as we see again and again in these plays. Yet if waiting for God or worldly authorities to take action appears fruitless, a victim is likely to feel compelled by grief and a sense of injury to take up the cause of revenge – even while painfully conscious that to do so may be to flout the laws of both heaven and earth. In the founding work of the genre, *The Spanish Tragedy*, these pressures produce outpourings of grief that became both popular and notorious on the Renaissance stage. Hieronimo mourns his murdered son: 'O eyes, no eyes, but fountains fraught with tears; / O life, no life, but lively form of death; / O world, no world, but mass of public wrongs, / Confused and filled with murder and misdeeds'.[8] This heightened rhetoric invites the audience to relish its artifice, and was easy to parody: by 1598, when Kyd's play was a decade or so old, Jonson made a foolish character in *Every Man in his Humour* a fan:

> Indeede, here are a number of fine speeches in this booke: *Oh eyes, no eyes but fountaines fraught with teares*; there's a conceit: Fountaines fraught with teares. *Oh life, no life, but lively forme of death*: is't not excellent? *Oh world, no world, but masse of publique wrongs*; O Gods mee: *confusde and fild with murther and misdeeds*. Is't not simply the best that ever you heard?[9]

Clearly Jonson means to mock, but this passage also tells us how very popular and familiar *The Spanish Tragedy* was over a long period. Indeed, Jonson himself, who acted for a time in his early career, seems to have played Hieronimo in the early 1590s, and some ten years on, in 1601 and 1602, accepted payments from Philip Henslowe for writing additions to this very play.[10] Henslowe's diary records twenty-nine performances of *The Spanish Tragedy* between 1592 and 1597 alone, and it continued in repertory through to the 1640s. This enduring success evidently owed much to the emotional appeal of its grieving protagonist; in fact it was often known simply as *Hieronimo*.

The moral and emotional pressures on Hieronimo drive him to madness, which became another stock feature of revenge tragedy. Ferdinand in *The Duchess of Malfi* has been consumed by lubricious obsession with his sister's sexuality; news of her death tips him over the brink of sanity into lycanthropia, which his doctor explains in a wonderfully macabre and surreal passage:

> In those that are possessed with't there o'erflows
> Such melancholy humour, they imagine
> Themselves to be transformèd into wolves,

Steal forth to churchyards in the dead of night,
And dig dead bodies up; as two nights since
One met the Duke, 'bout midnight in a lane
Behind Saint Mark's church, with the leg of a man
Upon his shoulder; and he howled fearfully;
Said he was a wolf, only the difference
Was a wolf's skin was hairy on the outside,
His on the inside.
    (5.2.8–18)

To sum up, the ingredients that characterised Elizabethan and Jacobean revenge tragedy and sustained its popularity over a long period included artful modes of death, dismembered body-parts, ghosts, ingenious villainy, moral ambivalence, emotional excess, and madness. Already by 1599 the genre was sufficiently formulaic to be parodied:

some damnd tyrant to obtaine a crowne,
Stabs, hangs, impoysons, smothers, cutteth throats,
And then a Chorus too comes howling in,
And tels us of the worrying of a cat,
Then of a filthie whining ghost,
Lapt in some fowle sheete, or a leather pelch,
Comes skreaming like a pigge halfe stuckt,
And cries *Vindicta*, revenge, revenge.[11]

However, the fact that its excess often tipped over into absurdity does not seem in any way to have affected the popularity of revenge tragedy; if anything, the opposite is true. Many revenge tragedies even acknowledge their own comic potential by moving towards self-parody, or incorporate comic elements in order to intensify their horrific effects.

UNEASY LAUGHTER

There is something ridiculous as well as sinister about the description of the lycanthropic Ferdinand in *The Duchess of Malfi*: a howling Duke with a dismembered leg slung over his shoulder. It is in keeping with Ferdinand's earlier tricks – while still nominally sane – with dead men's hands and corpse-effigies, which were a savage kind of practical joke. Revenge tragedy in fact often teeters on the brink of comedy. Criminals in *The Spanish Tragedy* and *The Revenger's Tragedy* jest and pun impudently on their way to the gallows, thinking they are going to be saved by a last-minute intervention by their confederates, only to discover abruptly that they are mistaken (*Spanish Tragedy*, 3.6; *Revenger's Tragedy*, 3.4). Such moments apply comic techniques of trickery, misunderstanding and mistiming to tragic situations. At other times, revenge tragedy is self-conscious about the comic potential of its tendency to excess, dealing as it does in deranged behaviour, inflated rhetoric, perverse spectacles of death, and piles of corpses. The bombastic style of *The Spanish Tragedy* lent itself to parody; subsequent plays often pre-empt mockery by engaging in self-parody. Thus the debauched courtly brothers of *The Revenger's Tragedy*, having failed to intercept the order for their brother's execution, receive his severed head in camp and farcical style:

AMBITIOSO: Whose head's that then?
OFFICER: His whom you left command for, your own brother's.
[*He takes the head from the bag and displays it*]
AMBITIOSO: Our brother's!
O furies!
SUPERVACUO: Plagues!
AMBITIOSO: Confusions!
SUPERVACUO: Darkness!
AMBITIOSO: Devils!
SUPERVACUO: Fell it out so accursedly?
AMBITIOSO: So damnedly?
SUPERVACUO [*to Officer*]: Villain, I'll brain thee with it.
OFFICER: O, my good lord.
   (4.1.72–7)

The above scene is likely to provoke in an audience a slightly queasy laughter, self-conscious of its own impropriety. A decade or so earlier Shakespeare had already explored the potential of uneasy laughter in *Titus Andronicus*, and indeed had pushed it much further, combining excessive horror with dark mirth to powerful effect. Titus has been confronted with the spectacle of his daughter Lavinia, who has been raped and whose tongue and hands have been amputated by her rapists. Titus's sons are about to be executed; he is told that if he cuts off his own hand and sends it to the king, they will be spared. He duly severs and sends his hand, but they are executed anyway, and a messenger returns with both the hand and their two heads. Titus's reaction is simply laughter: 'Ha, ha, ha!' It is one of the most shocking and disturbing moments in this notoriously shocking play. His brother asks 'Why dost thou laugh? It fits not with this hour.' Titus replies, 'Why, I have not another tear to shed' (3.2.263–4). Revenge tragedy understands the close proximity of horror and absurdity; its characters and situations are driven beyond the normal boundaries of decorum, and genre, to a place where grief and laughter meet in a profoundly uncomfortable blend. Its characteristic mode is the reckless embrace of extremity.[12]

WOMEN: HEROINES OR WHORES?

Revenge tragedy is also marked by strong interest in the characters and moral dilemmas of women, and by the complex views which it develops of the female sex. Webster, for instance, placed women at the centre of his two greatest plays, *The White Devil* and *The Duchess of Malfi*. In the first of these the heroine, Vittoria Corombona, is the 'white devil' of the title: not merely a fair villainess, but a compelling mixture of contradictory character traits. She is an adulteress who is implicated in murder, a woman of profound immorality, yet she wins the audience's admiration and even sympathy by means of her courage and rhetorical skill. In Webster's next work, the Duchess of Malfi breaks social codes in her forward wooing and in marrying her steward against the wishes of her male relatives, yet the audience cannot resist the endearing sincerity and warmth of her relationships with her husband and children, and her dignity and steadfastness in the face of persecution. The more her increasingly crazed brother torments her with corpse-effigies, a masque of madmen, and threats of painful death, the more noble and emotionally authentic she becomes, declaring 'I am Duchess of Malfi still' (4.2.134).

Revenge tragedy often celebrates strong women like these, and also develops sympathy for the way in which women are treated as commodities in a marriage-market. Isabella in *Women Beware Women*, for example, compelled by her father to marry a boorish and idiotic but wealthy suitor, laments, 'O, the heart-breakings / Of miserable maids where love's enforced! / . . . Men buy their slaves, but women buy their masters' (1.2.168–9, 178). Yet at the same time revenge tragedy also produces some of the most bitter misogyny to be found in Renaissance drama. Even the Duchess of Malfi, though generally presented as attractive and heroic, is made the victim of a coarse practical joke. To expose her first pregnancy, Bosola brings her early-ripened apricots to satisfy her cravings; she gorges herself on them, only to learn that they were ripened in horse-dung, and she leaves the stage to be sick. Her vomiting brings on her labour, and throughout the episode the pregnant female body seems to be viewed as an object of mockery and disgust (2.1.121–66). The main action of the play is punctuated by Bosola railing against women: 'There was a lady in France that, having had the smallpox, flayed the skin off her face to make it more level; and whereas before she looked like a nutmeg-grater, after she resembled an abortive hedgehog' (2.1.24–7). He upbraids an old lady for using cosmetics, and tells her, 'I would sooner eat a dead pigeon, taken from the soles of the feet of one sick of the plague, than kiss one of you fasting' (2.1.34–6).[13] In passages like these women are identified with the flesh, and are made to personify a moral equation, fundamental to revenge tragedy, between sex and death. Deep-rooted iconography reaching back to the Fall is invoked, as in a passage from *Women Beware Women*: 'When I behold a glorious dangerous strumpet / Sparkling in beauty, and destruction too, / Both at a twinkling, I do liken straight / Her beautified body to a goodly temple / That's built on vaults where carcasses lie rotting' (3.1.95–9).

Revenge tragedy, then, seems deeply divided and even self-contradictory in its view of women; yet it is undeniably fascinated by the female sex. Many of the most memorable scenes in the genre are profound explorations of women's moral dilemmas and inner turmoils. A powerful example is Beatrice-Joanna in *The Changeling* (1622) by Thomas Middleton and William Rowley. She pays her servant De Flores to murder the man to whom she is betrothed so that she can marry Alsemero, with whom she has fallen in love at first sight. De Flores has a badly blemished face, and is regarded by Beatrice-Joanna with violent disgust; when she drops a glove and he picks it up, she gives him the pair, saying, 'They touch my hand no more: / . . . Take 'em and draw thine own skin off with 'em' (1.1.232–4). She sees De Flores merely as an appropriate tool to carry out the dark deed of murder, and has no idea that there might be any further consequences for her. De Flores presents her with the dead man's severed finger, one of those bodily fragments charac-teristic of revenge tragedy which are laden with meaning and foreboding; in this case it is phallic as well as macabre. Beatrice is shocked, and when De Flores is offended by her attempts to pay him off, she can only reply, 'I understand thee not' (3.4.30, 70). When he further makes clear that he intends to deflower her, she feebly attempts to take refuge in feminine decorum, and in rank: 'Thy language is so bold and vicious / I cannot see which way I can forgive it / With any modesty . . . / Think but upon the distance that creation / Set 'twixt thy blood and mine, and keep thee there' (3.4.126–8, 133–4).

In this masterfully orchestrated scene, Beatrice-Joanna's hypocrisy and affectation turn De Flores, a vicious murderer and potential rapist, into a victim of injustice and the voice of truth and honesty, even as at the same time we feel her fear of this deeply sinister figure, and her desperation as she wriggles on a hook of her own making. Finally, she is forced to acknowledge that she is, as De Flores states, 'a woman steeped in blood' and 'the deed's creature' (3.4.129, 140); her actions have made them equals and bound them together irrevocably. From this point she is inexorably set on a pathway to hell, as she and De Flores become partners in further crimes. She ends the play with a devastating speech of self-loathing and self-annihilation, addressed to her father, in which she reduces herself to an agent of pollution and disease, to be expelled as mere bodily waste: 'O come not near me, sir. I shall defile you. / I am that of your blood was taken from you / For your better health. Look no more upon't, / But cast it to the ground regardlessly; / Let the common sewer take it from distinction' (5.3.149–53). Beatrice-

Joanna is represented in terms which clearly draw upon a misogynistic tradition of woman as duplicitous and prone to depravity; yet the psychological depth and complexity of her representation also create a compelling dramatic role.

Intense and impressive female roles like the ones discussed here become even more remarkable when we remember that they were played by boy actors, a phenomenon that will be discussed below in chapter 8.

WHY REVENGE TRAGEDY?

We may well feel a need to account in some way for the efflorescence of revenge on the Renaissance stage, and for the particular morbidity, sensationalism, and moral turbulence of this group of plays. Some have seen them as a reflection of the religious turmoils of the late sixteenth and early seventeenth centuries. It can be argued that they express a kind of Calvinist fatalism, a belief that each individual is inexorably predestined by divine decree to end up in heaven or hell, and that attempts to influence events by the exercise of individual will are delusory and doomed. This way of thinking seems to fit many of Middleton's tragedies, and also Webster's: the Duchess of Malfi dies with her eyes firmly upon heaven's gates, and is presumably one of the elect (4.2.224), whereas other characters die 'in a mist', in a state of blindness and confusion that suggests an opposite destination (*White Devil*, 5.6.259; *Duchess of Malfi*, 5.5.93). Vittoria in *The White Devil* declares that 'My soul, like to a ship in a black storm, / Is driven I know not whither' (5.6.247–8), while Bosola in *The Duchess* proclaims, 'O, this gloomy world! / In what a shadow, or deep pit of darkness, / Doth, womanish and fearful, mankind live!' (5.5.99–101).[14]

Certainly revenge plays evince a strong anti-Catholicism: they tend to be set in Italy or Spain and to feature adulterous and Machiavellian Cardinals. English Protestant vilification of Catholics as idolaters of the Whore of Babylon created a xenophobic reputation for Catholic courts and cities as dens of vice. This is amplified in these plays to produce a nightmarish fantasy-world of unbridled self-indulgence, ruthless self-advancement, and dark deeds of cruelty.[15]

Yet at the same time this may be read as a veiled commentary on the English court, especially in plays written after the accession of James I, who was regarded by some Protestants as over-friendly to Catholic nations in his foreign policy, and whose court was perceived as morally dissolute by comparison with Elizabeth's. A description by Sir John Harington of a masque performed in 1606 to entertain King James and his visiting brother-in-law, King Christian IV of Denmark, sounds uncannily like the over-blown and calamitous masque that ends *Women Beware Women* (as mentioned earlier), though in the real-life case the participants fell down drunk rather than dead. A lady playing the Queen of Sheba approached the two monarchs to present them with gifts, but tripped on the steps and fell on top of King Christian, covering his garments with her offerings of 'wine, cream, jelly, beverage, cakes, spices, and other good matters'. The king tried to dance with her but fell over, and was led away to lie down. Ladies representing Hope and Faith came next, but forgot their lines, and staggered away; Charity managed a few incoherent words, then rejoined Hope and Faith who were 'both sick and spewing in the lower hall'. Peace 'most rudely made war with her olive branch, and laid on the pates of those who did oppose her coming'. Harington clearly enjoyed the comedy of the spectacle, but at the same time, although himself hardly of an ascetic disposition, he sounded an admonitory note: 'we are going on, hereabouts, as if the devil was contriving every man shoud [*sic*] blow up himself, by wild riot, excess, and devastation of time and temperance'.[16]

More seriously, incidents like the murder of Sir Thomas Overbury did irrevocable damage to the reputation of the court. Overbury was a friend and confidant of James's favourite Robert Carr. Carr took as his mistress Frances Howard, Countess of Essex, and her marriage was annulled, on entirely unconvincing grounds, in proceedings which attracted much prurient interest. Carr married her, against Overbury's advice, and was raised by James to the title of Earl of Somerset. On James's orders, Overbury was consigned to the Tower of London, where he mysteriously died in September 1613. Rumours built up and in 1616 James was compelled to order an investigation, which found that Overbury had been poisoned on the Countess of Somerset's command, and that her husband had been involved in the plot. Royal authority itself was severely damaged by the scandal, not only because James's antipathy towards Overbury had been apparent, but also because the king's public behaviour towards Carr, ever since his rise to prominence in 1607, had made it obvious that he was infatuated with him, and now provoked a new wave of ribald comment.[17] It is far from unlikely, then, that plays such as *The Duchess of Malfi*, first performed in spring 1614 and opening with a procession of the leading figures of the court of Malfi which provokes caustic commentary, included a strong measure of reaction to the current state of the English court.[18] Antonio declares that 'a prince's court / Is like a common fountain, whence should flow / Pure silver drops in general; but if't chance / Some cursed example poison't near the head, / Death, and diseases through the whole land spread' (1.1.11–15).

Thus it is not difficult to find in revenge tragedies veiled critique of topical events. Jonathan Dollimore has gone further, finding in Renaissance tragedy an endemic radicalism: 'a subversive knowledge of political domination, a knowledge which interrogated prevailing beliefs, [and] submitted them to a kind of intellectual vandalism'.[19] For all its fantastical and nightmarish qualities, revenge tragedy can be understood as a response to ideological pressures in the real world of its time.

7

PLAYING WITH GENRE: CITY COMEDY, DOMESTIC TRAGEDY, TRAGICOMEDY

As we have seen, Renaissance playwrights always wrote with an awareness of generic conventions, whether they were keeping to the rules (as Jonson tended to do) or breaking them (as Shakespeare often did). Revenge tragedy was also a kind of generic hybrid, full of mordant wit, and often relying upon gruesome laughter for its most unsettling effects.

As Renaissance drama developed, generic experimentation and innovation became increasingly sophisticated. By the early seventeenth century, recognised genres included not only comedy and tragedy, but also historical drama and pastoral, and various mixed combinations of all of these. Polonius exaggerates only a little when he says that a good Renaissance playing company could offer 'tragedy, comedy, history, pastoral, pastorical-comical, historical-pastoral, tragical-historical, tragical-comical-historical-pastoral, scene individable or poem unlimited' (*Hamlet*, 2.2.379–82).

This chapter will explore some of the most significant subgenres of the late sixteenth and early seventeenth centuries, namely city comedy, domestic tragedy, and tragicomedy. Its purpose is to investigate how Renaissance playwrights stretched and mingled dramatic conventions and moulded them into new forms.

CITY COMEDY

While revenge tragedy may have included critique of the English court in the veiled form of Machiavel-ridden courts of Italy and Spain, other plays presented the citizens of London to themselves. This did not necessarily entail realism: Thomas Heywood's *The Four Prentices of London* (*c.*1594) showed four brothers, a mercer, a goldsmith, a haberdasher, and a grocer, who go on chivalric adventures ranging across Europe and even as far as Jerusalem. They win military glory and one of them gains the hand of a princess. Francis Beaumont parodied this type of story, which became popular in prose fiction as well as on stage, in his comedy *The Knight of the Burning Pestle* (1607). This is a sophisticated metadrama, opening with two disgruntled audience members, a London grocer and his wife, interrupting a performance of a play-within-the-play named *The London Merchant*. They demand that the performance should instead depict their apprentice, Rafe, as the hero of a series of fairy-tale-like episodes, suggested by them:

> WIFE: George, let Rafe travel over great hills, and let him be very weary, and come to the King of Cracovia's house, covered with velvet, and there let the king's daughter stand in her window, all in beaten gold, combing her golden locks with a comb of ivory, and let her spy Rafe, and fall in love with him.[1]

While ranging less far afield, Thomas Dekker's *Shoemaker's Holiday* (1599) also combined realism and romance (that is, fantastical qualities), using the streets and workshops of London as the setting for a Dick-Whittington-like plot of a shoemaker's rise to be Mayor, and a general celebration of urban festivity.

Jonson's humours plays worked rather differently, demonstrating the satirical potential of the urban scene and urban character-types. This was explored further not only in his own plays such as *The Alchemist* (1610) and *Bartholomew* Fair (1614), but also in the works of Thomas Middleton (1580–1627), one of the main proponents of city comedy (also known as 'citizen comedy'). Such plays were set among the real streets and landmarks of London and peopled by recognisable contemporary urban types, drawn mainly from the middling and lower classes: merchants, shopkeepers, and craftsmen; their wives, sons and daughters, and apprentices; and opportunists, petty criminals, and women of dubious virtue.

We encountered Middleton in chapter 6 as an author of revenge tragedy. He was a dramatist of notable range and achievement: Gary Taylor, the editor of Middleton's Collected Works for Oxford University Press, points out that he shares with Shakespeare alone the distinction of having created plays still considered masterpieces across all four genres of comedy, history, tragedy, and tragicomedy. Middleton was also the only playwright trusted by Shakespeare's company to adapt Shakespeare's plays after his death, and wrote successful plays for more different theatrical venues than any other of his contemporaries. Indeed, he had the biggest dramatic hit of the Renaissance period, the topical and controversial satire *A Game at Chess* (1624).[2] His achievement in writing both revenge tragedy and city comedy shows consistency as well as range, since these two genres share febrile energy and moral bleakness, and are equally characterised by complex plots driven by devious individuals in greedy pursuit of ambition, lust, and wealth.

A good example is Middleton's *A Chaste Maid in Cheapside* (1613), whose four interlocking plots make one of the most technically impressive of Renaissance plays. In the first plot, Yellowhammer, a goldsmith, is trying to marry his son Tim, a Cambridge student, to a Welsh heiress, and his daughter Moll to a wealthy knight, Sir Walter Whorehound. Meanwhile, in the second plot, Sir Walter has a mistress, Mrs Allwit, whose husband complacently allows Sir Walter to beget many illegitimate children with Mrs Allwit in return for a financial subsidy and a comfortable life. In the third plot, Touchwood Senior and his wife are forced to separate because he is so potent that she repeatedly falls pregnant, draining their finances. Incidentally, Touchwood's younger brother, Touchwood Junior, is in love with Moll Yellowhammer (from plot 1), and schemes to elope with her. Finally, Sir Oliver and Lady Kix are in despair because of their inability to conceive a child. This and the other plot impasses are conveniently resolved when Touchwood Senior offers to share with them a highly efficacious 'potion' that will make Lady Kix with child. He sleeps with Lady Kix and impregnates her; the Kixes pay him, enabling him to return to his wife; Sir Walter, who was the Kixes' heir, is disinherited, and thrown out by both the Allwits and the Yellowhammers; and Moll, after various vicissitudes, gets to marry her lover, Touchwood Junior.

This is more than just a virtuoso exercise in plotting: it also makes clear at every turn the inextricability of money and sex in London life. Marriage is all about money, both for middle-aged couples making sexual compromises in order to maintain themselves, and for young people whose parents try to trade them on the marriage market. Extra-marital sex is even more a matter of money, as is made starkly clear when Touchwood Senior is solicited for help by a 'wench' carrying a baby, fathered by him. He explains that he has nothing to give, and suggests that 'There's tricks enough to rid thy hand on't' (2.1.96). Two 'promoters' are introduced, officials charged with confiscating illicit meat during Lent. This brings another item into the equation between money and sex: flesh. Flesh, as in the sexualised body, is what everyone desires; flesh, as in meat, is craved by women made pregnant by sex; and flesh is what makes the promoters fat and rich, as they either seize meat for their own use or accept bribes to overlook it. The baby, too, the physical outcome of sex, is identified with flesh: the wench cunningly hides it in a basket, allows the promoters to think that it is smuggled mutton, and dumps it on them. The vignette entertains us as the grasping promoters get their come-uppance, but we hear their point of view too: 'SECOND PROMOTER: Life, had she none to gull but poor promoters / That watch hard for a living? / FIRST PROMOTER: Half our gettings must run in sugar-sops / And nurses' wages now' (2.2.172–5). We are left in no doubt that everyone is struggling to survive in this world of financial insecurity.

The well-oiled and intricate plot-mechanisms of city comedy suggest the fast-paced and acquisitive nature of urban life, while episodes like this give us snapshots of city characters and street practices. Another city comedy, *The Roaring Girl* (1611), which Middleton co-wrote with Thomas Dekker, even represented on stage a whole London street of shops, as a stage direction specifies:

The three shops open in a rank: the first a pothecary's shop, the next a feather shop, the third a sempster's shop. Mistress Gallipot in the first, Mistress Tiltyard in the next, Master Openwork and his wife in the third. To them enters Laxton, Goshawk, and Greenwit.

MISTRESS OPENWORK: Gentlemen, what is't you lack? What is't you buy? See fine bands and ruffs, fine lawns, fine cambrics. What is't you lack, gentlemen, what is't you buy?

(3.1–4)

The scene exploits the inherent theatricality of an urban shopping street: the shops are places of display, where traders perform in order to attract attention and sales, while customers make public displays of their wealth and taste. Jack Dapper, a Jacobean dandy, announces that he intends to spend at least an hour choosing the right feather for his hat; it must be spangled, but ahead of the general fashion (3.154–62, 225–6). Meanwhile, the depiction of three shops side-by-side enables dramatic counterpoint between three parallel scenes; and each shop also has a front-of-house and back-of-house, a division between public and private space, which facilitates plots of seduction and deceit.

In chapter 5 we saw that in the Prologue to *The Alchemist* Jonson drew attention to its London setting, and that the action of the play was precisely set in the Blackfriars district, where the play was performed at the Blackfriars playhouse. In many ways it seems appropriate to think of city comedies as holding up a mirror to their audiences and to the real urban world that they inhabited. In the case of *The Roaring Girl* the relation between the play and reality seems particularly close, since the cross-dressing, free-wheeling female character of the title, Moll Cutpurse, was based on a real and notorious London character, Mary Frith. Frith herself even appears to have performed a song on the stage of the Fortune playhouse where *The Roaring Girl* was staged.[3] However, the relation between the plays and the real lives of their audiences may have been a little more complex than just reflection and symmetry. For one thing, a number of early city comedies were first performed by boys' companies at private theatres, and may therefore represent a stylised version of

Moll Cutpurse, from the title page of *The Roaring Girl* by Thomas Middleton and Thomas Dekker, 1611.

middle- and lower-class London that was presented to elite spectators for their entertainment.[4] Moreover, even in later plays like *The Roaring Girl*, there is evidence of some gaps between the stage-world and the world of the audience. One scene showcases 'canting', the supposed street-slang of lowlife criminals and vagabonds. A character named Trapdoor demonstrates: 'Ben mort, shall you and I heave a booth, mill a ken, or nip a bung? And then we'll couch a hogshead under the ruffmans, and there you shall wap with me, and I'll niggle with you'. Moll Cutpurse translates: 'good wench . . . shall you and I rob a house, or cut a purse? . . . and then we'll lie under a hedge'. Wapping and niggling, unsurprisingly, are indecent suggestions (10.192–218). This may look like documentary representation of urban culture; yet Trapdoor's and Moll's canting dialogue is a performance, and evidently required translation for the audience, supporting other evidence that canting may to some extent have been a literary invention.

In fact the relative realism of city comedy often incorporates various less than realistic features. It seems that the real Mary Frith was already to some extent a focus of urban myth even before *The Roaring Girl* was written, and the play takes this further, depicting Moll Cutpurse as a benevolent folkloric outlaw who sorts out everyone's problems, like a metropolitan Robin Hood or fairy godmother. In many city comedies young lovers use tricks and the help of friends to fight off the dragons and giants of avaricious parents and grasping old suitors so that love wins out in the end. City comedy turns city life into drama, and in so doing mythologises and idealises as well as satirising. Despite their apparent cynicism and gritty realism, Middleton's city comedies are less of a departure from *The Four Prentices of London* and the chivalric adventures of its citizen-heroes than might at first sight appear. Middleton's plays too, though in more subtle ways, make use of fantastical romance ingredients.

DOMESTIC TRAGEDY

City comedy, then, could accommodate fantastical elements, but nevertheless was based in an idea of urban realism. Another genre which purported to represent real or realistic settings and events was 'domestic tragedy', a genre defined in 1943 by H.H. Adams. This group of plays is characterised by native, bourgeois, homely settings and characters.[5] They are not without lurid elements, depicting sexual crimes and murders, but these are set in the humdrum households of sturdy English citizens. Whereas city comedy is much concerned with the latest trends in metropolitan dress, speech, and manners, domestic tragedy is generally set in provincial towns or rural households, in settings that must have appeared to London audiences distinctly unfashionable and even backward. It was thus a departure both from the metropolitan scene of city comedy, and from the exotic Italian and Spanish courtly settings of revenge tragedy, and indeed from the principles of classical tragedy, in which protagonists possessed both high birth and heroic greatness.

The earliest such play is the anonymous *Arden of Faversham* (1592), which concerns the murder of Arden by two villains, Black Will and Shakebag, hired by Mistress Arden and her lover Mosby. It was based on a real murder case of 1551 that had been related in Holinshed's *Chronicles*. Other domestic tragedies include *A Warning for Fair Women* (anonymous, published 1599), which similarly concerned adultery and murder, and *A Yorkshire Tragedy* (1606, probably by Middleton), which related the murder of two young children by their father in a violent fit of rage. Both of these plays were based on sensational real cases which had been reported in pamphlets; they are related to an emergent news-culture and a taste for real-life, close-to-home scandal.

A Woman Killed With Kindness (1603) by Thomas Heywood (?1574–1641) is a slightly different case since it drew on literary sources, most notably William Painter's *Palace of Pleasure* (1566–7), a very popular and influential collection of *novelle* (racy short stories with Italian and French sources); this furnished the sub-plot and some ingredients of the main plot.[6] Yet Heywood adapted these literary sources to the rural English scene and plain style of domestic tragedy, and in so doing created a masterpiece of the genre. In the main plot, John Frankford marries Anne, and soon afterwards befriends Wendoll, inviting him to share his home. In John's absence, Wendoll seduces Anne and initiates an affair. Frankford discovers them in bed together, but instead of killing Anne outright – as the play makes clear he is expected and entitled to do – he decides to 'kill her with kindness', by banishing her to another manor house that he owns, separating her from their children, and vowing never to see her again. Full of remorse, Anne starves herself to death, and in so doing becomes a saintly figure who is reconciled with her husband on her deathbed. Meanwhile, in the subplot, Sir Charles Mountford falls into debts, and Sir Francis Acton, who is attracted to Mountford's sister Susan, pays them off in order to compel Mountford to give Susan to him as his wife.

Clearly the play has much to say about the complicated relations between women and property in this period. When Frankford claims Wendoll as his friend and companion, he urges him to 'use my table and my purse, / They are yours', and tells his wife, 'Prithee Nan, / Use him with all thy loving'st courtesy'.[7] Anne herself tells Wendoll, after Frankford's departure on business, that her husband left instructions for his friend 'To make bold in his absence and command / Even as himself were present in the house, / For you must keep his table, use his servants, / And be a present Frankford in his absence' (6.75–8). Anne was legally her husband's possession; the play therefore poses a question as to how far hospitality extends, and whether in enjoying all the comforts of Frankford's house, Wendoll might not naturally be tempted to enjoy his wife as well. Anne's own feelings in the matter remain somewhat opaque, as befits a piece of property: when Wendoll declares his love for her, she briefly resists, but then succumbs with the indecipherable words 'O Master Wendoll, O' (6.151). Meanwhile, in the sub-plot, Mountford is unable to countenance losing the house which 'successively / Hath 'longed to me and my progenitors / Three hundred year' (7.15–17). Rather than give up 'This virgin title never yet deflowered' (7.23) he 'trick[s]' up his sister in a wedding dress and jewels, and offers her to Acton to rape or marry as he pleases, despite Susan's fervent protestations that she would rather her brother 'Rip up my breast, and with my bleeding heart / Present him as a token' (14.1, 58–9).

Anne's body, in particular, is closely identified with her husband's house. Frankford, having been informed of his wife's infidelity by a servant, has copies of the house-keys made by pressing them into wax. This gesture is redolent of sexual ownership and invokes the proverbial association in this period between wax and women's moral pliancy (compare Viola in *Twelfth Night*: 'How easy is it for the proper false / In women's waxen hearts to set their forms!', 2.2.27–8). Frankford lays a trap for Wendoll and Anne by appearing to ride away on business, then returning secretly at night to catch them in bed together. As he unlocks and enters each portal of the house – 'This is the key that opes my outward gate; / This is the hall door; this my withdrawing chamber' (13.8–9) – these too are sexually charged actions, as he re-asserts his possession of both his wife's body and his household by means of an act of re-penetration.

The play is thus deeply interested in the meanings and materiality of domestic space. The house is vividly realised as the setting for the main events, from the opening communal festivities of Frankford and Anne's wedding celebration, to jocular below-stairs scenes among the servants, to the nocturnal exposure of the lovers. Several scholars have even seen the house as itself one of the principal characters.[8] It is certainly a living space, with its physical detail and social rituals precisely evoked by the stage directions: 'Enter three or four servingmen, one with a voider[9] and a wooden knife[10] to take away all, another the salt and bread, another the table-cloth and napkins, another the carpet. Jenkin with two lights after them' (8.0 s.d.). As Frankford enters to receive the revelation of Anne's adultery, he is specified to be 'as it were brushing the crumbs from his clothes with a napkin, and newly risen from supper' (8.22 s.d.). The news he is about to hear is all the more shocking against this backdrop of recognisable, ordinary, everyday life.

In keeping with this domesticity of setting, the language of the play is also pared-back and plain. The prologue sets the tone: 'Look for no glorious state, our muse is bent / Upon a barren subject, a bare scene' (0.3–4). We are alerted to 'Our poet's dull and earthy muse' (0.11). Accordingly, there is very little figurative language or elaborate rhetoric; instead the style is often almost primitive in its simplicity, yet this creates a ruggedness and restraint which is often intensely moving. As Frankford banishes Anne from the house, he says, 'Come, take your coach, your stuff; all must along. / Servants and all make ready, all be gone. / It was thy hand cut two hearts out of one' (13.184–6). The shift from practical instructions to a terse statement of blame suggests a deep hinterland of pent-up agony and fury. Similarly, just before she dies, Anne is asked, in the manner of commonplace conversation, 'How do you feel yourself?' She answers simply 'Not of this world' (17.113–14), conveying in just four brief words her mortal weakness, her pious purgation of her guilty flesh by self-starvation, and an ethereal other-worldliness as she becomes almost a living ghost.

The moral themes of the play are also less simple than first appearances might suggest. Adams wrote of the sermonising qualities of domestic tragedy, and there are elements of this in *A Woman Killed With Kindness*: Anne, for instance, having been caught in adultery, admonishes, 'O women, women, you that have yet kept / Your holy matrimonial vow unstained, / Make me your instance' (13.142–4). Frankford is praised by other characters for his kindness and mildness towards his erring wife. Yet at the same time the play seems to question the virtue of kindness. Frankford adopts this policy because 'I'll not martyr thee, / ... but with usage / Of more humility torment thy soul, / And kill thee, even with kindness' (13.154–7). His intention is to destroy Anne more effectively than with the sword, while retaining the moral high ground; this is clearly kindness as cruelty. It seems especially questionable given that arguably it was Frankford's own reckless kindness to Wendoll that pushed the lovers towards adultery in the first place. In the sub-plot, it is Acton's apparent kindness to Mountford in paying off his debts that places Mountford under obligation and compels him to prostitute his sister. Mountford laments: 'His kindness like a burden hath surcharged me, / And under his good deeds I stooping go, / Not with an upright soul' (14.63–5). Kindness is exposed as potentially an extreme form of oppression. Thus *A Woman Killed With Kindness* uses the confined scale and familiar world of the domestic to explore troubling and provocative themes.

TRAGICOMEDY

Even the sombre emotional landscape of *A Woman Killed With Kindness* has comic moments, as down-to-earth servants quarrel, dance, and make wry comments on the main action. As discussed in chapter 4, in the 1580s Sir Philip Sidney deplored the mingling of 'kings and clowns' and 'hornpipes and funerals' which he thought made 'neither right tragedies, nor right comedies'.[11] We have now seen, however, that over the decades which followed Sidney's death in 1586 English dramatists boldly experimented with the mingling of comic and tragic materials. Revenge tragedy, for instance, depended for some of its most troubling and dramatic effects upon comic ingredients, while city comedy often shared the bleak and cynical world-view of revenge tragedy.

Moreover, by the early seventeenth century tragicomedy had become a recognised and valued genre in its own right. English writers became aware of the Italian author Giovanni Battista Guarini (1538–1612), who had written a pastoral tragicomedy called *Il Pastor Fido* (*c*.1585) and a defence of this genre, *Compendio Della Poesia Tragicomica* (1601). In the latter Guarini explained that he who makes a tragicomedy does not intend to compose separately either a tragedy or a comedy, but from the two a third thing that will be perfect of its kind and may take from the others the parts that with most verisimilitude can stand together ... [Tragicomedy] is the mingling of tragic and comic pleasure, which does not allow hearers to fall into excessive tragic melancholy or comic relaxation ... And truly if today men understood well how to compose tragicomedy (for it is not an easy thing to do), no other drama should be put on the stage, for tragicomedy is able to include all the good qualities of dramatic poetry and to reject all the bad ones.[12]

Tragicomedy, then, could facilitate the representation of truth, subvert audience expectations, and produce sophisticated modulations of mood and tone. It could be understood as something more sophisticated than, say, the alternation of tragic and comic scenes, or a play which begins with tragic potential then ends happily (John Florio, for instance, in 1598 had defined tragicomedy as 'halfe a tragedie, and halfe a comedie').[13] Instead it could be a 'third thing', suspended somewhere between tragedy and comedy. As such, Guarini suggested, it was not merely a legitimate and independent genre, but perhaps even the highest of genres.

Meanwhile, as we saw in chapter 4, Shakespeare was increasingly experimenting with transgressions of generic boundaries. The 'problem plays' *Measure for Measure* (1604) and *All's Well That Ends Well* (1605) each swerved from a tragic trajectory to a comic ending, while he introduced a Fool into a tragedy in *King Lear* (1605). His 'late plays' or 'romances' like *The Winter's Tale* (1610) and *The Tempest* (1611) moved further towards the 'third thing' commended by Guarini, offering a more sustained exploration of a mixed mood, neither comic nor tragic but poised unsettlingly somewhere between the two. This ambiguous tone dominates much of the action, and creates beneath the nominally happy endings undercurrents of loss and of problems still unresolved.

Meanwhile John Fletcher (1579–1625) wrote *The Faithful Shepherdess* (*c.*1608–09), a pastoral tragicomedy strongly influenced by Guarini. It was a failure on stage, but Fletcher used a preface to the published edition to offer an explanation of his generic intentions:

'A tragi-comedie is not so called in respect of mirth and killing, but in respect it wants [i.e. lacks] deaths, which is inough to make it no tragedie, yet brings some neere it, which is inough to make it no comedie'.[14] Shakespeare's three final works, after his sole-authored late plays, were collaborations with Fletcher: *Henry VIII* (also known as *All is True*, 1612), the lost play *Cardenio* (1612–13), and *The Two Noble Kinsmen* (1613). The two of these plays that survive create an ongoing mood of moral and emotional ambiguity, in which particular moments provoke conflicting responses. In *The Two Noble Kinsmen*, for instance, the Jailer's Daughter runs mad for love of Palamon. Her deranged behaviour combines bawdy with pathos in a manner that recalls Ophelia, but sometimes tends more towards comic absurdity. A Doctor advises that sex will cure her; encouraged by him and the girl's father, a Wooer courts her by pretending to be Palamon. He succeeds, and her story ends like this:

> DOCTOR: Let's get her in.
> WOOER [*to the JAILER'S DAUGHTER*]:
>   Come, sweet, we'll go to dinner,
> And then we'll play at cards.
> JAILER'S DAUGHTER: And shall we kiss too?
> WOOER: A hundred times.
> JAILER'S DAUGHTER: And twenty.
> WOOER: Ay, and twenty.
> JAILER'S DAUGHTER: And then we'll sleep together.
> DOCTOR [*to the WOOER*]:   Take her offer.
> WOOER [to the JAILER'S DAUGHTER]:
> Yes, marry, will we.
> JAILER'S DAUGHTER: But you shall not hurt me.
> WOOER: I will not, sweet.
> JAILER'S DAUGHTER: If you do, love, I'll cry. *Exeunt.*
>   (5.4.107–112)

Is this a conventional happy ending in marriage, or a tragic misunderstanding? Is it a comical trick of disguise, or a tragic act of deception? A cure, or an appalling act of exploitation, even a rape?

The audience is likely to feel all these jarring responses at once, creating a profoundly uncertain mood.

Fletcher went on to become the principal playwright of the King's Men after Shakespeare, and by his own death in 1625 had written or had a hand in over 50 plays, many of them written with Francis Beaumont or other collaborators, and many of them tragicomedies. It has been asserted that 'tragicomedy was arguably the single most important dramatic genre of the period 1610–50'.[15] There is agreement, however, that the term was broad, continuing to encompass tragic plays with comic endings as well as those in a sustained mixed mood. Some tragicomedies used pastoral settings and Italianate influences to appeal to a mainly courtly audience, whereas others drew more upon Spanish chivalric romance. What all Jacobean and Caroline tragicomedies shared, however, was a certain edginess which was artistically productive and which extended English drama's persistent fascination with breaking generic boundaries.

We have seen that Renaissance authors and audiences had an advanced understanding of the rules of genre, and of how these could be broken, played with, and used to create hybrid works of great originality and ingenuity. The history of Renaissance drama is often a story of the mingling of comedy and tragedy, realism and romance, and of diverse generic variants, combinations, and inventions. It was often in the places where apparently opposed genres met that Renaissance playwrights created their most innovative and compelling works.

8

PLAYING WITH GENDER: BOY ACTORS, FEMALE PERFORMERS, FEMALE DRAMATISTS

Renaissance England was in a state of ideological ferment in relation to sexuality and gender. We saw in chapter 3 that Marlowe
explored homoeroticism in his works and was rumoured to be a
lover of boys, and that such charges were made as part of general
denigrations of this author as an atheist and a dangerously seditious
thinker. Sodomy was a capital offence, and yet the classical literature and art that were such important sources and influences were
full of images of lovely boys and same-sex desire. Meanwhile women
were represented by boys in the public playhouses, avoiding what
was deemed to be immodest self-exposure by women, but potentially foregrounding the androgynous boy heroine as simply another
kind of troubling object of desire. Women themselves were enjoined
by conduct-books – manuals of correct godly behaviour – to be
chaste, silent and obedient; yet from 1558 to 1603 England was
ruled by a queen who was a consummate performer and a very
public example of independent female will. Daughters of royal and
aristocratic families received an impressive humanist education in
languages, literature, and rhetoric, yet moralists condemned authorship and publication by women as unfeminine and improper. As we
saw in chapter 6 in relation to revenge tragedy, Renaissance culture
often expressed a complex and self-contradictory view of women,
alternating between celebrating their nobility of character and vilify-
ing them for embodying sexual temptation. These many tensions

and cultural cross-currents were played out on stage and in dramatic writings.

In the playhouses, boy-heroine roles often involved cross-dressing in which the female character adopted male disguise, creating possibilities for the exploration not only of same-sex desire but also of the ambiguity of gender identity, and even implying that it was merely a matter of performance rather than of an individual's essential being. Meanwhile, women were not absent from dramatic activity. Although they did not act in the commercial playhouses, they did perform at court and in aristocratic households. Several women also translated and wrote plays, in so doing often using drama to reflect upon the social position of women and the nature of female heroism. This chapter will explore how the participation of boys and women in Renaissance drama exposed fault-lines in contemporary ideologies of gender and sexuality, and thereby created highly charged and innovative works.

BOYS PLAYING WOMEN

One of the most widely known facts about Renaissance drama is that at the public playhouses female roles were taken by boy actors, usually aged between around ten and eighteen. There was no law against women appearing on stage; it was simply a social convention which appears to have been universally accepted and upheld. However, even if there was general assent that women should not act in public, their representation by boys was far from uncontroversial. As we learned in chapter 1, the opening of the first commercial playhouses in the 1570s provoked condemnation from Puritan writers like John Northbrooke, Stephen Gosson and Phillip Stubbes. One of Gosson's chief objections was that the impersonation of women by boys dangerously blurred the boundaries of gender:

> The Law of God very straightly[1] forbids men to put on womens garments, garments are set downe for signes distinctive betwene sexe and sexe, to take unto us those garments that are manifest signes of another sexe, is to falsifie, forge, and adulterate, contrarie to the expresse rule of the worde of God.[2]

For Gosson, costume was not merely an outside; it had the troubling power to change and corrupt the inner being of the wearer. Stubbes, meanwhile, complained about playhouse practices as follows:

> such wanton gestures, such bawdie speaches: such laughing and fleering: such kissing and bussing: such clipping and culling: Suche winckinge and glancinge of wanton eyes, and the like is used, as is wonderfull to behold. Than these goodly pageants being done, every mate sorts to his mate, every one bringes another homeward of their way verye freendly, and in their secret conclaves (covertly) they play the *Sodomits,* or worse.[3]

Elsewhere in his tract Stubbes uses the term 'sodomy' to refer to fornication and adultery between men and women, but it seems likely that in this passage he meant to include sex between men; it was certainly taken in this sense by William Prynne, a couple of generations later, who wrote *Histrio-Mastix* (1633), a work arguing 'That popular stage-playes ... are sinfull, heathenish, lewde, ungodly spectacles, and most pernicious corruptions'.[4] Prynne cites Stubbes as an authority:

> Yea witnes ... M[aster] *Stubs,* his *Anatomy of Abuses* ... where he affirmes, that Players and Play-haunters in their secret conclaves play the Sodomites: together with some moderne examples of such, who have beene desperately enamored with Players Boyes thus clad in womans apparell, so farre as to sollicite them by words, by Letters, even actually to abuse them. (pp. 211–12)[5]

Attacks like these drew forth defences. Thomas Heywood, author of *A Woman Killed with Kindness* and, by his own estimate, writer of or contributor to no fewer than 220 plays (see chapter 2 above), published *An Apology for Actors* in 1612. Interestingly, he attributed less power to theatre than did its detractors, denying its ability to transform boys into women (or woman-like objects of male lust):

> Yea (but say some) you ought not to confound the habits of either sex, as to let your boyes weare the attires of virgins, &c. ... But to

see our youths attired in the habit of women, who knowes not what their intents be? who cannot distinguish them by their names, assuredly knowing, they are but to represent such a Lady, at such a time appoynted?[6]

Heywood attributes imagination to the playhouse audiences, and an ability to discriminate between reality and theatrical illusion. Two passages from the works of Lady Mary Wroth (1587?–1651/1653) support Heywood's view. Wroth was a member of the Sidney family, arguably the most accomplished literary dynasty of the English Renaissance. She had extensive experience of drama: she performed in masques at court; she was an important patron to Ben Jonson, who dedicated *The Alchemist* to her; and she wrote her own play, *Love's Victory* (see below). In 1621 she published the first prose romance in English by a woman, *The Countess of Montgomery's Urania*, which included an observation on boy actors. A male character who is pursued by a sexually domineering woman is said to be 'unmoveable' and 'no further wrought, then if he had seene a delicate play-boy acte a loving womans part, and knowing him a Boy, lik'd onely his action'.[7] This implies that boys playing women have gestural skills that are aesthetically pleasing, but are emotionally unconvincing. Wroth then wrote a manuscript sequel to the *Urania*, in which she described a duplicitous and overbearing woman as

> for her over-acting fashion more like a play-boy dressed gawdely up to shew a fond, loving, woemans part then a great Lady; soe busy, so full of taulke, and in such a sett formallity, with soe many framed lookes, fained smiles, and nods, with a deceiptfull downe-cast looke, insteed of purest modesty and bashfulness.[8]

For Wroth, the boy playing a woman stands for affectation and inauthenticity.

This selection of contemporary views suggests a wide range of response to boy-players: for Gosson they become female, or at least hermaphroditic, when they put on female clothing; for Heywood they become female characters when they act, but only temporarily and by means of the audience's assent to the illusion; but for Wroth they are mere posers, unable to portray women convincingly. If we turn to Renaissance plays themselves for evidence of the dramatic effects of boy-players, the evidence is similarly contradictory. On the one hand Renaissance drama contains so many richly drawn female roles, where indeed womanliness is often very much to the fore, and these suggest that many boy actors must have been highly gifted at representing women. Examples include Titania in *A Midsummer Night's Dream*, Gertrude in *Hamlet*, Hermione in *The Winter's Tale*, the Duchess of Malfi, Beatrice-Joanna in *The Changeling*, and many more. For each of these plays to succeed it seems essential that the audience should have believed in these female characters as women. Presumably audiences who were accustomed to the impersonation of women by boys willingly suspended their disbelief and accepted these figures as female for the duration of the play. In fact we have an example of a Jacobean playgoer who was evidently engaged and moved in just this way. A spectator at a performance of *Othello* by the King's Men at Oxford in 1610 particularly praised the boy who played Desdemona:

> [N]ot only by their speech but by their deeds they drew tears. – But indeed Desdemona, killed by her husband, although she always acted the manner very well, in her death moved us still more greatly; when lying in bed she implored the pity of those watching with her countenance alone.[9]

The telling details of this passage are the female pronouns, as the boy actor *becomes* Desdemona for this enthralled audience-member.

In other cases, however, female roles may have gained an extra frisson from the audience's awareness of the boy within the costume. The defeated Cleopatra, imagining how Octavius will lead her in triumph through Rome and humiliate her, foresees that 'The quick comedians / Extemporally will stage us, and present / Our Alexandrian revels. Antony / Shall be brought drunken forth, and I shall see / Some squeaking Cleopatra boy my greatness / I'th'posture of a whore' (*Antony and Cleopatra*, 5.2.212–17). It is difficult to know how to read this moment. In the Renaissance playhouse, did the mention of a boy actor draw attention to the fact that Cleopatra was, in fact, at this very moment being impersonated on stage by a boy, perhaps raising an ironic laugh? Or did this mention of an imaginary incompetent boy actor conceal the real, skilful boy playing Cleopatra even deeper within his costume, assuming and enhancing the audience's belief in him as the 'real' Cleopatra? Was it even perhaps possible to sustain both these apparently contradictory responses at once?

Even less obviously self-conscious moments could touch on gender in a way which had a similarly ambiguous effect. When Lady Macbeth called on evil spirits to 'unsex me here ... And take my milk for gall', were Renaissance audiences aware that the figure speaking was already a boy-woman of uncertain gender (*Macbeth*, 1.5.39–46)? Or did the idea of 'unsexing' rely upon, and reinforce, their acceptance that this was a definitely female figure now wilfully disrupting conventions of gender? When Webster's Duchess of Malfi went into labour and had to be rushed off stage to give birth, was the comic grotesqueness of the moment intensified by the audience's awareness that this was a boy impersonating a heavily pregnant woman, or was this awareness suppressed in willing submission to the fiction of the play? These are perplexing questions which it may not be possible to answer at a distance of four centuries from the original performers and spectators, and they remind us that the Renaissance experience of public theatre was in this respect essentially different from our own. There have been some recent productions that have experimented with all-male casts, but fascinating as these are, they cannot have the same effect as original Elizabethan and Jacobean productions in their own time, since we bring to them a completely different mentality. Modern all-male productions in the professional theatre are self-consciously exceptional and experimental; we do not go to a play in an expectation that women will always be played by men. Although we can perhaps sometimes get near to this Elizabethan and Jacobean experience in settings like boys-only schools, boys playing women are not part of our usual experience of drama. Modern professional productions which have made the provocative choice of all-male casting also inevitably bring into play modern attitudes to homosexuality, which, as we saw in chapter 3, was not named or understood in the same way in the sixteenth and seventeenth centuries. When looking back at Renaissance drama, then, perhaps the most we can say with certainty is that the use of boy-actors in female roles created opportunities for sophisticated play not only with gender and sexuality, but also with the illusionism of theatre.

BOYS PLAYING WOMEN PLAYING BOYS

It seems more obvious that Renaissance audiences had some metadramatic awareness of the boy behind the female role when we turn to the many cases of cross-dressed heroines in Renaissance drama. Michael Shapiro has identified no fewer than 79 such plays between 1570 and 1642.[10] Cross-dressing required boys dressed as women to dress as boys, thus casting attention onto their under-lying gender, but also arguably going beyond this to explore the fluidity and arbitrariness of gender-identity. Indeed, cross-dressing heroines were far from being merely a dramatic expedient to make boy-actors more comfortable and natural in their roles; they were rife in non-dramatic Renaissance culture, suggesting an endemic interest in the flexibility of boundaries of gender identity and in their potential for transgression.

Even before the Renaissance, there was a tradition of saints' lives in which a holy woman disguised herself as a man in order to preserve her chastity and seclude herself in monastic life.[11] Chivalric romance and romantic epic then developed traditions of the warrior-woman, whose armour often represents militant chastity, and the female page, who disguises herself as a boy in order to accompany her beloved on his adventures. In England, Sidney and Spenser worked variations on these themes: Sidney's *New Arcadia* (published 1590) includes a warrior-woman in the person of Parthenia, who disguises herself as a knight in order to avenge her husband's death, and a love-lorn female page, Zelmane, who disguises herself as a boy in order to serve her beloved Pyrocles on his quests.[12] In Spenser's *Faerie Queene* (1590) Britomart, a virtuous virgin questing in search of her true love, is the armed warrior-woman. Meanwhile, many shorter works of non-dramatic fiction also included cross-dressed heroines. Barnabe Riche's *Farewell to Military Profession* (1581) was a collection of *novelle* – a genre of short fictions, often about clever devices or scandalous behaviour in love affairs, derived from Italian and French sources. Riche included several stories of cross-dressing, among them 'Apolonius and Silla', the source for *Twelfth Night*. Thomas Lodge's *Rosalynde* (1590) placed a cross-dressing heroine in a pastoral setting, and gave Shakespeare the source for *As You Like It*. Cross-dressing women were all over the place in Renaissance literature, even in lyric poetry, where John Donne implored his lover 'Be my true mistress still, not my feigned page'. He fears that if she travels with him in male dress, 'Men of France . . . Will quickly know thee, and know thee' (that is, sexually), while 'Th'indifferent Italian, as we pass / His warm land, well content to think thee page, / Will hunt thee with such lust, and hideous rage, / As Lot's fair guests were vexed' (that is, sodomitic intent).[13]

The cross-dressed woman was thus a profoundly ambiguous figure: sometimes personifying virginity; sometimes suffering for the cause of true love; and sometimes an object of both hetero- and homosexual lust. These mixed meanings carried over into the playhouse and were compounded by the extra layer of gender provided by the boy actor within the female/male disguise. Some cross-dressing heroines, like Moll Cutpurse in *The Roaring Girl* or Bess Bridges in Heywood's *Fair Maid of the West* (part 1, c.1600; part 2, c.1630) were bold, swaggering proto-feminists, related to the warrior-women of romance. Moll trounces would-be rakes who prey upon women, and declares, 'I have no humour to marry. I love to lie o' both sides o'th'bed myself; and again o'th'other side, a wife, you know, ought to be obedient, but I fear me I am too headstrong to obey, therefore I'll ne'er go about it' (4.37–41). The equally spirited Bess Bridges sets sail in a pirate ship to rescue her lover and has adventures ranging as far afield as Morocco. Other cross-dressed heroines fell into the type of the love-lorn and pitiful female page, while others again were characterised as pert and cheeky pages.

Shakespeare was of course one of the leading creators of cross-dressed heroines, using them in five plays,[14] and working creative variations on the motif. Julia in *The Two Gentlemen of Verona* (1590–91) evokes the pathos of the female page as her fickle lover Proteus employs her in his wooing of another woman. *The Merchant of Venice* (1596) then has no fewer than three cross-dressed female characters, setting Jessica's use of disguise to elope in counterpoint against Portia's and Nerissa's use of male disguise to act as men and solve their husband's problems. Jessica is coy yet sexy in her male disguise – her lover Lorenzo calls it 'the lovely garnish of a boy' (2.6.45) – whereas Portia as the lawyer Balthasar displays not only the legal wit and rhetorical skill of a young prodigy, but a degree of professional dignity as well.

Next, in *As You Like It* (1599), Shakespeare adds further complications again by making his boy actor playing a woman disguise 'herself' as a boy and then in turn pretend to be a woman. The disguised Rosalind encounters her lover Orlando in the Forest of Arden and impersonates herself in scenes of mock-wooing. Here three layers of identity (boy playing woman playing boy) become four (boy playing woman playing boy playing woman). At times this layered role-play draws attention to sexual ambiguity and homoeroticism. Rosalind in disguise is named Ganymede, after Jove's cup-bearer and boy lover; the term was also common slang for boy prostitutes in Elizabethan England. In role as Ganymede she/he seems to equate women and boys as objects of male love, describing how she/he cured a man of love:

> He was to imagine me his love, his mistress; and I set him every day
> to woo me. At which time would I, being but a moonish youth, grieve,
> be effeminate, changeable, longing and liking, proud, fantastical,
> apish, shallow, inconstant, full of tears, full of smiles; for every passion
> something, and for no passion truly anything, as boys and women
> are for the most part cattle of this colour. (3.2.364–70)

At moments like this, the Ganymede identity is foregrounded as an erotically playful boy. Yet nothing is ever simple in the world of boy-heroines; at other points in the play our attention is drawn to the 'woman' within the disguise. Rosalind is excited to discover that Orlando is in the forest and writing love poems to her, exclaiming to her cousin and confidante Celia, 'Dost thou think, though I am caparisoned like a man, I have a doublet and hose in my disposition?' (3.2.177–8). When she sees a cloth stained with Orlando's blood, she nearly reveals her true identity by fainting, and has to claim, ironically, to be counterfeiting (4.3.156–80). Finally, she speaks the Epilogue to the play, partly staying in role as Rosalind – 'It is not the fashion to see the lady the epilogue' – and partly stepping out of it – 'If I were a woman I would kiss as many of you as had beards that pleased me, complexions that liked me, and breaths that I defied not' (Epilogue, 1–2, 14–16). Or, is this the pert Ganymede again? Whether Ganymede or boy-player, it seems clear that he is flirting with the men in the audience here, though the final lines of the Epilogue add yet more ambiguity: 'And I am sure, as many as have good beards, or good faces, or sweet breaths, will for my kind offer, when I make curtsy, bid me farewell (17–19).

Shakespeare uses the multiple ambiguities of Rosalind/Ganymede to unleash same-sex desire within the plot: Phoebe thinks she is falling in love with a boy (Ganymede) but is really wooing a woman (Rosalind), while Orlando falls more deeply in love with Rosalind by sparring and flirting with her in her Ganymede role. Shakespeare took this further in *Twelfth Night* (1601), where Viola/Cesario's extended scenes of intimacy with both Orsino and Olivia represent both male-male and female-female desire with unprecedented emotional depth. Olivia falls in love with Viola/Cesario when she/he speaks eloquently and passionately of love:

> VIOLA: If I did love you in my master's flame,
> With such a suff'ring, such a deadly life,
> In your denial I would find no sense,
> I would not understand it.
> OLIVIA: Why, what would you?
> VIOLA: Make me a willow cabin at your gate
> And call upon my soul within the house,
> Write loyal cantons of contemnèd love,
> And sing them loud even in the dead of night;
> Halloo your name to the reverberate hills,
> And make the babbling gossip of the air
> Cry out 'Olivia!' O, you should not rest
> Between the elements of air and earth
> But you should pity me.
> OLIVIA: You might do much.
>   (1.5.233–46)

We know by now that the name Viola really wishes to cry out in desire is 'Orsino!' Her frustrated longing for him produces this pure verbal jet of passion which inadvertently strikes Olivia, creating the love-triangle that lies at the centre of the play. This triangle is formed not only by misunderstandings – Olivia falls in love with a woman thinking that she is a man – but also symmetries – Olivia falls in love with Viola because she speaks so eloquently of female desire, and as a result Olivia herself becomes the unrequitedly desiring woman of Viola's speech.

Meanwhile, Viola/Cesario's scenes with Orsino are even more emotionally charged, as the Duke declares that 'I have unclasped / To thee the book even of my secret soul' (1.5.12–13). Viola's disguise, in creating intimacy with her master, at once offers opportunities for her to confess her feelings, and compels her to do so in encoded fashion. Her fictional veiling of her true identity and desires is however so thin that it trembles constantly on the brink of revelation, as when she narrates the tale of her 'sister' who 'sat like patience on a monument, / Smiling at grief' (113–14). Orsino for his part draws closer to Cesario in the belief that he is a boy. Although the page is revealed as Viola in the play's final scene, she does not revert to women's clothes, and Orsino continues to address her as 'Boy' and 'Cesario' even while declaring his love for her (5.1.260, 372). His assertion that 'You shall from this time be / Your master's mistress' (5.1.314–15) creates a link to the lovely boy of Shakespeare's Sonnets, who is addressed in similar terms in Sonnet 20: 'A woman's face with nature's own hand painted / Hast thou, the master-mistress of my passion' (lines 1–2).

Portia and Rosalind take command of the action of their plays and are the principal agents of the final resolution in each case. This creates opportunities for modern readers and spectators, who usually see them acted by women, to respond to them as proto-feminist heroines who are emancipated by their male clothing. Viola is not quite the same: although she displays wit and spirit, she feels herself to be trapped by her disguise – 'O time, thou must untangle this, not I. / It is too hard a knot for me t'untie' (2.2.38–9). Shakespeare's final boy-heroine, Imogen in *Cymbeline* (1609), shares this sense of powerlessness at the hands of fate. Thus Shakespeare deploys the cross-dressed boy-heroine in a wide range of different ways. However, all these characters share the fact that they work supremely well on stage. One reason for this is that the heroine in disguise has a secret that she shares with the audience, gaining our complicity and sympathy, and also creating entertaining opportunities for dramatic irony. The use of disguise can also assist the dramatist in simulating the interiority of the character. Hamlet claims that 'I have that within which passeth show', pointing to his mourning clothes – 'These but the trappings and the suits of woe' – to draw a contrast with the infinitely deeper grief and melancholy that lie behind them, invisible and unspeakable. In a similar way the presentation of a female character dressed as a boy can set up a distinction between a public and private self, an outer male self which is merely a performance and an inner female self which is implied to be in some sense 'true'. Yet the presence of a boy actor behind that female identity sets up another layer again. Sometimes this is suppressed; at other times attention is called to it, but even this can also draw the audience in by acknowledging the illusionism of theatre and soliciting their collaboration in it. The layerings of identity in these figures can both gesture towards a mysterious interiority and draw attention to their own artifice, once again enabling sophisticated experimentation not only with gender identity and different permutations of sexual desire, but also with the complex relation between stage and reality.

WOMEN AND DRAMATIC PERFORMANCE

Although female parts were taken by boys in the commercial playhouses, women themselves were actively involved in drama in a number of ways. Women appear to have made up a significant proportion of the playhouse audience. John Rainoldes, in a 1599 attack on theatre, condemned 'flocking and gadding' to playhouses, and deplored a gentlewoman who spoke in defence of theatre, swearing 'by her troth that she was as much edified at a play as ever she was at any sermon'.[15] Women were also involved in the management of playhouses at several levels: royal women were patrons of playing companies; some women of the trading classes invested in playhouses; and women sometimes acted as 'gatherers', collecting money from spectators.[16]

Meanwhile away from the playhouses there was a tradition of female patronage of drama at court and in aristocratic households,[17] and there were many times and places where women actually performed. Women took part in disguisings and mummings at court from the reign of Henry VIII onwards.[18] As we learned in chapter 1, Elizabeth I herself was a theatrical performer on occasions like her coronation pageants; she also blurred the roles of spectator and performer at the many courtly entertainments, such as Sidney's *Lady of May* or Peele's *Arraignment of Paris*, that required her to participate in the fiction to make a judgement or receive a gift. Meanwhile the pageants laid on for her during her progresses sometimes used a combination of professional actors and courtiers, especially members of the host families, and these sometimes included female performers. When Elizabeth visited Bisham in Berkshire in 1592, her host was Lady Elizabeth Russell (1528–1609), a formidable figure and a notable translator, composer of epitaphs, and literary patron, who may well have taken a leading hand in the planning and writing of the entertainment. Her two daughters, Elizabeth (18) and Anne (16) took prominent roles; Lady Russell was eager to show off their accomplishments in hope that they would become maids of honour to the queen and make advantageous marriages. As the queen and her entourage approached the house, they encountered the two girls, dressed as shepherdesses, sitting on a hillside and sewing samplers. The sisters fended off the wooing of Pan and spoke in praise of women's chastity and constancy, developing from this a long oration in praise and welcome of the queen. The queen was then greeted by Ceres, goddess of harvest, who was almost certainly played by a boy actor. Thus three types of theatrical representations of femaleness were brought together in one performance: a professional male performer impersonating a woman; the queen as public performer, processing in splendour; and, perhaps most significantly, aristocratic women as amateur performers, a practice that was evidently not considered unusual in court circles.[19]

As we saw in chapter 5, performance by women became an even more marked feature of court life during the reign of James I, when the queen, Anne of Denmark, regularly commissioned masques and performed with her ladies. Between 1604 and 1611 she took part in six masques at Hampton Court and Whitehall, four by Jonson and two by Daniel, most of them designed by Inigo Jones. Jonson attributed to Anne such important and innovative features as the 'blackamoor' theme of *The Masque of Blackness* and the 'antimasque' of *The Masque of Queens*, suggesting her active creative engagement in devising the masques.[20] They evidently encouraged dramatic participation by other women, such as a performance for the queen in 1617 of Robert White's *Cupid's Banishment* by 'the young Gentlewomen of the Ladies Hall in Deptford' (a private academy for girls of noble families), partly organised by Lucy Russell (née Harington), Countess of Bedford, who had been one of the leading performers in Queen Anne's masques.[21] The daughters of Sir John Crofts also performed at court, in a masque now known as *The Visit of the Nine Goddesses*.[22]

Female performance at court was promoted even more in the reign of Charles I by his controversial French queen Henrietta Maria. In 1626 she and her ladies performed a pastoral play, Racan's *Artenice*, with an all-female cast. Whereas Anne of Denmark had played silent and mainly symbolic roles in her masques, the new queen attracted attention and criticism by acting a speaking part. The female-only casting also necessitated cross-dressing, with some of the women on stage even wearing beards.[23] Women-actors were already accepted in continental countries such as France and Italy, but when a French troupe including actresses attempted to perform in London in 1629 they were 'hissed, hooted, and pippin-pelted from the stage'.[24] Undeterred, Henrietta Maria commissioned and performed in four masques from 1631 to 1638 asserting the power of female beauty and chastity,[25] and in 1633 once again led her ladies in a pastoral play, Walter Montagu's *The Shepherd's Paradise*, in which nine out of the thirteen actresses played male roles. At around the same time William Prynne published *Histrio-Mastix*, which not only attacked cross-dressing boy-actors as an incitement to sodomy, but asserted that women-actors were even worse. According to Prynne the women-actors in ancient Greece and Rome 'were all notorious impudent, prostituted strumpets', while those in the present day 'infuse so great lasciviousness into the minds of hearers and spectators that all may seem, even with one consent, to extirpate all modesty out of their minds, to disgrace the female nature, and to satiate their lusts with pernicious pleasure'. Their performances, he raged, were 'obscene' and 'full of filthy wantonness'.[26] Prynne's stance was perceived as an attack on the royal court and its culture, with the result that he found himself on trial in Star Chamber for sedition, and was punished by having his ears cropped.

Female performance at court persisted regardless. Performances by women in private country-house settings also continued and developed in complexity, as in the example of Milton's *Comus* (also known as *A Masque Presented at Ludlow Castle*, 1634), in which the fifteen-year-old daughter of the house, Lady Alice Egerton, took a large and challenging speaking and singing role.[27] Moreover, these kinds of private, domestic performances had by now become an important medium for dramatic writing by women.

FEMALE DRAMATISTS

For a Renaissance woman to write drama required no less boldness than standing up on a stage to act, given that many male writers of the period expressed views on female authorship like the following, from Thomas Salter's *Mirror of Modesty* (1579):

> suche as compare the small profit of learnyng with the great hurt and domage that commeth to them [i.e. women] by the same shall sone perceive (although that they remaine obstinate therein) how far more convenient the Distaffe, and Spindle, Nedle and Thimble were for them with a good and honest reputation, then the skill of well using a penne or wrighting a loftie vearce with diffame and dishonour, if in the same there be more erudition then vertue.[28]

It is not surprising, then, that just as women did not act at the public playhouses, they did not write for them either. However, from the mid sixteenth century plays began to be written by aristocratic women, with the support and encouragement of their families, in a form usually known in modern times as 'closet drama'. This term until recently tended to be used disparagingly, to suggest plays written to be read not performed, aimed at a coterie readership of immediate family and friends, and characterised by social and intellectual elitism. Unfavourable comparisons were made with plays written for the commercial playhouses by Shakespeare and the other professional male dramatists of the period.[29] However, it has become increasingly understood that this is an inappropriate and unproductive comparison, and closet dramas by women have begun to be discussed in terms of their own aesthetic principles and objectives. The frequent moral earnestness of these plays must be understood as defensive in relation to views like Salter's, while their erudition was intrinsic to their purpose of displaying the costly and impressive humanist education received by daughters of aristocratic families. Nor should it be assumed that they are dry or lifeless, or constrained by their relatively secluded setting. In fact writing within a circle of approving family and friends seems to have been liberating to women writers, as does the fact that their plays often circulated only in the relatively private medium of manuscript, escaping both the censure sometimes incurred by the self-exposure of print, and the censorship applied to printed works and the public stage. Their plays often engage in lively and provocative debate about both personal and political issues.[30]

Moreover, the idea that 'closet plays' were written only to be read, not performed, may be mistaken. They may have been used in group readings in aristocratic households, with individuals taking different parts, or they may have been partly or fully staged. Alison Findlay, Stephanie Hodgson-Wright, and others have successfully mounted performances of Renaissance plays by women, and have also found some evidence of performance in details of the texts. They suggest that we approach them with an assumption that the woman dramatist's script 'was written with a theatrical arena in mind, whether or not evidence of a production has survived in documentary form'.[31] Supporting this approach is the exciting recent discovery of a portrait of a Jacobean lady, possibly Lady Anne Clifford (1590–1676), dressed as Cleopatra and accompanied by verses from Samuel Daniel's play of that name (a closet drama commissioned by Mary Sidney Herbert, Countess of Pembroke; see below).

This suggests that aristocratic women may have acted out costumed roles in household performances, or at the very least staged themselves in dramatic personae in static tableaux or portraits based on scripted roles.[32] In this social milieu, drama was evidently a significant form of female self-expression.

As mentioned, several early dramas by women exist only in manuscript, and it may well be that women wrote more manuscript plays that are now lost to us. The earliest surviving drama by a Renaissance Englishwoman is *The Tragedy of Iphigenia* by Lady Jane Lumley (1537–1578), a translation of Euripides (possibly via Erasmus's Latin version). Lumley was the daughter of Henry Fitzalan, Earl of Arundel, a prominent politician at the courts of Edward VI and Mary I. He owned one of the most impressive libraries in England, and had ensured that his daughter received a fine humanist education. Her *Iphigenia* may be understood as designed to display this, to enhance the prestige of the family, and to celebrate daughterly affection, virtue, and obedience. Indeed, the plot of the play takes this to extremes that are somewhat disturbing: Iphigenia must be sacrificed to the goddess Diana by her father Agamemnon in order to secure the safe journey of the Greek fleet to Troy. Iphigenia first resists her fate then willingly embraces it, and is miraculously saved by Diana, who at the very moment of sacrifice on the altar transports the girl to heaven and substitutes a white hart in her place.

Clearly this play must be understood in the context of filial allegiance to dynastic and factional ambitions. Any modern reader searching the text for signs of early feminism will be startled to find Iphigenia voicing such sentiments as 'do you not thinke it to be better that I shulde die, then so many noble men to be let of their journey for one womans sake? for one noble man is better than a thousande women.'[33] Nevertheless Iphigenia does in a sense choose her fate and exercise an autonomous will, while other characters vacillate and agonise around her. Her scenes with her father are touching. Even before her first entrance, Agamemnon torments himself by imagining what she will say to him: 'I have pitie of the litell gerle, for I knowe she will speake thus unto me, O father will you kill me? if you forsake me, of whom shall I aske remedie?' (p. 17, lines 305–06). The echoes here of Christ's cry from the cross underline the Christian as well as classical iconography of sacred martyrdom that runs through the narrative. When Iphigenia actually enters, her very innocence exacerbates Agamemnon's guilt: 'What is the cause father, that you seame to be so sadde, seinge you saye, you are so joyfull at our comminge?' (p. 19, lines 384–5). Even her cleverness, which was previously a delight to him, becomes galling: 'Trulye daughter the more wittely you speake, the more you troble me' (p. 19, lines 398–9).

The play's date is uncertain, but its subject-matter may relate not only to Lumley's demonstration of her duty to her father, but also to the fate of her cousin, Lady Jane Grey. At the death of Edward VI, the Duke of Northumberland, who had been Lord President of the privy council and in effect ruler of England during Edward's minority, tried to cling to power by marrying his son to Lady Jane Grey, who had royal blood, and declaring her queen. Arundel at first supported Jane's accession, but rapidly changed sides, becoming one of the first of the Privy Council to ride to Mary Tudor and join her cause, for which Mary rewarded him with high office. Lady Jane Grey had been forced to marry Northumberland's son and become a pawn in the aborted coup by her ambitious and domineering parents. If Lumley's play was written after Lady Jane Grey's execution, its narrative of filial submission and sacrifice must have carried uncomfortable resonances, to say the least.[34]

Lady Jane Grey was renowned for her erudition, and her cousin Lady Jane Lumley was presenting herself in a similar light, as an exemplary highly educated noblewoman, in undertaking a translation of a classical text. Indeed in exercising her skill as a translator Lumley was participating in a favoured literary activity for Renaissance women. It showed skill in languages, it could claim a virtuous purpose of making improving works available to a wider readership, and it positioned the female translator as a subordinate handmaiden to the original male author. Nevertheless, a woman's choice of work to translate could be laden with meaning, and she often put an individualistic stamp on the text in the process of translation. Elizabeth I was a keen translator throughout her life, and in her later years often undertook manuscript translations of classical texts for her own pleasure and recreation. In 1589 she translated a

181

Chorus spoken by women from *Hercules Oetaeus*, a play attributed to Seneca.[35] The text is characteristic of many of Elizabeth's writings in dwelling stoically on the vicissitudes of fortune and the insecurities of rule; it may also, in its nautical imagery and reference to the River Tagus in Portugal, form a literary response to the disastrous 'English Armada' of 1589 which failed in its attempted assaults on Spain and Portugal.

In the following year Mary Herbert, Countess of Pembroke (1561–1621) – usually referred to as Mary Sidney – translated a French classical-style tragedy by Robert Garnier, *The Tragedy of Antony*, which she went on to publish in 1592 and 1595. Mary was the sister of Sir Philip Sidney, the iconic Elizabethan courtier-poet who had died in 1586. She wrote a number of works, many in translation, and many in tribute to and mourning for her brother: noble deaths, and stoicism in the face of loss, are recurrent themes. Her version of *Antony* is notable for its characterisation of Cleopatra, who elevates her love for Antony above all else, even her children, and becomes a heroic martyr to this cause. Yet she is sensual too: 'most happie in this happles case, / To die with thee, and dieng thee embrace: / My bodie joynde with thine, my mouth with thine, / My mouth, whose moisture burning sighes have dried'.[36] It is more than possible that Shakespeare was aware of Mary Sidney's play when writing his own *Antony and Cleopatra* (1606).

We saw that topical comment may have been present in Lumley's *Iphigenia* and Elizabeth I's Chorus from *Hercules Oetaeus*. Mary Sidney's works often express political views in encoded form, reflecting her affiliation with a court faction which favoured a more assertive promotion of Protestantism at home and abroad, and her self-appointed role of chief mourner and literary executor to her brother Philip, who died fighting Catholic Spain in the Netherlands.[37] In common with other Roman plays, translations and histories produced in the last years of Elizabeth I's reign, *Antony* may well be using Roman history to consider alternative models of government and to glance obliquely at contemporary events, such as the instability created by rival courtiers and their factions, anxiety over the succession after Elizabeth's death, and the likely accession of James of Scotland (perhaps figured as Octavius Caesar).[38]

Another striking feature of the play is the quality of Mary Sidney's poetry, and her skilful experimentation with different rhyme-schemes and metres. This is in keeping with her translation of the Psalms (which revised and completed a project begun by her brother Philip) where, again, she clearly relished playing inventively with poetic form. Some of the most elaborate verse-patterning in *Antony* is in the Choruses, such as this extract from one addressed to the Nile:

> Nought thee helps thy hornes to hide
>   far from hence in unknown grounds,
>   that thy waters wander wide,
>   yerely breaking banks, and bounds.
>   and that thy Skie-coullor'd brooks
>   through a hundred peoples passe,
>   drawing plots for trees and grasse
>   with a thousand turns and crookes,
>   whome all weary of their way
>   thy throats which in widenesse passe
>   powre into their mother Sea.
>   (2.551–62)

The rhyme-scheme is ababcddcede, intricately twining and looping back on itself to mimic the 'turns and crookes' of the river.

Closet drama was written by men too, especially in the circle associated with the Sidney family. Mary Sidney commissioned Samuel Daniel to write a *Tragedy of Cleopatra* (published 1594) as a counterpart to her *Antony*. Fulke Greville, a close friend of Philip Sidney's and another guardian of his political and literary legacy, wrote three closet plays, *Mustapha*, *Alaham*, and *Antony and Cleopatra*, between about 1595 and 1600; he then destroyed the latter play, fearing that it would be seen as controversial in relation to events leading to the Essex Rebellion of 1601. Daniel did indeed fall into the kind of trouble that Greville feared: in 1605 another closet drama by him, *Philotas*, was performed for King James, but was deemed to be a seditious reflection on the fall of Essex, and Daniel was called before the privy council to answer charges. Evidently closet drama could be incendiary, and was not necessarily a 'safe' or socially irrelevant medium in which for women to write.

The first woman to write original plays in English was Lady Elizabeth Cary (1585–1639), whose *Tragedy of Mariam* was composed around 1602–04 (soon after her marriage) and published in 1613. A earlier play by her, apparently set in Syracuse, is lost. *Mariam* concerns the wife of Herod, King of the Jews, who struggles with her divided feelings towards him: she loves him, but also hates him because he condemned to death her brother and grandfather, to secure his hold on the throne. At the beginning of the play Herod, who has been absent in Rome, is believed to be dead; however, he returns, and he and Mariam explore their conflicting emotions toward one another. Finally Salome, Herod's promiscuous and deceitful sister, tricks him into believing that Mariam has tried to poison him; Mariam is executed, and Herod is consumed by regret.

The play has received much interest from modern critics because of its complex female characters. Salome is clearly condemned for her immoral behaviour, yet is given an eloquent defence of a woman's equal right to divorce:

> Why should such priviledge to man be given?
> Or given to them, why bard from women then?
> Are men then we in greater grace with Heaven?
> Or cannot women hate as well as men?
> Ile be the custome-breaker: and beginner
> To shew my Sexe the way to freedomes doore.[39]

Meanwhile Mariam is torn not only between love and hate for Herod, but also between impulses towards obedience and rebellion. She is acutely aware of her own inconsistency, confessing that 'I did this morning for his death complaine, / And yet doe mourne, because he lives ere night' (3.3.36–7). Restraint makes her crave freedom; she recognises that 'hee by barring me from libertie, / To shunne my ranging, taught me first to range' (1.1.25–6). The Chorus, often the moral centre of classical tragedy, criticises her unfixity, and advocates absolute wifely submission: wives not only give their bodies in marriage, but 'sure, their thoughts no more can be their owne'

(3.3.120). Yet Mariam's inability to subject her will to her husband's often appears as noble integrity, in such statements as, 'I cannot frame disguise, nor never taught / My face a looke dissenting from my thought' (4.3.58–9). She is finally vindicated after her death by Herod's elegiac tribute, which celebrates the purity of both her body and her mind. He laments, 'now I see that heav'n in her did linke, / A spirit and a person to excell' (5.1.245–6).

It is tempting to try to read back into *Mariam* the events of Lady Elizabeth Cary's later life. Her husband, Sir Henry Cary, was an ambitious courtier and politician who in 1620 became Viscount Falkland. They had eleven children, but the marriage became increasingly troubled, and broke down irrevocably in 1626 when Elizabeth converted to Catholicism. She was held under house arrest for six weeks by royal command, rejected by both her husband and mother, and reduced to severe poverty. All these events happened at least twenty years after the composition of *Mariam*, and so cannot be directly connected with it. However, it is possible to assert that Cary's play and her life suggest a consistent interest in female autonomy and its costs, and in conflicts between obedience and conscience. In *Mariam*, the heroine's death is announced with the words 'Her body is divided from her head' (5.1.90). The image of the state as a body – the body politic – with the monarch as its head was a commonplace in this period, and reminds us that Mariam's rebelliousness is directed not only at her husband but also at her king. Mariam's story, then, may be seen as one of politics as much as marriage, with implications for all subjects in society: who should be obeyed in a contest between an ordained authority (such as a husband, father, or king), and individual conscience?

Cary's *Mariam*, although an original work, is very much in the classical dramatic tradition in which Jane Lumley, Elizabeth I and Mary Sidney had also written: tragic, heroic, peopled by characters of high status and noble stature, and marked by lofty rhetoric and earnest moral purpose. The next English drama to be written by a woman was a departure: a comedy, *Love's Victory*, by Lady Mary Wroth (1587?–1651/1653). Wroth was Mary Sidney's niece, and thus a member of the most notable literary dynasty of the English Renaissance. She was the most prolific and innovative female writer of her age, ignoring the conventions which limited women mainly to religious writing or translation. She produced the first English prose romance by a woman, *The Countess of Montgomery's Urania*, published in 1621, and followed by an unpublished manuscript sequel. She also wrote the first English sonnet sequence by a woman (*Pamphilia to Amphilanthus*, published with the *Urania* in 1621), and, in *Love's Victory*, the first comedy by an Englishwoman. Not surprisingly, her literary exploits were controversial: Edward Denny, Baron of Waltham, took offence at parts of the *Urania* which he took to be a veiled satire against himself and his family, and attacked Wroth as a 'hermophradite' and a 'monster'. He admonished her to 'leave idle bookes alone / For wise and worthyer women have writte none'.[40] Wroth also courted controversy in her life, engaging in an adulterous affair of long duration with her promiscuous cousin William Herbert, Earl of Pembroke (Mary Sidney's son); this produced two illegitimate children, and seems to be shadowed by several of the characters and narratives of her fictional works.[41]

Wroth took a keen interest in drama. She performed at court in *The Masque of Blackness* and *The Masque of Beauty*, and included masques and masque-like incidents in the *Urania*. As mentioned above, at two points in the *Urania* she took occasion to comment on the inauthenticity of boys acting female roles. Ben Jonson dedicated *The Alchemist* to her, as well as two epigrams and a sonnet, and she was widely praised for her literary patronage. Her own play, *Love's Victory*, is set among shepherds, and concerns several couples and their fortunes and misfortunes in love.[42] It is written in rhyming couplets, which create a light-hearted and comical mood rather like the speeches of the young Athenian lovers in *A Midsummer Night's Dream*. There is little action for the first four acts, as characters declare their loves, discuss various love-triangles and other obstacles to desire, and play riddling love-games. Women play a prominent part in these activities, and to some extent this part of the play is a feminised dramatisation of the pastoral world presented in the *Arcadia* by Wroth's uncle Philip Sidney, a world which she also explored and developed in her prose romance, the *Urania*. In Act 5, however, the play moves into the fashionable genre of pastoral tragicomedy. Philisses and Musella are in love, but she is destined to marry the boorish Rustic. On the wedding day, Philisses and Musella go to the Temple of Love, intending to stab themselves. Silvesta intervenes to give them a potion which merely simulates death. Their bodies are laid on the altar of the temple, and everyone expresses their grief, including Musella's mother, who repents of preventing Musella's marriage to Philisses. The couple rise from the altar, and the goddess Venus appears to explain that Silvesta acted as her agent. She blesses the marriage, all the other couples pair off happily, and the play ends in a celebration of love's victory.

There are echoes here not only of *Romeo and Juliet* (with the tragic miscommunications and mistimings removed) but other plays too; Middleton's *Chaste Maid in Cheapside*, for instance, ends with a thwarted young couple (Touchwood Junior and Moll Yellowhammer) supposedly dead, only for them to rise from their coffins and have their union blessed by their penitent parents. Wroth evidently knew of this tradition, whether from Shakespeare or Middleton or their sources, but placed it in the private setting of a closet drama, where her play may well have taken on additional intense resonances from references to, and performances by, real people in her circle. Philisses and Musella in some ways resemble the lovers Astrophil and Stella of Philip Sidney's sonnet sequence of that name, who in turn in some ways resemble Philip himself and Lady Penelope Rich. At the same time Musella and Philisses also in some respects seem to figure Wroth herself and her lover William Herbert. Further correspondences are implied between other characters and other relations and friends of Wroth, but, as in all her works, she avoids exact one-to-one matches to create more subtle effects. The *Urania*, for instance, also seems to draw on incidents and relationships from Wroth's life, but transmutes and recasts them in multiple inset narratives; they are thereby reviewed from a number of oblique angles, and used to generate layered, reverberative effects rather than simple and direct parallels to reality. *Love's Victory*, similarly, draws in the reader or spectator with suggestive hints towards real-life referents, but at the same time creates its own world of dramatic fiction which resists reductive interpretations.

Love's Victory is a good example of how closet drama facilitated sophisticated artistic effects not feasible in the public playhouses.

For all the women surveyed here, drama was important as a means of displaying their knowledge and exercising their literary skill, but it was also more than this: they used drama to explore the nature of female heroism, to investigate the relations between life and art, and to reflect on controversial issues in both personal relations and politics. Closet drama is being increasingly recognised as an important Renaissance genre, and it is one in which women made some of the most notable contributions.

One of the most distinctive features of the Renaissance public playhouses was the performance of female roles by boy actors. As we have seen, this generated a cloud of turbulent issues around these sexually ambiguous figures, but it did not entail the absence of women from participation in drama. Over the period until the closure of the theatres by Parliament in 1642, women were increasingly active as performers at court and in domestic settings, and as authors of drama. When the theatres re-opened with the Restoration of the monarchy, women would be prominent as performers and authors, and the foundations for this were laid in the pre-Civil-War period.

Epilogue

THE AFTERLIVES OF RENAISSANCE DRAMA

This book has mainly concentrated on drama of the late Elizabethan and Jacobean periods (*c.*1585–1625), because these are the years that produced most of the plays that continue to be widely read and performed today. However, drama continued to thrive through the reign of Charles I (1625–42). As we have seen in the previous chapter, dramatic performance was an important part of court culture, enthusiastically encouraged by Queen Henrietta Maria and also by Charles himself. Unlike her royal predecessors, Henrietta Maria even visited playhouse performances, attending the Blackfriars no fewer than four times. The fact that she felt it not indecorous to do this was partly because London theatre had become increasingly polarised, with the 'private' playhouses (the Blackfriars, Phoenix, and Salisbury Court) catering increasingly to court taste, while the 'public' playhouses (the Globe, Fortune, and Red Bull) were frequented by less elite audiences, often watching revivals of old favourites. Dramatic innovation took place mainly in the private playhouses, where playwrights like Richard Brome, William Davenant, Philip Massinger and James Shirley developed romantic-heroic plays of love and honour and comedies depicting fashionable London life.[1]

The year 1642 brought radical change, as the Civil War broke out and the Puritan-led parliament took power. They issued an order closing all the playhouses, since they offered 'Spectacles of Pleasure, too commonly expressing lascivious Mirth, and Levitie' which were

189

discordant with 'Publike Calamities' and 'Seasons of Humiliation'.[2] This was initially a temporary edict, but it was followed by the demolition of the Globe playhouse in 1644 'to make tennements', further legal measures against players and playing in the late 1640s, and the destruction of more playhouses in 1649.[3] Drama did not cease entirely: drolls, or short playlets, continued at the Red Bull, and some plays were performed in schools and other private settings.[4] Writers also continued to compose drama, with over 108 plays known to have been written over the period 1642–60, many of which were published.[5] Each side in the Civil War produced pamphlet dialogues in dramatic form in support of their cause. Meanwhile Margaret Cavendish, Duchess of Newcastle, was a prolific author of plays not intended for performance; as she explained, 'some of my Thoughts make Playes, and others Act those Playes on the Stage of Imagination, where my Mind sits as a Spectator'.[6] Nevertheless, despite the persistence of all these forms of drama, the genre existed under conditions of suppression until 1660, when the Restoration of the monarchy brought the re-opening of the playhouses.

However, this did not restore the theatrical conditions that had operated before 1642. Only two companies were issued with royal patents and permitted to produce plays, the King's Company under Thomas Killigrew and the Duke's Company under Sir William Davenant, and these two merged, in 1682, into the United Company. London theatre was thus less diverse in its locations and audiences than in the pre-Civil-War period. At the same time it set several conventions which continue in modern theatre. Women, of course, played female parts, and women such as Aphra Behn, Susanna Centlivre, Delariviere Manley, and Mary Pix pursued careers as professional playwrights. There were seats in the pit, and this became the main seating area, with the addition of boxes containing the most expensive seats, while the least affluent theatre-goers were removed from the standing pit of the Elizabethan playhouse to cheap seats in the gallery. The proscenium arch was introduced; most of the acting took place on a fore-stage extending towards the audience, but the area behind the proscenium arch was used for movable scenery, to create an illusionistic setting.[7]

There is therefore some degree of continuity in the history of English theatre from 1660 to the present day. What has not been continuous over that period, however, is the popularity of Renaissance drama. Today Shakespeare is the most performed playwright in the world, with numerous productions running at any one time in English-speaking nations, and a high profile too in many non-Anglophone cultures (as witnessed by Shakespeare's Globe's 2012 season of 37 plays in 37 languages by different international companies). His works are at the core of the curriculum of English Literature at both school and university level, and many plays by his contemporaries are also widely studied and enjoy regular revivals on stage. Yet in 1660 it was by no means apparent that Renaissance drama, even including Shakespeare's works, would endure to achieve such levels of popularity and cultural value. This epilogue to the *Short History of English Renaissance Drama* will briefly trace the history of Renaissance drama after its own time, and will consider why it continues to be of such interest and appeal today.

SHIFTING TASTES IN THE EIGHTEENTH AND NINETEENTH CENTURIES

Revivals of Renaissance plays formed a significant proportion of the repertoire of the Restoration theatres. Beaumont and Fletcher were the most popular Renaissance playwrights; Shakespeare had not yet achieved his ascendancy, and was less popular and highly regarded than either of these authors or Ben Jonson. Revenge tragedies and city comedies were performed fairly frequently in the 1660s, but declined in favour over ensuing decades.[8] When Shakespeare plays were performed, they were often in adapted form, such as Davenant and Dryden's *The Tempest; or the Enchanted Island* (1667), which added a musical setting and four new characters including a sister for Miranda and a love-interest for Ariel; or Nahum Tate's *King Lear* (1681), which notoriously added a happy ending.[9]

Over the course of the eighteenth century Shakespeare rose in esteem, assisted by a series of prestigious editions of his collected works by editors like Nicholas Rowe (in 1709), Alexander Pope (1725), and Samuel Johnson (1765). In 1741 his statue was erected in Poets' Corner in Westminster Abbey, while at Drury Lane David

Garrick (1717–1779), the foremost actor of his generation, staged and starred in numerous productions of Shakespeare's plays. Garrick promoted himself as well as Shakespeare by means of events like the Shakespeare Jubilee of 1769, a three-day festival in Stratford-upon-Avon. Shakespeare's works were also popular because they harmonised with the literature of sentiment that became fashionable from the 1740s onwards. Jonson's works, however, did not suit this development in taste, and were increasingly disparaged in order to praise Shakespeare by contrast, although Garrick made a great success of the role of Abel Drugger in an adaptation of *The Alchemist*.[10] Some other city comedies continued to be performed, and in 1744 Robert Dodsley published *A Select Collection of Old English Plays* in twelve volumes. However, on the whole other Renaissance dramatists were reduced to little more than footnotes to Shakespeare, and many disappeared from view almost entirely.[11] Marlowe, for instance, was not performed at all in London throughout the eighteenth century, nor was Webster after 1707.[12] One notable exception, however, was Philip Massinger's *A New Way to Pay Old Debts* (1625), a play which is hardly performed or studied today. It tells the story of a grasping businessman, Sir Giles Overreach, who accrues wealth by ruining others and finally goes mad. It was revived several times by Garrick and became a regular feature of the repertoire after John Henderson triumphed in the role of Overreach in 1781, establishing it as a starring role; Edmund Kean created even more of a sensation in 1816.[13]

The late eighteenth and early nineteenth centuries saw adulation of Shakespeare rise to unprecedented heights, as he was held to personify the Romantic idealisation of the artist as a divinely inspired genius. Other Renaissance playwrights began to regain attention thanks to the efforts of Charles Lamb, who in 1808 published *Specimens of the English Dramatic Poets who Lived about the Time of Shakespeare*, offering appreciative discussions of extracts from Renaissance plays. Lamb also provided William Hazlitt with materials to write his lectures on the *Dramatic Literature of the Age of Elizabeth* (delivered 1819, published 1820). Hazlitt praised the artless yet 'truly English' vitality of the Elizabethan and Jacobean playwrights, seeing them as 'a bold, vigorous, independent race of thinkers, with prodigious strength and energy'.[14] He particularly extolled Marlowe as a kind of forerunner of the Romantic anti-hero, with 'a lust for power in his writings, a hunger and thirst after unrighteousness, a glow of the imagination, unhallowed by any thing but its own energies'.[15]

A gradual re-awareness of non-Shakespearean Renaissance drama was assisted by the growth of antiquarianism and of literary scholarship as a profession, leading to the publication of editions. John Ford's works appeared in 1811 and 1827 and Marlowe's in 1818 and 1826. Alexander Dyce was an important editor, producing editions of Webster (1830), Middleton (1840) and Marlowe (1850). He was followed by F.J. Furnivall, whose Early English Text Society (founded 1864) and New Shakspere Society (founded 1873) sponsored editions and scholarship. A.H. Bullen followed with a series called English Dramatists which included editions of Marlowe (1885), Middleton (1886), Marston (1887), and Peele (1888), and with a seven-volume *A Collection of Old English Plays* (1882–90) which included a number of plays never published before. Mermaid editions, published from the late 1880s onwards, were significant in making Renaissance plays available to a wider audience.

Meanwhile the Shakespeare industry continued to grow, powered by star performances by great Victorian actor-managers like William Charles Macready (1793–1873) and Henry Irving (1838–1905), popular editions, the growth of Stratford-on-Avon as a tourist centre, and the rise of English Literature as a subject of academic study. Colonialism also played a part, as Shakespeare was carried to the outposts of the Empire as the epitome of all that was great about Britain and as a supposedly civilising influence.[16] America too, over the course of the nineteenth century and into the twentieth, increasingly embraced Shakespeare as a hero of democratic values.[17]

RENAISSANCE DRAMA IN THE TWENTIETH CENTURY

In 1894 William Poel founded the Elizabethan Stage Society, which was dedicated to stripping away the lavish and spectacular trappings of most Victorian productions of Shakespeare, attempting instead to recreate a more authentic style of staging. The Society also revived a number of plays by Shakespeare's contemporaries, including Marlowe, Jonson, and Beaumont and Fletcher. It was succeeded in 1919 by the Phoenix Society, whose express purpose was to revive neglected Renaissance plays. This growing interest in Renaissance drama received a significant boost from T.S. Eliot, who in 1920, on the brink of great fame as the defining poet of the modern age, published a volume of criticism, *The Sacred Wood*, which included essays on *Hamlet*, Marlowe, Jonson and Massinger. These, together with Eliot's 1921 essay on 'The Metaphysical Poets', and more on drama in his volume *Elizabethan Essays* (1934), were instrumental in redefining the canon of English literature, shifting attention away from the Romantics and their successors and back to relatively neglected Renaissance authors. For Eliot the English Renaissance was not a golden age, but an age 'of anarchism, of dissolution, of decay', and it was this that gave it a particular resonance with the modern condition.[18] He therefore relished the neurotic and morbid qualities of Renaissance drama, especially revenge tragedy, declaring in 'Whispers of Immortality' (1920) that 'Webster was much possessed by death / And saw the skull beneath the skin'.[19] *The Waste Land* (1922), the work which established Eliot's reputation, persistently echoes and alludes to Renaissance plays.

Eliot has often been seen as voicing a general feeling of disillusionment and nihilism in the wake of the horrors of the First World War, and it may well be that the many atrocities of the twentieth century help to account for a new fascination with the more violent and shocking varieties of Renaissance drama. F.L. Lucas, who edited Webster's works in 1927, wrote of the 'exaggerated fuss' made 'about the dead man's hand in *The Duchess of Malfi*. Too many of the present generation have stumbled about in the darkness among month-old corpses on the battlefields of France to be much impressed by the falsetto uproar which this piece of "business" occasioned in nineteenth-century minds.'[20] Renaissance audiences may have been habituated to horror by gruesome executions at Tyburn, deaths by plague, and experiences of war, and perhaps even found it in some sense therapeutic to see similar horrors reproduced in the safe space of the stage. Something like this seems to have happened in the twentieth century, not only after the First World War but also after the Second. Wendy Griswold has found from a statistical study of revivals of Renaissance plays on the London stage that from 1955 on, 'previously neglected revenge tragedies received multiple productions: three productions of *Titus Andronicus* in 1957, seven Webster productions from the late fifties through the seventies, and long-ignored masterpieces like *The Revenger's Tragedy* and *Women Beware Women* back on the stage.'[21] These plays spoke to generations who had made devastating discoveries of the extreme acts of cruelty which human beings are capable of inflicting upon one another: S. Gorley Putt wrote in 1970 that

> We, who have heard of doctors reading by the light of lampshades made of the skin of their human victims need not shudder when the Duke in . . . *The Revenger's Tragedy* is made to kiss a poisoned skull. And before the incineration of Hiroshima, Marlowe's Tamburlaine himself would have turned pale.[22]

The popularity of revenge tragedy in the decades after the Second World War may then be partly accounted for by a pervasive cultural sense that power can easily fall into the hands of evil, that the forces of justice and social good may prove weak when confronted with such forces, and that the right course of action for the individual in such a crisis is hard to determine – all themes that are well to the fore in Renaissance revenge plays. The director Tony Richardson, writing in 1961 about his production of *The Changeling*, cited the 'extraordinary existentialism of the theme . . . the idea that you are solely and wholly responsible for your actions' as one of the factors that made the play 'tremendously in tune with the contemporary theatre audience'.[23] If individualism and its anxieties link revenge tragedy with modern concerns, so too does the graphic and often perverse sexuality of the genre. Richardson also wrote of Middleton's 'understanding of a certain kind of sexual violence' as prescient of modernity.[24] It is more than possible that the sex and violence of revenge tragedy appealed to a culture trembling on the brink of the 'permissive society'.

The idea of relevance to the modern age was not confined to revenge tragedy. Jan Kott in 1961 published *Shakespeare our Contem-*

porary, which was hugely influential on a generation of directors. Marlowe too was claimed as 'singularly of the twentieth century' because he was 'fascinated by power' and saw 'the ancient moral and religious limitations giving way'.[25] Subversion, then, and the questioning of established belief systems could be found in Renaissance drama; along with other issues that struck chords from the 1960s onwards, such as race, gender, and sexuality. Racial tensions could be thought-provokingly explored through revivals of plays like *The Jew of Malta*, *The Merchant of Venice*, and *Othello*. Meanwhile, as we saw in several of the chapters of this book, numerous Renaissance plays offered strong and complex female roles that were a gift to modern star actresses, and that could be used to address feminist issues. Cross-dressing heroines, too, could be used to assert female independence, or to explore homoeroticism in ways full of interest for the newly tolerant and sexually aware society of the twentieth century's later decades.

In practical terms, the rise and rise of Renaissance drama was assisted by the establishment of the Arts Council in 1947 and by its financial subsidy from the 1950s onwards of the Royal Shakespeare Company and the National Theatre. Increasing access to education and the growth of English Literature as a university subject – usually with Shakespeare and Renaissance drama prominent in the curriculum – also produced directors, actors and audiences with an enthusiasm for Renaissance plays. There was a brief moment in the 1980s and early 1990s when some iconoclastic academics questioned the dominance of Shakespeare in the literary canon, and the ideological and commercial interests that had grown up around him. Books such as *Political Shakespeare* (edited by Jonathan Dollimore and Alan Sinfield, 1985), *The Shakespeare Myth* (edited by Graham Holderness, 1988), and Gary Taylor's *Reinventing Shakespeare* (1990) invited readers to re-examine Shakespeare's cultural pre-eminence and challenge 'Bardolatry'. To some extent other Renaissance dramatists benefited from this; Taylor, for instance, made a case for Middleton to be regarded as no less significant than Shakespeare, and set about editing an Oxford University Press *Collected Works* of Middleton (published 2007), similar in format to the Oxford Shakespeare which he had co-edited. However, if there had been any intention of pushing Shakespeare off his pedestal, it was frustrated.

One important phenomenon that these academic iconoclasts largely ignored was the reach of Shakespeare beyond the UK and US, and the increasing importance of this as culture became globalised. Many different cultures have found, and continue to find, Shakespeare's plots and characters adaptable to their interests and concerns, producing a long and rich history of Shakespeare performance all over the world. To name just a few examples: Italy has a notable history of Shakespeare productions, including Giorgio Strehler's experimental and influential *Tempest* of 1978; in Eastern Europe Shakespeare plays were used as a dissident medium during the period of Communist oppression; and former British colonies such as India adapted Shakespeare to indigenous theatrical traditions.[26] Meanwhile cinema increasingly became the medium in which many viewers encountered Shakespeare, not only in Hollywood adaptations, but also in non-Anglophone versions such as the Japanese director Akira Kurosawa's *Throne of Blood* (based on *Macbeth*, 1957) and *Ran* (based on *King Lear*, 1985).

Shakespeare's centrality to British culture also continued. By the end of the twentieth century he was a greater cultural presence than ever, on school and university syllabuses and on the professional and amateur stage. In 1997 a reconstruction of Shakespeare's Globe opened on Bankside in London, and has continued ever since to offer annual seasons of plays without any public funding. Its first two seasons included two city comedies by Middleton: *A Chaste Maid in Cheapside* (1997) and *A Mad World, My Masters* (1998). It is not hard to understand why: just as in their own time these plays aimed to hold up a mirror to the social aspirations, sexual greed, and financial acquisitiveness of their original London audiences, so at the end of the twentieth century they spoke to current urban cultural concerns. Renaissance drama, then, continued to be seen as relevant. Indeed, it became positively fashionable in the wake of two major cinema films. Baz Luhrmann's *Romeo + Juliet* (1996) updated Shakespeare's play to a setting of urban gang warfare, and added pop-video styling and Leonardo di Caprio to achieve huge success with young audiences. Two years later, *Shakespeare in Love* cleverly combined parodic wit with a kind of authenticity, not only in its look but also in its use of Shakespearean motifs like thwarted love and cross-dressing. It was a worldwide cinematic hit, and as the twenty-first century began, Shakespeare was a bigger cultural presence than ever.

RENAISSANCE DRAMA IN THE TWENTY-FIRST CENTURY

Luhrmann's *Romeo + Juliet* was followed by a string of American high-school rom-coms based on Shakespearean plots, including *10 Things I Hate About You* (1999, based on *The Taming of the Shrew*), *Get Over It* (2001, based on *A Midsummer Night's Dream*), and *She's the Man* (2006, based on *Twelfth Night*). International films based on Shakespeare have also proliferated and are becoming increasingly visible to UK and US audiences. A Maori version of *The Merchant of Venice* (*Te Tangata Whai-Rawa o Weniti*) was made in 2002, while Bollywood has produced Shakespeare adaptations including *Maqbool* (based on *Macbeth*, 2003) and *Omkara* (based on *Othello*, 2006). In China, *The Banquet* (2006) converted *Hamlet* into a martial arts film, while *Prince of the Himalayas* (also 2006) relocated the same play to ancient Tibet. Critics debate whether such films represent the homogenisation and suppression of local cultures by a commercially driven global culture, or subversive retorts to global culture by developing nations and previously disenfranchised communities. Either way, twenty-first Shakespeare on film is frequently concerned with multiculturalism, creatively exploring tensions between the global and the local, and using Shakespeare's plays to communicate local traditions and languages to a wide audience. Experiences of displacement and of friction between communities are frequent themes, and are readily found in plays such as *Romeo and Juliet*, *The Merchant of Venice*, and *Othello*.[27] At the same time for the UK, and for England in particular, Shakespeare will always be bound up with ideas of national identity and national pride. In 2009 he was voted Britain's greatest national treasure,[28] and his plays and related events were at the centre of the cultural festival that accompanied the 2012 London Olympics.

It is hard to find a time when there is not at least one Shakespeare production running on the London stage. Some of these, especially at the Globe, foreground authenticity and participate in Britain's very successful heritage and tourist industries, but at the same time Shakespeare continues to be claimed as our contemporary. In 2005, for instance, the BBC screened a series of television plays titled *Shakespeare Re-Told*. These were adaptations of four Shakespeare plays to present-day settings, aimed at demonstrating his enduring interest and relevance. Many other Renaissance plays also continue to be revived, especially revenge tragedies, and for these too relevance to modern life continues to be a touchstone. Few playgoers now have direct experience of the kinds of atrocities of war that could be invoked to explain the success of revenge tragedy in the twentieth century; rather than being enured to horrors as were soldiers returning from the First World War trenches, audiences today are perhaps more likely to be seeking sensationalism in order to enliven their relatively tame lives. Yet at the same time revenge tragedy does still seem to offer a form of catharsis, and to speak to cultural anxieties around sexuality, violence, and the costs of individualism. The plays lend themselves to addressing twenty-first-century concerns about the consequences of unbridled self-interest, materialism, violent crime, gang rivalries, and the sexualisation of culture, and productions often make imaginative links between the disturbing world of revenge tragedy and some of the edgier forms of modern popular culture. In 2008 two productions of *The Revenger's Tragedy* opened in the same week, one at the National Theatre in London, the other at the Royal Exchange Theatre in Manchester. The National production was praised as 'the precursor of Tarantino's *Pulp Fiction* or Coppola's *The Godfather*' (*The Mail on Sunday*), while Charles Spencer's review in *The Daily Telegraph* was headed 'the enduring appeal of nastiness and perversity'.[29]

Renaissance drama, then, continues to thrive, to enthrall and provoke, and to address ever wider audiences. We can only speculate as to the new and diverse forms it will take and the unexpected responses it will inspire as the twenty-first century progresses. It is an exciting prospect.

Notes

Introduction

1   William Shakespeare, *As You Like It* (2.7.138). All references to Shakespeare's works are to *The Norton Shakespeare*, ed. Stephen Greenblatt et al., 2nd edn (New York: Norton, 2008), unless otherwise stated.
2   Dressing rooms.
3   Gerald Bullett ed., *Silver Poets of the Sixteenth Century* (London: Dent, 1947), p. 296.
4   Ann Jennalie Cook, 'Audiences: investigation, interpretation, invention', in John D. Cox and David Scott Kastan eds, *A New History of Early English Drama* (New York: Columbia UP, 1997), p. 314.
5   Andrew Gurr, *The Shakespearean Playing Companies* (Oxford: Oxford UP, 1996), pp. 26–7.
6   *Oxford English Dictionary*, www.oed.com, accessed 27 April 2011. All further references to the OED will be to this online edition.
7   Jacob Burckhardt, *The Civilization of the Renaissance in* Italy (1860), trans. S.G.C. Middlemore, introd. Peter Burke (London: Penguin, 2004), pp. 99, 103, 101. For more on the history of the idea of the Renaissance, see Margreta de Grazia, 'World pictures, modern periods, and the early stage', in Cox and Kastan, *New History*, pp. 9–13.
8   See Joan Kelly, 'Did Women Have a Renaissance'?, in *Women, History and Theory: The Essays of Joan Kelly* (Chicago: U of Chicago P, 1984), pp. 19–51.
9   Erasmus, *Praise of Folly* (1511), trans. Betty Radice, introd. A.H.T. Levi (1971; rev. edn London: Penguin, 1993), pp. 86–8.
10 John Donne, 'An Anatomy of the World: The First Anniversary', in *The*

Complete English Poems, ed. A.J. Smith (Harmondsworth: Penguin, 1971), lines 205–8, 213–19.

11 From the website of the British Humanist Association, www.humanism.org.uk/home, accessed 16 April 2011.

12 For a fuller definition and discussion of Renaissance humanism, see Diarmaid MacCulloch, *Reformation: Europe's House Divided* (2003; London: Penguin, 2004), pp. 76–87.

13 John Milton, *Paradise Lost*, ed. Alastair Fowler (London: Longman, 1971), VIII:259–82.

14 William Harrison, 'Of Universities', in *The First and Second Volumes of Chronicles*, ed. Raphael Holinshed (London, 1587), Bk. 2, Ch. 3, p. 151. In the 1577 edition the passage appears in Bk. 3, Ch. 4.

15 Baldesar Castiglione, *The Book of the Courtier*, trans. George Bull (1967; rev. edn Harmondsworth: Penguin, 1976), pp. 338, 340.

16 Stephen Greenblatt, *Renaissance Self-Fashioning: From More to Shakespeare* (Chicago: U of Chicago P, 1980), p. 256.

17 Francis Barker, *The Tremulous Private Body: Essays on Subjection* (Ann Arbor: U of Michigan P, 1995), pp. 8, 55.

18 For a detailed history of the Reformation, see MacCulloch, *Reformation*.

19 David Lawrence Smith, *A History of the Modern British Isles, 1603–1707: The Double Crown* (Oxford: Wiley-Blackwell, 1998), p. 37.

20 Sir Philip Sidney, 'The Defence of Poesy', in *The Oxford Authors: Sir Philip Sidney*, ed. Katherine Duncan-Jones (Oxford: Oxford UP, 1989), p. 248.

21 John Jewel, 'The Third Part of the Sermon Against Peril of Idolatry', in *The Second Tome of Homilies* (London, 1571), pp. 130–31.

22 Mary Herbert, Countess of Pembroke, is usually known as Mary Sidney. For more on her writings, see chapter 8 below.

23 Edmund Spenser, Sonnet LXVIII, *Amoretti*, in *The Shorter Poems*, ed. Richard A. McCabe (London: Penguin, 1999), p. 421.

24 There were subsequent revised and expanded editions in 1570, 1576, and 1583.

25 For a judicious account, see Alison Shell, *Shakespeare and Religion* (London: Arden, 2010).

26 See Stephen Greenblatt, *Hamlet in Purgatory* (Princeton: Princeton UP, 2001).

27 See Paul Whitfield White, 'Theater and Religious Culture', in Cox and Kastan, *New History*, pp. 133–51.

28 For a more detailed account of the cultural and historical background to English Renaissance drama, see Julia Briggs, *This Stage-Play World: English Literature and Its Background, 1580–1625* (Oxford: Oxford UP, 1983).

Chapter 1

1 Katherine Duncan-Jones, *Shakespeare: Upstart Crow to Sweet Swan, 1592–1623* (London: Methuen, 2011), p. 9.

2 See Helen Hackett, *Shakespeare and Elizabeth: The Meeting of Two Myths* (Princeton: Princeton UP, 2009), pp. 54–55, 114–20.

3 *Everyman and Mankind*, ed. Douglas Bruster and Eric Rasmussen (London: A & C Black, 2009), pp. 76–81.

4 René Weis, *Shakespeare Revealed: A Biography* (London: John Murray, 2007), pp. 64, 83.

5 *Everyman and Mankind*, ed. Bruster and Rasmussen, p. 5.

6 See John M. Wasson, 'The English church as theatrical space', in Cox and Kastan, *New History*, pp. 26–37.

7 Charles W. Whitworth, Jr. ed., *Three Sixteenth-Century Comedies: 'Gammer Gurton's Needle', 'Roister Doister', 'The Old Wife's Tale'* (London: Ernest Benn, 1984), p. xx.

8 The terms 'ministry' and 'métier' are related to the term 'mystery'; see *OED*.

9 Paul Whitfield White, 'Theater and religious culture', in Cox and Kastan, *New History*, pp. 135, 139; Michael D. Bristol, 'Theater and popular culture', in Cox and Kastan, *New History*, p. 240; Richard Dutton, 'Censorship', in Cox and Kastan, *New History*, pp. 290–91.

10 Richard Beadle and Pamela M. King eds, *York Mystery Plays: A Selection in Modern Spelling* (Oxford: Oxford UP, 1995), p. x.

11 Jean MacIntyre and Garrett P.J. Epp, '"Cloathes worth all the rest": costumes and properties', in Cox and Kastan, *New History*, p. 271.

12 Beadle and King, *York Mystery Plays*, pp. 23–7. All references are to this edition.

13 Coventry Shearmen and Taylors' Play, s.d. at line 783; William Tydeman, 'An introduction to medieval English theatre', in Richard Beadle ed., *The Cambridge Companion to Medieval English Theatre* (Cambridge: Cambridge UP, 1994), p. 28.

14 For more on the York cycle see Beadle and King, *York Mystery Plays*, pp. ix–xxx; and Richard Beadle, 'The York cycle', in Beadle, *Medieval English Theatre*, pp. 85–108.

15 Beadle, *Medieval English Theatre*, p. 61, fig. 8.

16 Meg Twycross, 'The theatricality of medieval English plays', in Beadle, *Medieval English Theatre*, pp. 56–83.

17 *Mankind*, in *Everyman and Mankind*, ed. Bruster and Rasmussen, p. 107, lines 194–6. All references are to this edition.

18 *Everyman*, in *Everyman and Mankind*, ed. Bruster and Rasmussen, p. 190, lines 122–3. All references are to this edition.

19 Pamela M. King, 'Morality Plays', in Beadle, *Medieval English Theatre*, p. 257.

20 For more on morality plays, see G.A. Lester ed., *Three Late Medieval Morality Plays: Mankind, Everyman, Mundus et Infans* (1981; rpt. London: A. & C. Black, 2002), pp. xi–xxxvii; King, 'Morality Plays', in Beadle, *Medieval English Theatre*, pp. 240–64.

21 *Gammer Gurton's Needle*, in Whitworth, *Three Sixteenth-Century Comedies*, 1.5.53–4, 2.1.107–8. All references are to this edition.

22 Wager.

23 Thou horse, thou [unspecific term of abuse], thou privy.

24 One afflicted with a scabby disease of the scalp.

25 I'll back you to win this contest.

26 Whitworth, *Three Sixteenth-Century Comedies*, p. xxxi.

27 *Roister Doister* in Whitworth, *Three Sixteenth-Century Comedies*, 4.4.17–20, 4.7.59–72, 4.8. All references are to this edition.

28 I have removed the line-divisions from the verse to clarify the punctuation.

29 Christopher Marlowe, *Edward II*, in *Doctor Faustus and Other Plays*, ed. David Bevington and Eric Rasmussen (Oxford: Oxford UP, 1995), 5.4.6–16.

30 Thomas Sackville and Thomas Norton, *Gorboduc, or Ferrex and Porrex*, ed. Irby B. Cauthen, Jr. (London: Edward Arnold, 1970), 1.2.388–93. All references are to this edition.

31 For more on *Gorboduc*, see Peter Happé, *English Drama Before Shakespeare* (London: Longman, 1999), pp. 101–5, and Sackville and Norton, *Gorboduc*, pp. xi–xxviii.

32 For more on early developments in English Renaissance comedy and tragedy, see A. R. Braunmuller and Michael Hattaway eds, *The Cambridge Companion to English Renaissance Drama*, 2nd edn (Cambridge: Cambridge UP, 2003), pp. 256–60, 302–03.

33 John Leland and Nicholas Udall, pageant verses for the coronation procession of Anne Boleyn, British Library Royal MS 18.A.lxiv, ff. 1–16; John Leland and Nicholas Udall, 'Leland's and Udall's verses before the coronation of Anne Boleyn', in F.J. Furnivall ed., *Ballads from Manuscripts* (London, 1868–73), vol. 1, pp. 364–401.

34 See Lawrence Manley, *Literature and Culture in Early Modern London* (Cambridge: Cambridge UP, 1995), pp. 212–93; Gordon Kipling, '"Wonderfull spectacles": theater and civic culture', in Cox and Kastan, *New History*, pp. 153–71.

35 Manley, *Literature and Culture*, p. 223.

36 Leland and Udall, BL Royal MS 18.A.lxiv, ff. 8v-9r.

37 Leland and Udall, BL Royal MS 18.A.lxiv, ff. 8v, 9v, 13r-v, 16r.

38 Richard Mulcaster, *The Queen's Majesty's Passage* (1559), in Arthur F. Kinney ed., *Renaissance Drama: An Anthology of Plays and Entertainments* (Oxford: Blackwell, 1999), p. 22. All references are to this edition.

39 Elizabeth I, *Collected Works*, ed. Leah S. Marcus, Janel Mueller, and Mary Beth Rose (Chicago: U of Chicago P, 2000), p. 194; see also pp. 189, 383.

40 Tydeman, 'Introduction', in Beadle, *Medieval English Theatre*, pp. 15–16; R. Mark Benbow, Introduction to *The Araygnment of Paris*, in George Peele, *Dramatic Works*, ed. R. Mark Benbow, Elmer Blistein, and Frank S. Hook (New Haven: Yale UP, 1970), p. 29.

41 Sir Philip Sidney, *The Lady of May*, in Kinney ed., *Renaissance Drama*, p. 41. All references are to this edition.

42 Andrew Gurr, *The Shakespearean Stage 1574–1642*, 3rd edn (Cambridge: Cambridge UP, 1992), pp. 32–3; Peele, *Dramatic Works*, pp. 25, 39.

43 Peele, *Dramatic Works*, *Araygnment of Paris* 5.1.1147–52, 1170–73, 1240 s.d.

44 See Louis Adrian Montrose, 'Gifts and reasons: the contexts of Peele's *Araygnment of Paris*', *English Literary History* 47.3 (Autumn 1980), pp. 433–61.

45 John Lyly, *Endymion*, ed. David Bevington (Manchester: Manchester UP, 1996), 3.4.165–8. All references are to this edition.

46 See Helen Hackett, 'Dream-visions of Elizabeth I', in Katharine Hodgkin, Michelle O'Callaghan and S.J. Wiseman eds, *Reading the Early Modern Dream: The Terrors of the Night* (New York: Routledge, 2008), pp. 45–66.

47 W.R. Streitberger, 'Personnel and professionalization', in Cox and Kastan, *New History*, p. 341.

48 Peele, *Dramatic Works*, p. 24.

49 Recent scholarship suggests that large indoor rooms were used for performance at inns rather than the inn-yards. See John Orrell, 'The Theaters', in Cox and Kastan, *New History*, p. 103.

50 Gurr, *Shakespearean Stage*, p. 8.

51 Gurr, *Shakespearean Stage*, p. 27; Peter H. Greenfield, 'Touring', in Cox and Kastan, *New History*, p. 259; Streitberger, 'Personnel', p. 343.

52 Gurr, *Shakespearean Stage*, p. 30.

53 Michael Wood, *In Search of Shakespeare* (London: BBC Worldwide, 2003), pp. 105–6.

54 Weis, *Shakespeare Revealed*, p. 83; Katherine-Duncan Jones, *Ungentle Shakespeare: Scenes from his Life* (London: Arden Shakespeare, 2001), pp. 27–53.

55 Gurr, *Shakespearean Stage*, p. 118–19.

56 Gurr, *Shakespearean Stage*, p. 31.

57 Jean Howard, *The Stage and Social Struggle in Early Modern England* (London: Routledge, 1994), p. 25.

58 Howard, *Stage and Social Struggle*, p. 40.

59 Gurr, *Shakespearean Stage*, p. 31.

60 For more on the anti-theatrical controversy in relation to boy actors and cross-dressing, see chapter 8 below.

Chapter 2

1 Liza Picard, *Elizabeth's London: Everyday Life in Elizabethan London* (London: Weidenfeld & Nicholson, 2003), pp. 15, 28.

2 James Howell, *Londinopolis: An Historical Discourse or Perlustration of the City of London* (London, 1657), pp. 20, 22.

3 Picard, *Elizabethan London*, p. 22.

4 See Brian Crockett, *The Play of Paradox: Stage and Sermon in Renaissance England* (Philadelphia: U of Pennsylvania P, 1995); Arnold Hunt, *The Art of Hearing: English Preachers and Their Audiences, 1590–1640* (Cambridge: Cambridge UP, 2012).

5 Thomas Middleton and Thomas Dekker, *The Roaring Girl* (1611), 3.1–4. All quotations from Thomas Middleton's works are from *The Collected Works*, gen. eds Gary Taylor and John Lavagnino (Oxford: Oxford UP, 2007), unless otherwise stated. For more on this passage, see chapter 7 below.

6 Embroidered border (*OED* n.[1] I.1).

7 Collar, necklace, or covering for the throat (*OED* n.[1] 1b, 2, 3).

8 Isabella Whitney, 'The Manner of her Will, and What she Left to London', in Isabella Whitney, Mary Sidney and Aemilia Lanyer, *Renaissance Women Poets*, ed. Danielle Clarke (London: Penguin, 2000), pp. 19–28, lines 41–74.

9 Gurr, *Shakespearean Stage*, p. 213; Picard, *Elizabeth's London*, pp. xxii, 31.

10 Picard, *Elizabeth's London*, p. 118.

11 A lumbering cart, often a dung-cart (*OED* n.1 3).

12 Carters (*OED* n.1).

13 Presumably a knight whose valour lies mainly in prodigious drinking.

14 'Score': credit account at the ale-house, recorded by a row of marks on a board, slate, or door (*OED* n.10a). Everard Guilpin, *Skialetheia, or, A Shadow of Truth, in Certain Epigrams and Satires* (London, 1598), Satire 5, sigs D4r-D7r.

15 Picard, *Elizabeth's London*, p. 50.

16 Picard, *Elizabeth's London*, p. 35.

17 Picard, *Elizabeth's London*, pp. 30–31.

18 Ben Jonson, 'On the Famous Voyage', in *The Complete Poems*, ed. George Parfitt (London: Penguin, 1988), pp. 86–92, lines 124–48.

19 Picard, *Elizabeth's London*, p. 90.

20 Picard, *Elizabeth's London*, pp. 90–93.

21 H.H. Lamb, *Climate: Present, Past and Future*, vol. 2 (London: Methuen, 1977), pp. 568–70.

22 A game in which balls were bowled at targets (*OED* n.3).

23 Joseph P. Ward, 'The Taming of the Thames: Reading the River in the Seventeenth Century', *Huntington Library Quarterly* 71.1 (March 2008), pp. 55–75; John Taylor, *The Colde Tearme, Or, The Frozen Age, Or, The Metamorphosis of The River of Thames* (London, 1621).

24 Henry Machyn's diary, quoted in John Nichols ed., *The Progresses and Public Processions of Queen Elizabeth*, 3 vols (London, 1823), vol. 1, p. 67.

25 Picard, *Elizabeth's London*, p. 219.

26 Gurr, *Shakespearean Stage*, pp. 47, 117.

27 Tiffany Stern, *Documents of Performance in Early Modern England* (Cambridge: Cambridge UP, 2009), pp. 36–62.

28 Gurr, *Shakespearean Stage*, pp. 117–18.

29 Gurr, *Shakespearean Stage*, pp. 121–54; Andrew Gurr, 'Shakespeare's Globe: a history of reconstructions and some reasons for trying', in J.R. Mulryne and Margaret Shewring eds, *Shakespeare's Globe Rebuilt* (Cambridge: Cambridge UP, 1997), pp. 27–47; John Orrell, 'The Theaters', in Cox and Kastan, *New History*, pp. 102–12.

30 Gabriel Egan, 'Reconstructions of the Globe: a retrospective', *Shakespeare Survey* 52 (1999), pp. 1–16.

31 Ann Jennalie Cook, 'Audiences: investigation, interpretation, invention', in Cox and Kastan, *New History*, p. 314.

32 Gurr, *Shakespearean Stage*, p. 213.

33 John Davies, 'In Cosmum', in *The Poems of Sir John Davies*, ed. Robert Kruger (Oxford: Oxford UP, 1975), p. 136.

34 Michael Drayton, *Idea* 47, in Maurice Evans ed., *Elizabethan Sonnets* (London: Dent, 1977), p. 107.

35 Edmund Gayton, *Pleasant notes upon Don Quixot* (London, 1654), p. 271.

36 John Marston, *Jacke Drums Entertainment* (London, 1601), sig. H3v.

37 Gurr, *Shakespearean Stage*, p. 182. See chapter 6 below for more on the use of body-parts in revenge tragedy.

38 Gurr, *Shakespearean Stage*, p. 198.

39 Gurr, *Shakespearean Stage*, pp. 187–8.

40 Gurr, *Shakespearean Stage*, p. 191.

41 Gurr, 'Shakespeare's Globe', in Mulryne and Shewring, *Shakespeare's Globe Rebuilt*, p. 27.

42 The Fortune was a square building.

43 For more on this passage, see chapter 4 below.

44 Gurr, *Shakespearean Stage*, p. 78.

45 Gurr, *Shakespearean Stage*, pp. 33, 49–55; Orrell, 'The Theaters', in

Cox and Kastan, *New History*, pp. 98–9; Streitberger, 'Personnel', in Cox and Kastan, *New History*, p. 350.

46 Antonia Southern, *Player, Playwright and Preacher's Kid: The Story of Nathan Field, 1587–1620* (London: Athena Press, 2009), pp. 11–12.

47 Ben Jonson, 'Epitaph on S.P., a Child of Q[ueen] El[izabeth's] Chapel', *Complete Poems*, ed. Parfitt, p. 81.

48 Gurr, *Shakespearean Stage*, pp. 154–63; Orrell, 'Theaters', in Cox and Kastan, *New History*, pp. 98–102.

49 John Webster, *The Duchess of Malfi*, in *The Duchess of Malfi and Other Plays*, ed. René Weis (Oxford: Oxford UP, 1996), 4.1.53.

50 See *The Chamber of Demonstrations: Reconstructing the Jacobean Indoor Playhouse*, http://www.bristol.ac.uk/drama/jacobean/project1.html, accessed 13 Aug 2012.

51 Tiffany Stern, *Making Shakespeare: From Stage to Page* (London: Routledge, 2004), p. 30.

52 Mulryne and Shewring, *Shakespeare's Globe Rebuilt*, pp. 189–91.

53 Revision to Stowe's *Annales* for 5th edition (1631), as quoted in E.K. Chambers, *The Elizabethan Stage*, 4 vols (Oxford: Clarendon, 1623), vol. 2, pp. 373–4.

54 Gurr, *Shakespearean Stage*, p. 215.

55 Gurr, *Shakespearean Stage*, pp. 45–6. For more on the formation of the Lord Chamberlain's Men, see Streitberger, 'Personnel', in Cox and Kastan, *New History*, pp. 345–7.

56 'Robert Greene on Shakespeare (1592)', in *Norton Shakespeare*, ed. Greenblatt et al., pp. 3299–300; Jonson, *Timber: or Discoveries*, in *Complete Poems*, ed. Parfitt, p. 394.

57 James Shapiro, *1599: A Year in the Life of William Shakespeare* (London: Faber, 2005), pp. 12–13.

58 Streitberger, 'Personnel', p. 354.

59 See chapter 4 below for more on Shakespeare's witty fools.

60 Ben Jonson, 'Explorata: Or Discoveries', in *The Complete Poems*, ed. George Parfitt (London: Penguin, 1988), p. 398.

61 James Wright, *Historia Histrionica* (London, 1699), p. 5.

62 John Webster, 'An excellent Actor', in *New Characters (Drawne to the Life)*, attrib. Sir Thomas Overbury (London, 1615), sig. M6r; Thomas May, *The Heire* (London, 1622), sig. B1r.

63 Stern, *Making Shakespeare*, p. 63.

64 See Simon Palfrey and Tiffany Stern, *Shakespeare in Parts* (Oxford: Oxford UP, 2007).

65 Thanks to Nick Hutchison for pointing out this example.

66 Webster, 'Excellent Actor', sig. M5v. See Andrew Gurr, 'Who strutted and bellowed?', *Shakespeare Survey* 16 (1963), pp. 95–102.

67 For more on Jonson's publication of his Works, see chapter 5 below.

68 For traces of *Cardenio* in an eighteenth-century play, see *Double*

Falsehood or the Distressed Lovers, ed. Brean Hammond (London: Arden Shakespeare, 2000).

69 Brian Vickers, *Shakespeare, Co-Author: A Historical Study of Five Collaborative Plays* (Oxford: Oxford UP, 2002).

70 William Shakespeare, *The RSC Shakespeare: Complete Works*, ed. Jonathan Bate and Eric Rasmussen (Basingstoke: Macmillan, 2007), pp. 2464–8.

71 Emma Smith, 'Chettle, Henry (*d.* 1603x7)', *Oxford Dictionary of National Biography* (Oxford: Oxford UP, 2004), http://www.oxforddnb.com/view/article/5245, accessed 30 June 2011.

72 Thomas Heywood, *The English Traveller* (London, 1633), sig. A3r.

73 See William Shakespeare and John Fletcher, *The Two Noble Kinsmen*, ed. N.W. Bawcutt, introd. Peter Swaab (London: Penguin, 2009), pp. xxxvi–xlvi.

74 For more on *The Two Noble Kinsmen*, see chapter 7 below.

75 Compare William Shakespeare and John Fletcher, *King Henry VIII*, ed. Gordon McMullan (London: Arden Shakespeare, 2000) with John Fletcher and William Shakespeare, *The Two Noble Kinsmen*, ed. Lois Potter (London: Arden Shakespeare, 1997).

76 Marlowe, *Faustus and Other Plays*, pp. xvi–xvii, xxvi–xxviii.

77 Eric Rasmussen, 'The revision of scripts', in Cox and Kastan, *New History*, p. 459.

78 Thomas Middleton, *The Collected Works*, gen. eds Gary Taylor and John Lavagnino (Oxford: Oxford UP, 2007), pp. 1165–1201.

79 William Shakespeare, *Hamlet: The Texts of 1603 and 1623*, ed. Ann Thompson and Neil Taylor (London: Arden Shakespeare, 2006), 7. 115–22.

80 Stern, *Making Shakespeare*, pp. 151–52.

81 Stern, *Making Shakespeare*, pp. 141–58.

82 Stern, *Documents of Performance*.

Chapter 3

1 Prologue, *Tamburlaine the Great, part 1*, lines 1–6, in Marlowe, *Doctor Faustus and Other Plays*, ed. Bevington and Rasmussen, p. 3. All further references to Marlowe's plays are to this edition unless otherwise stated.

2 See Roma Gill, 'Christopher Marlowe', in Fredson Bowers ed., *Dictionary of Literary Biography: Elizabethan Dramatists* (Detroit: Gale, 1987), vol. 62, p. 212.

3 Park Honan, *Christopher Marlowe, Poet and Spy* (Oxford: Oxford UP, 2005), p. 377.

4 William Vaughan, 'Of Atheists', in *The Golden Grove* (London, 1600), sigs C4v-C5r, quoted in J. A. Downie, 'Reviewing what we think we

know about Christopher Marlowe, again', in Sarah K. Scott and M.L. Stapleton eds, *Christopher Marlowe the Craftsman: Lives, Stage, and Page* (Farnham: Ashgate, 2010), p. 43.

5   Honan, *Christopher Marlowe*, p. 376.

6   Charles Nicholl, *The Reckoning: The Murder of Christopher Marlowe* (1992; paperback, London: Picador, 1993).

7   Rosalind Barber, 'Was Marlowe a Violent Man?', in Scott and Stapleton, *Marlowe the Craftsman*, pp. 47–59.

8   Lisa Hopkins, *Christopher Marlowe, Renaissance Dramatist* (Edinburgh: Edinburgh UP, 2008), p. 9.

9   Honan, *Christopher Marlowe, Poet and Spy*, pp. 374–75.

10 Honan, *Christopher Marlowe, Poet and Spy*, p. 381.

11 Harry Levin, *The Overreacher: A Study of Christopher Marlowe* (London: Faber, 1954); A.L. Rowse, *Christopher Marlowe: A Biography* (London: Macmillan, 1964), p.150.

12 Downie, 'Reviewing what we think we know', in Scott and Stapleton, *Marlowe the Craftsman*, p. 44.

13 GAVESTON: 'Come not here to scoff at Gaveston, / Whose mounting thoughts did never creep so low / As to bestow a look on such as you' (*Edward II*, 2.2.76–8).

14 See Hopkins, *Christopher Marlowe*, p. 24.

15 Ben Jonson, 'To the memory of my beloved, the author Mr William Shakespeare: and what he hath left us', in *Complete Poems*, ed. Parfitt, pp. 263–5, line 30. As noted in chapter 1 above, earlier plays like *Gorboduc* had used iambic pentameter and blank verse, but it was Marlowe who conclusively established these as standard for English Renaissance drama.

16 Russ McDonald, 'Marlowe and style', in Patrick Cheney ed., *The Cambridge Companion to Christopher Marlowe* (Cambridge: Cambridge UP, 2004), p. 66.

17 *On the Dignity of Man*, as quoted in Jonathan Dollimore, *Radical Tragedy: Religion, Ideology and Power in the Drama of Shakespeare and his Contemporaries* (1984; 2nd edn, Hemel Hempstead: Harvester Wheatsheaf, 1989), p. 112.

18 One example of parody is Shakespeare's *Henry IV part 2*, where the bombastic Pistol speaks of 'hollow pampered jades of Asia' (2.4.141).

19 Mark Thornton Burnett, '*Tamburlaine the Great, Parts 1 and 2*', in Cheney, *Cambridge Companion*, p. 142.

20 Prologue, line 11. All quotations from *Doctor Faustus* are from the A-text.

21 Romans 6: 23. Faustus quotes the Latin Vulgate Bible with his own English translation; the missing part of the verse is quoted here from the Geneva Bible, the English Bible in most widespread use in Elizabethan England. *The Geneva Bible: A Facsimile of the 1560 Edition*, introd. Lloyd E. Berry (Madison: U of Wisconsin P, 1969).

22 'Despair', in *The Catholic Encyclopedia*, www.newadvent.org/cathen/04755a.htm, accessed 13 Aug 2012.
23 Chambers, *Elizabethan Stage*, vol. 3, pp. 423–24.
24 William Prynne, *Histriomastix* (London, 1633), f. 556r, quoted in Chambers, *Elizabethan Stage*, vol. 3, pp. 423–4.
25 Christopher Marlowe, *Doctor Faustus*, ed. David Bevington and Eric Rasmussen, Revels Plays (Manchester: Manchester UP, 1993), p. 49.
26 Alan Bray, *Homosexuality in Renaissance England* (1982; 2nd edn, London: Gay Men's Press, 1988), pp. 62, 67, 70, 71; Bruce R. Smith, *Homosexual Desire in Shakespeare's England: A Cultural Poetics* (1991; pbk, Chicago: U of Chicago P, 1994), pp. 11, 41; *OED*, definitions of 'homosexual', 'buggery', 'sodomy'.
27 Bray, *Homosexuality*, p. 65.
28 In myth, Pelops had an ivory shoulder, having been dismembered by his father and reassembled by the gods. Ovid, *Metamorphoses*, trans. David Raeburn (London: Penguin, 2004), 6.401–11.
29 David Norbrook and H.R. Woudhuysen eds, *The Penguin Book of Renaissance Verse 1509–1659* (London: Penguin, 1992), p. 268, lines 63–9.
30 Christopher Marlowe, *The Tragedie of Dido, Queene of Carthage*, in *The Complete Works of Christopher Marlowe*, ed. Fredson Bowers, 2 vols, (1973; 2nd edn, Cambridge: Cambridge University Press, 1981), vol. 1, pp. 1–70, 1.1.1.s.d, 1.1.46–8.
31 Raphael Holinshed, *The Third Volume of Chronicles* (London, 1586), p. 341.
32 Downie, 'Reviewing what we think we know', in Scott and Stapleton, *Marlowe the Craftsman*, p. 38; Laurie E. Maguire, 'Marlovian texts and authorship', in Cheney, *Cambridge Companion to Marlowe*, pp. 43–4, 55.
33 Honan, *Christopher Marlowe, Poet and Spy*, pp. 183, 185, 219–21, 264; Thomas Healy, '*Doctor Faustus*', in Cheney, *Cambridge Companion to Marlowe*, p. 179.
34 Robert A. Logan, 'Marlowe scholarship and criticism: the current scene', in Scott and Stapleton, *Marlowe the Craftsman*, p. 18.

Chapter 4

1 'Robert Greene on Shakespeare (1592)', in *Norton Shakespeare*, ed. Greenblatt et al., pp. 3299–300.
2 For an account of Shakespeare's reputation up to the publication of the First Folio in 1623, see Duncan-Jones, *Shakespeare: Upstart Crow*.
3 William Shakespeare, *The Tempest*, ed. Stephen Orgel (Oxford: Oxford UP, 1994), 4.1.148–58n, 152–3n.

4 Jonson, 'To the memory of my beloved', *Complete Poems*, ed. Parfitt, pp. 263–5, lines 47–50.

5 Alexander Pope ed., *The Works of Shakespeare, Collected and Corrected* (1765), quoted in Brian Vickers ed., *Shakespeare: The Critical Heritage: Vol. 2: 1693–1733* (London: Routledge, 1974), pp. 403–4.

6 'Preface', in Samuel Johnson ed., *The Plays of William Shakespeare, in Eight Volumes* (1765), quoted in Brian Vickers ed., *Shakespeare: The Critical Heritage: Vol. 5: 1765–1774* (London: Routledge, 1979), p. 57.

7 Blackbird, i.e. a woman of dark colouring, considered less attractive than fair colouring.

8 One of the less prestigious legal colleges.

9 See L.C. Knights, 'How many children had Lady Macbeth?', in *Explorations: Essays in Criticism Mainly on the Literature of the Seventeenth Century* (London: Chatto & Windus, 1946), pp. 1–39.

10 For more on this, see chapter 8 below.

11 Sidney, *Defence of Poesy*, pp. 243–44.

12 Richard Dutton, *Ben Jonson: Authority: Criticism* (Basingstoke: Macmillan, 1996), pp. 106–08.

13 For more on Shakespeare's mixing of genres in his late plays, including his tragicomedies written in collaboration with John Fletcher, see chapter 7 below.

14 See chapter 2 above for discussion of Robert Armin's contribution to Shakespeare's development of the witty fool.

15 All references here to *King Lear* are to the Conflated Text in *The Norton Shakespeare*, ed. Greenblatt.

Chapter 5

1 I.e. foreigners.

2 Richard West, 'On Mr. Ben. Johnson', from *Jonsonus Virbius* (1638), quoted in D.H. Craig ed., *Ben Jonson: The Critical Heritage* (London: Routledge, 1990), p. 210.

3 Though the first to hold this title officially was Jonson's successor William Davenant, appointed in 1638. For all biographical information on Jonson in this chapter, please see Ian Donaldson, *Ben Jonson: A Life* (Oxford: Oxford UP, 2011).

4 See James A. Riddell, *Jonson's Folio of 1616*, in Richard Harp and Stanley Stewart eds, *The Cambridge Companion to Ben Jonson* (Cambridge: Cambridge UP, 2000), pp. 152–62.

5 'An Ode. To Himself', Jonson, *Poems*, ed. Parfitt, pp. 160–61.

6 Ben Jonson, *The Alchemist and Other Plays*, ed. Gordon Campbell (Oxford: Oxford UP, 1995), p. 9.

7 Induction to *Bartholomew Fair*, in Jonson, *Alchemist and Other Plays*, ed. Campbell, p. 32.

8 Ben Jonson, *Every Man out of his Humour*, in *Ben Jonson*, ed. C.H. Herford and Percy Simpson, 11 vols (Oxford: Clarendon, 1925–52), vol. 4, 'After the Second Sounding', p. 432, lines 105–09. See also Dutton, *Ben Jonson: Authority: Criticism*, pp. 115–23 for a helpful discussion of Jonsonian 'humours'.

9 Ben Jonson, *Cynthia's Revels*, in *Jonson*, ed. Herford and Simpson, vol. 4, p. 43, 'Prologue', lines 10–11, 13, 16–17.

10 See Leah Marcus, 'Jonson and the court', in Harp and Stewart, *Cambridge Companion to Jonson*, pp. 31–3.

11 Ben Jonson, *Sejanus, His Fall*, ed. Philip J. Ayres (Manchester: Manchester UP, 1990), p. 49.

12 Ben Jonson, *The Masque of Blackness*, in David Lindley ed., *Court Masques: Jacobean and Caroline Entertainments 1605–1640* (Oxford: Oxford UP, 1995), p. 1. All further references are to this edition.

13 Quoted in Clare McManus, '"Defacing the carcass": Anne of Denmark and Jonson's *The Masque of Blackness*', in Julie Sanders, Kate Chedgzoy and Susan Wiseman eds, *Refashioning Ben Jonson: Gender, Politics, and the Jonsonian Canon* (Basingstoke: Macmillan, 1998), pp. 94–5.

14 For more on female performance in courtly and aristocratic settings, see chapter 8 below.

15 Ben Jonson, 'The Masque of Queens', in Lindley, *Court Masques*, pp. 35, 43–4.

16 Jonson, 'Masque of Queens', in Lindley, *Court Masques*, p. 35.

17 Ben Jonson, *Hymenaei* (London, 1606), sig. A3r.

18 Stephen Orgel, *The Illusion of Power: Political Theater in the English Renaissance* (Berkeley: U of California P, 1975), pp. 10–16.

19 See Dutton, *Ben Jonson: Authority: Criticism*, Ch. 3.

20 Ben Jonson, 'Pleasure Reconciled to Virtue', in Lindley, *Court Masques*, p. 123.

21 'An Epistle to Master John Selden', in *Poems*, ed. Parfitt, pp. 147–49, lines 19–22.

22 Ben Jonson, *Volpone*, in *Alchemist and Other Plays*, ed. Campbell, 1.5.56–9. All further references are to this edition.

23 Ben Jonson, *The Alchemist*, in *Alchemist and Other Plays*, ed. Campbell, Prologue, lines 7–8. All further references are to this edition.

24 *The Alchemist* was first performed in Oxford, in September 1610, since the plague had forced the closure of the London playhouses, but it was probably performed at the Blackfriars soon after they re-opened in November.

25 Concubines.

26 A fish which has fleshy filaments hanging from its mouth.

27 A toy weapon; a battle-axe with a sharp-ended staff.

28 Dolls.

29 Ben Jonson, *Bartholomew Fair*, in *Alchemist and Other Plays*, ed. Campbell, 2.2.28–32. All further references are to this edition.

30 Watering-can.

31 Martin Butler, 'Jonson's London and its theatres', in Harp and Stewart, *Cambridge Companion to Jonson*, pp. 24–5; Sir Thomas Bodley, *Letters of Sir Thomas Bodley to Thomas James, First Keeper of the Bodleian Library*, ed. G.W. Wheeler (Oxford: Clarendon, 1926), p. 219, and see pp. 221–2.

32 *Wits Recreations. Selected from the Finest Fancies of Moderne Muses* (London, 1640), sig. G3v.

33 Dutton, *Ben Jonson: Authority: Criticism*, p. 51.

34 'Conversations with William Drummond', in Jonson, *Poems*, ed. Parfitt, pp. 479–80.

35 A tun is a large cask or barrel used for wine or beer. Jonson, 'My Picture Left in Scotland', in *Poems*, ed. Parfitt, p. 140; 'Induction', *The Staple of News*, Herford and Simpson vol. 6, p. 281, lines 62–3.

36 Anne Barton, *Ben Jonson, Dramatist* (Cambridge UP, 1984), pp. 300–320.

37 Donaldson, *Ben Jonson*, p. 416; Julie Sanders, 'Print, popular culture, consumption and commodification in *The Staple of News*', in Sanders, Chedgzoy and Wiseman, *Refashioning Ben Jonson*, pp. 183–207.

38 Donaldson, *Ben Jonson*, p. 399.

39 Ben Jonson, 'Prologue', *Every Man in his Humour*, folio text, *Jonson*, ed. Herford and Simpson, vol.3, p. 303, lines 3–4, 13–14. All further references are to this edition.

40 Jonson, *Timber: or Discoveries*, in *Complete Poems*, ed. Parfitt, p. 394.

41 Jonson, *Every Man Out*, in *Jonson*, ed. Herford and Simpson, vol. 3, p. 515, 3.6.195–201.

Chapter 6

1 Thomas Middleton, *The Revenger's Tragedy*, in *Collected Works*, gen. eds Taylor and Lavagnino, 3.5.130–223. All further references to Middleton's works are to this edition. *The Revenger's Tragedy* used to be attributed to Cyril Tourneur but is now thought to be by Middleton.

2 John Webster, *The White Devil*, in *The Duchess of Malfi and Other Plays*, ed. René Weis (Oxford: Oxford UP, 1996), 5.3.1–40; *The Duchess of Malfi*, in *The Duchess of Malfi and Other Plays*, ed. Weis, 5.2.271–85. All further references to Webster's plays are to this edition.

3 John Ford, *'Tis Pity She's a Whore*, ed. Derek Roper (Manchester: Manchester UP, 1997), 5.6.10.

4 See, for instance, Ashley H. Thorndike, 'The relations of *Hamlet* to

contemporary revenge plays', *PMLA* 17. 2 (1902): 125–220.

5 See chapter 2 above on how the shock-value of this moment would have been enhanced by the particular lighting conditions of a Jacobean indoor playhouse.

6 On the importance of memory in revenge tragedy, see John Kerrigan, *Revenge Tragedy: Aeschylus to Armageddon* (Oxford: Clarendon, 1996), Ch. 7.

7 Prologue, *The Jew of Malta*, lines 14–15, in Marlowe, *Doctor Faustus and Other Plays*, ed. Bevington and Rasmussen, p. 251.

8 Thomas Kyd, *The Spanish Tragedy* (*c*.1587), in *Four Revenge Tragedies*, ed. Katharine Eisaman Maus (Oxford: Oxford UP, 1995), 3.2.1–4. All further references are to this edition.

9 Ben Jonson, *Every Man in his Humour* (1598), quarto of 1601, in *Ben Jonson*, ed. C.H. Herford and Percy Simpson, 11 vols (Oxford: Clarendon, 1925–52), vol.3, pp. 191–289, 1.3.134–40.

10 Donaldson, *Ben Jonson*, pp. 105–06; Barton, *Ben Jonson, Dramatist*, pp. 13–28.

11 *A Warning for Fair Women* (London, 1599), sig. A2v.

12 For more on laughter in revenge tragedy, see Kerrigan, *Revenge Tragedy*, Ch. 8, and Nicholas Brooke, *Horrid Laughter in Jacobean Tragedy* (London: Open Books, 1979).

13 Pigeons were applied to plague-sores to draw out the infection.

14 See Margot Heinemann, *Puritanism and Theatre: Thomas Middleton and Opposition Drama under the Early Stuarts* (Cambridge: Cambridge UP, 1980); Thomas Middleton, *Women Beware Women and Other Plays*, ed. Richard Dutton (Oxford: Oxford UP, 1999), pp. xii–xvi.

15 See Alison Shell, *Catholicism, Controversy and the English Literary Imagination, 1558–1660* (Cambridge: Cambridge UP, 1999), Ch. 1.

16 Sir John Harington, *Letters and Epigrams*, ed. N.E. McClure (Philadelphia: U of Pennsylvania P, 1930), pp. 119–20.

17 Alan Stewart, *The Cradle King: A Life of James VI and I* (London: Chatto and Windus, 2003), pp. 258–9, 261, 278–80.

18 See Alastair Bellany, *The Politics of Court Scandal in Early Modern England: News Culture and the Overbury Affair, 1603–1666* (Cambridge: Cambridge UP, 2002).

19 Dollimore, *Radical Tragedy*, p. xxi. J.W. Lever in *The Tragedy of State* (London: Methuen, 1971) had previously emphasised the political force of revenge tragedy.

Chapter 7

1 Francis Beaumont, *The Knight of the Burning Pestle*, ed. Sheldon P. Zitner (Manchester: Manchester UP, 1984), 4.33–8.

2 Middleton, *Collected Works*, ed. Taylor and Lavagnino, p. 25.
3 Thomas Middleton, *The Roaring Girl*, ed. Elizabeth Cook (1976; London: A. & C. Black, 1997), pp. xvii-xxii.
4 Wendy Griswold, *Renaissance Revivals: City Comedy and Revenge Tragedy in the London Theatre, 1576–1980* (Chicago: U of Chicago P, 1986), pp. 15, 26, 29.
5 Henry Hitch Adams, *English Domestic or Homiletic Tragedy, 1575 to 1642* (New York: Columbia UP, 1943).
6 See Thomas Heywood, *A Woman Killed With Kindness*, ed. R.W. van Fossen (London: Methuen, 1961), pp. xvii–xxvii, 103–15.
7 Thomas Heywood, *A Woman Killed With Kindness*, ed. Brian Scobie (London: A & C Black, 1985), 4.65–7, 79–80. All further references are to Scobie's edition unless otherwise stated.
8 Yve Bescou, 1931, quoted in Heywood, *Woman Killed*, ed. van Fossen, pp. xxix–xxx; Heywood, *Woman Killed*, ed. Scobie, p. xv.
9 A tray, basket, or other vessel in which dirty dishes or utensils and leftover food were placed in clearing the table after a meal.
10 Probably to scrape off crumbs from the table-top.
11 Sidney, *Defence of Poesy*, pp. 243–4.
12 Giambattista Guarini, *The Compendium of Tragicomic Poetry*, in *Literary Criticism: Plato to Dryden*, ed. Allan H. Gilbert (New York: American Book Co, 1940), pp. 507, 512.
13 Quoted in Gordon McMullan and Jonathan Hope, 'Introduction: the politics of tragicomedy, 1610–50', in Gordon McMullan and Jonathan Hope eds, *The Politics of Tragicomedy: Shakespeare and After*, (London: Routledge, 1992), p. 1.
14 John Fletcher, 'To the Reader', in *The Faithful Shepherdess: A Critical Edition*, ed. Florence Ada Kirk (New York: Garland, 1980), pp. 15–16.
15 McMullan and Hope, 'Introduction', in *Politics of Tragicomedy*, p. 1.

Chapter 8

1 I.e. straitly, strictly.
2 Stephen Gosson, *Playes Confuted in Five Actions* (London, 1582), sig. E3v, quoted in Howard, *Stage and Social Struggle*, p. 40.
3 Phillip Stubbes, *The Anatomie of Abuses* (London, 1583), sig. L8r-v.
4 William Prynne, *Histrio-Mastix* (London, 1633), title page.
5 For more on the anti-theatrical tracts and Renaissance attitudes to gender, sexuality, identity, and theatre, see Laura Levine, *Men in Women's Clothing: Anti-Theatricality and Effeminization, 1579–1642* (Cambridge: Cambridge UP, 1994).

6 Thomas Heywood, *An Apology for Actors* (London, 1612), sig. C.3r-v.

7 Lady Mary Wroth, *The Countesse of Mountgomeries Urania* (London, 1621), p. 60; Lady Mary Wroth, *The First Part of the Countess of Montgomery's Urania*, ed. Josephine A. Roberts (Tempe, Arizona: Renaissance English Text Society, 1995), p. 73.

8 Lady Mary Wroth, *The Second Part of the Countess of Montgomery's Urania*, ed. Josephine A. Roberts, Suzanne Gossett and Janel Mueller (Tempe, Arizona: Renaissance English Text Society, 1999), p. 160.

9 Quoted by Gurr, *Shakespearean Stage*, p. 226.

10 Michael Shapiro, *Gender in Play on the Shakespearean Stage: Boy Heroines and Female Pages* (Ann Arbor: U of Michigan P, 1994), pp. 221–3.

11 See Michael Shapiro, *Gender in Play*, pp. 207–09.

12 Sir Philip Sidney, *The Countess of Pembroke's Arcadia*, ed. Maurice Evans (Harmondsworth: Penguin, 1977), pp. 366–7, 528.

13 Donne, 'Elegy 16: On his Mistress', *Complete Poems*, pp. 118–19.

14 Six if we include the lost *Cardenio*, co-authored by Shakespeare with John Fletcher. Traces of *Cardenio* in *The Double Falsehood* indicate that it included a cross-dressed heroine. See *Double Falsehood*, ed. Hammond.

15 John Rainoldes, *Th'Overthrow of Stage Playes* (1599), sigs A2r-A4r, quoted in S.P. Cerasano and Marion Wynne-Davies eds, *Renaissance Drama by Women: Texts and Documents* (London: Routledge, 1996), p. 162.

16 Cerasano and Wynne-Davies, *Renaissance Drama by Women*, pp. 158–9.

17 Suzanne Westfall, '"A commonty a Christmas gambold or a tumbling trick": household theatre', in Cox and Kastan, *New History*, p. 50.

18 Westfall, 'Commonty', in Cox and Kastan, *New History*, p. 45.

19 Jean Wilson, *Entertainments for Elizabeth* I (Woodbridge: Boydell and Brewer, 1980), pp. 43–7.

20 Lindley, *Court Masques*, pp. 1, 35. For more on Anne of Denmark's masques, see Clare McManus, *Women on the Renaissance Stage: Anna of Denmark and Female Masquing in the Stuart Court, 1590–1619* (Manchester: Manchester UP, 2002).

21 Alison Findlay and Stephanie Hodgson-Wright, with Gweno Williams, *Women and Dramatic Production 1550–1700* (Harlow: Pearson, 2000), pp. 47–8. A text of *Cupid's Banishment* is available at Cerasano and Wynne-Davies, *Renaissance Drama by Women*, pp. 76–89.

22 Findlay, Hodgson-Wright and Williams, *Women and Dramatic Production*, p. 48.

23 Sophie Tomlinson, '"She that plays the king": Henrietta Maria and the threat of the actress in Caroline culture', in McMullan and Hope, *Politics*

of Tragicomedy, p. 189; Cerasano and Wynne-Davies, *Renaissance Drama by Women*, p. 169.

24 Tomlinson, '"She that plays the king"', in McMullan and Hope, *Politics of Tragicomedy*, p. 195.

25 Findlay, Hodgson-Wright and Williams, *Women and Dramatic Production*, pp. 48–51.

26 Prynne, *Histrio-Mastix*, pp. 214–16, 414–15, quoted in Cerasano and Wynne-Davies, *Renaissance Drama by Women*, pp. 170–71.

27 For more on female performance in the Jacobean and Caroline periods, see Sophie Tomlinson, *Women on Stage in Stuart Drama* (Cambridge: Cambridge UP, 2005).

28 Thomas Salter, *A Mirrhor Mete for All Mothers, Matrones and Maidens, Intituled The Mirrhor of Modestie* (1579), quoted in Suzanne Trill, Kate Chedgzoy and Melanie Osborne eds, *Lay By Your Needles, Ladies, Take the Pen: Writing Women in England, 1500–1700* (London: Arnold, 1997), p. 47.

29 See Cerasano and Wynne-Davies, *Renaissance Drama by Women*, p. 16.

30 See Diane Purkiss, 'Introduction' to *Three Tragedies by Renaissance Women*, ed. Diane Purkiss (London: Penguin, 1998), pp. xi-xliii.

31 Findlay, Hodgson-Wright and Williams, *Women and Dramatic Production*, pp. 2–3, 23, 33–6.

32 Yasmin Arshad, 'The enigma of a portrait: Lady Anne Clifford and Daniel's *Cleopatra*', *British Art Journal* 11.3 (Spring 2011), pp. 30–36.

33 Jane, Lady Lumley, *The Tragedie of Iphigeneia*, in Purkiss, *Three Tragedies*, p. 31, lines 814–16. All further references are to this edition.

34 See Stephanie Hodgson-Wright, 'Jane Lumley's *Iphigenia at Aulis*: multum in parvo, or less is more', in S.P. Cerasano and Marion Wynne-Davies eds, *Readings in Renaissance Women's Drama: Criticism, History and Performance 1594–1998* (London: Routledge, 1998), pp. 129–41.

35 Elizabeth I, 'Translation of a Choral Ode from *Hercules Oetaeus*', in Elizabeth I, *Translations 1544–1589*, ed. Janel Mueller and Joshua Scodel (Chicago: U of Chicago P, 2009), pp. 437–56.

36 Mary, Countess of Pembroke, *The Tragedie of Antony*, in Purkiss, *Three Tragedies*, 5.171–4. All further references are to this edition.

37 See Margaret P. Hannay, *Philip's Phoenix: Mary Sidney, Countess of Pembroke* (Oxford: Oxford UP, 1990).

38 See Paulina Kewes, '"A Fit Memorial for the Times to Come . . .": Admonition and Topical Application in Mary Sidney's *Antonius* and Samuel Daniel's *Cleopatra*', *Review of English Studies* 63.259 (April 2012), pp. 243–64.

39 Elizabeth Cary, *The Tragedie of Mariam*, in Purkiss, *Three Tragedies*, 1.4.45–50. All further references are to this edition.

40 Lady Mary Wroth, *Poems*, ed. Josephine A. Roberts (Baton Rouge: Louisiana State UP, 1983), pp. 32–3.
41 See Margaret P. Hannay, *Mary Sidney, Lady Wroth* (Farnham: Ashgate, 2010).
42 The play is available in Cerasano and Wynne-Davies, *Renaissance Drama by Women*, pp. 91–126, and as Lady Mary Wroth, *Love's Victory: The Penshurst Manuscript*, ed. Michael G. Brennan (London: Roxburghe Club, 1988).

Epilogue

1   Martin Butler, *Theatre and Crisis 1632–1642* (Cambridge: Cambridge UP, 1984), pp. 33, 101, 2–3.
2   Quoted in Susan Wiseman, *Drama and Politics in the English Civil War* (Cambridge: Cambridge UP, 1998), p. 1.
3   Gary Taylor, *Reinventing Shakespeare: A Cultural History from the Restoration to the Present* (London: Hogarth, 1990), p. 7; Wiseman, *Drama and Politics*, p. 5.
4   Wiseman, *Drama and Politics*, p. 5; Griswold, *Renaissance Revivals*, p. 103.
5   Griswold, *Renaissance Revivals*, p. 103.
6   Margaret Cavendish, *CCXI Sociable Letters*, no. XXIX, p. 57, quoted in Sophie Tomlinson, '"My brain the stage": Margaret Cavendish and the fantasy of female performance', in Clare Brant and Diane Purkiss eds, *Women, Texts and Histories 1575–1760* (London: Routledge, 1992), p. 136.
7   See Edward A. Langhans, 'The theatre', in Deborah Payne Fisk ed., *The Cambridge Companion to English Restoration Theatre* (Cambridge: Cambridge UP, 2000), pp. 6–12.
8   Griswold, *Renaissance Revivals*, pp. 115–16.
9   See Michael Dobson, *The Making of the National Poet: Shakespeare, Adaptation and Authorship, 1660–1769* (Oxford: Clarendon, 1992).
10 Craig, *Jonson: Critical Heritage*, p. 2; Griswold, *Renaissance Revivals*, p. 120.
11 Griswold, *Renaissance Revivals*, p. 124; Martin White, *Renaissance Drama in Action* (London: Routledge, 1998), p. 202.
12 Griswold, *Renaissance Revivals*, p. 118.
13 Griswold, *Renaissance Revivals*, pp. 123, 142.
14 William Hazlitt, *Lectures on the Dramatic Literature of the Age of Elizabeth*, 2nd edn (London, 1821), p. 2.
15 Hazlitt, *Dramatic Literature of the Age of Elizabeth*, p. 56.
16 See, for instance, Jyotsna G. Singh, *Colonial Narratives/Cultural*

Dialogues: "Discoveries" of India in the Language of Colonialism (London: Routledge, 1996), pp. 120–52; Poonam Trivedi and Dennis Bartholomeusz eds, *India's Shakespeare: Translation, Interpretation and Performance* (Newark: U of Delaware P, 2005).

17 See Peter Rawlings ed., *Americans on Shakespeare 1776–1914* (Aldershot: Ashgate, 1999); Virginia Mason Vaughan and Alden T. Vaughan eds, *Shakespeare in American Life* (Washington, D.C.: Folger Shakespeare Library, 2007).

18 T.S. Eliot, 'Four Elizabethan dramatists', in *Elizabethan Essays* (London: Faber, 1934), p. 18.

19 T.S. Eliot, 'Whispers of Immortality', in *The Complete Poems and Plays of T.S. Eliot* (London: Faber, 1969), p. 52.

20 Quoted in White, *Renaissance Drama in Action*, p. 211.

21 Griswold, *Renaissance Revivals*, pp. 163–4.

22 Quoted in White, *Renaissance Drama in Action*, p. 211.

23 Quoted in White, *Renaissance Drama in Action*, p. 212.

24 Quoted in White, *Renaissance Drama in Action*, p. 212.

25 R.E. Knoll in 1969, quoted in MacLure, *Marlowe: Critical Heritage*, p. 23.

26 See Giorgio Strehler, 'Notes on *The Tempest*', trans. Thomas Simpson, *PAJ: A Journal of Performance and Art*, 24.3 (Sept 2002), pp. 1–17; Zdenek Stribrny, *Shakespeare and Eastern Europe* (Oxford: Oxford UP, 2000); and Trivedi and Bartholomeusz, *India's Shakespeare*.

27 See the two essays by Richard Burt in Richard Burt and Lynda E. Boose eds, *Shakespeare, The Movie, II* (London: Routledge, 2003); Sonia Massai ed., *World-Wide Shakespeares: Local Appropriations in Film and Performance* (London: Routledge, 2005); the essays by Caroline Silverstone and Carolyn Jess-Cooke in Mark Thornton Burnett and Ramona Wray eds, *Screening Shakespeare in the Twenty-First Century* (Edinburgh: Edinburgh UP, 2006); Dennis Kennedy, 'Found in Translation', *Around the Globe* 50 (Spring 2012), pp. 2–4; and Mark Thornton Burnett, *Shakespeare and World Cinema* (Cambridge: Cambridge UP, forthcoming, 2013).

28 Victoria Ward, 'William Shakespeare is voted Britain's greatest national treasure', *The Mirror*, 3 Jul 2009, http://www.mirror.co.uk/news/uk-news/william-shakespeare-is-voted-greatest-404099, accessed 21 Aug 2012.

29 *The Revenger's Tragedy*, press reviews, National Theatre website, https://microsites.nationaltheatre.org.uk/?lid=35417&dspl=reviews, accessed 21 Aug 2012; Charles Spencer, '*The Revenger's Tragedy*: the enduring appeal of nastiness and perversity', *The Telegraph*, 6 June 2008, http://www.telegraph.co.uk/journalists/charles-spencer/3553709/The-Revengers-Tragedy-the-enduring-appeal-of-nastiness-and-perversity.html, accessed 21 Aug 2012.

Bibliography

PRIMARY WORKS

Beadle, Richard and Pamela M. King eds, *York Mystery Plays: A Selection in Modern Spelling* (Oxford: Oxford UP, 1995).

Beaumont, Francis, *The Knight of the Burning Pestle*, ed. Sheldon P. Zitner (Manchester: Manchester UP, 1984).

Bodley, Sir Thomas, *Letters of Sir Thomas Bodley to Thomas James, First Keeper of the Bodleian Library*, ed. G.W. Wheeler (Oxford: Clarendon, 1926).

Bullett, Gerald ed., *Silver Poets of the Sixteenth Century* (London: Dent, 1947).

Castiglione, Baldesar, *The Book of the Courtier*, trans. George Bull (1967; rev. edn Harmondsworth: Penguin, 1976).

Cerasano, S.P., and Marion Wynne-Davies eds, *Renaissance Drama by Women: Texts and Documents* (London: Routledge, 1996), p. 162.

Coryate, Thomas, *Coryate's Crudities* (London, 1611).

Davies, John, *Poems*, ed. Robert Kruger (Oxford: Oxford UP, 1975).

Donne, John, *The Complete English Poems*, ed. A.J. Smith (Harmondsworth: Penguin, 1971).

Double Falsehood or the Distressed Lovers, ed. Brean Hammond (London: Arden Shakespeare, 2000).

Elizabeth I, *Collected Works*, ed. Leah S. Marcus, Janel Mueller, and Mary Beth Rose (Chicago: U of Chicago P, 2000).

Erasmus, *Praise of Folly* (1511), trans. Betty Radice, introd. A.H.T. Levi (1971; rev. edn London: Penguin, 1993).

Evans, Maurice ed., *Elizabethan Sonnets* (London: Dent, 1977).

Everyman and Mankind, ed. Douglas Bruster and Eric Rasmussen (London: A & C Black, 2009).

Fletcher, John, *The Faithful Shepherdess: A Critical Edition*, ed. Florence Ada Kirk (New York: Garland, 1980).

——, and William Shakespeare, *The Two Noble Kinsmen*, ed. Lois Potter (London: Arden Shakespeare, 1997).

Ford, John, *'Tis Pity She's a Whore*, ed. Derek Roper (Manchester: Manchester UP, 1997).

Gayton, Edmund, *Pleasant notes upon Don Quixot* (London, 1654).

Geneva Bible, The: A Facsimile of the 1560 Edition, introd. Lloyd E. Berry (Madison: U of Wisconsin P, 1969).

Guarini, Giambattista, *The Compendium of Tragicomic Poetry*, in *Literary Criticism: Plato to Dryden*, ed. Allan H. Gilbert (New York: American Book Co, 1940), pp. 504–33.

Guilpin, Everard, *Skialetheia, or, A Shadow of Truth, in Certain Epigrams and Satires* (London, 1598).

Harington, Sir John, *Letters and Epigrams*, ed. N.E. McClure (Philadelphia: U of Pennsylvania P, 1930).

Harrison, William, 'Description of England', in *The First and Second Volumes of Chronicles*, ed. Raphael Holinshed (London, 1587).

Heywood, Thomas, *An Apology for Actors* (London, 1612).

——, *The English Traveller* (London, 1633).

——, *A Woman Killed With Kindness*, ed. R.W. van Fossen (London: Methuen, 1961).

——, *A Woman Killed With Kindness*, ed. Brian Scobie (London: A & C Black, 1985).

Holinshed, Raphael, *The Third Volume of Chronicles* (London, 1586).

Howell, James, *Londinopolis: An Historical Discourse or Perlustration of the City of London* (London, 1657).

Jewel, John, 'The Third Part of the Sermon Against Peril of Idolatry', in *The Second Tome of Homilies* (London, 1571).

Jonson, Ben, *Hymenaei* (London, 1606).

——, *Ben Jonson*, ed. C.H. Herford and Percy Simpson, 11 vols (Oxford: Clarendon, 1925–52).

——, *The Complete Poems*, ed. George Parfitt (London: Penguin, 1988).

——, *Sejanus, His Fall*, ed. Philip J. Ayres (Manchester: Manchester UP, 1990).

——, *The Alchemist and Other Plays*, ed. Gordon Campbell (Oxford: Oxford UP, 1995).

Kyd, Thomas, *The Spanish Tragedy* (*c*.1587), in *Four Revenge Tragedies*, ed. Katharine Eisaman Maus (Oxford: Oxford UP, 1995).

Leland, John, and Nicholas Udall, pageant verses for the coronation procession of Anne Boleyn, British Library Royal MS 18.A.lxiv, ff. 1–16.

——, and ——, 'Leland's and Udall's verses before the coronation of Anne Boleyn', in F.J. Furnivall ed., *Ballads from Manuscripts* (London, 1868–73), vol. 1, pp. 364–401.

Lester, G.A. ed., *Three Late Medieval Morality Plays: Mankind, Everyman, Mundus et Infans* (1981; rpt. London: A. & C. Black, 2002).

Lindley, David ed., *Court Masques: Jacobean and Caroline Entertainments 1605–1640* (Oxford: Oxford UP, 1995).

Lyly, John, *Endymion*, ed. David Bevington (Manchester: Manchester UP, 1996).

Marlowe, Christopher, *The Tragedie of Dido, Queene of Carthage*, in *The Complete Works of Christopher Marlowe*, ed. Fredson Bowers, 2 vols, (1973; 2nd edn, Cambridge: Cambridge University Press, 1981), vol. 1, pp. 1–70.

——, *Doctor Faustus*, ed. David Bevington and Eric Rasmussen, Revels Plays (Manchester: Manchester UP, 1993).

——, *Doctor Faustus and Other Plays*, ed. David Bevington and Eric Rasmussen (Oxford: Oxford UP, 1995).

Marston, John, *Jacke Drums Entertainment* (London, 1601).

Middleton, Thomas, *Women Beware Women and Other Plays*, ed. Richard Dutton (Oxford: Oxford UP, 1999).

——, *The Collected Works*, gen. eds Gary Taylor and John Lavagnino (Oxford: Oxford UP, 2007).

——, and Thomas Dekker, *The Roaring Girl*, ed. Elizabeth Cook (London: A. & C. Black, 1997).

Milton, John, *Paradise Lost*, ed. Alastair Fowler (London: Longman, 1971).

Mulcaster, Richard, *The Queen's Majesty's Passage* (1559), in Arthur F. Kinney ed., *Renaissance Drama: An Anthology of Plays and Entertainments* (Oxford: Blackwell, 1999), pp. 17–34.

Norbrook, David, and H.R. Woudhuysen eds, *The Penguin Book of Renaissance Verse 1509–1659* (London: Penguin, 1992).

Ovid, *Metamorphoses*, trans. David Raeburn (London: Penguin, 2004).

Peele, George, *Dramatic Works*, ed. R. Mark Benbow, Elmer Blistein, and Frank S. Hook (New Haven: Yale UP, 1970).

Prynne, William, *Histrio-Mastix* (London, 1633).

Purkiss, Diane ed., *Three Tragedies by Renaissance Women* (London: Penguin, 1998).

Sackville, Thomas, and Thomas Norton, *Gorboduc, or Ferrex and Porrex*, ed. Irby B. Cauthen, Jr. (London: Edward Arnold, 1970).

Shakespeare, William, *The Tempest*, ed. Stephen Orgel (Oxford: Oxford UP, 1994).

——, *Hamlet: The Texts of 1603 and 1623*, ed. Ann Thompson and Neil Taylor (London: Arden Shakespeare, 2006).

——, *The RSC Shakespeare: Complete Works*, ed. Jonathan Bate and Eric Rasmussen (Basingstoke: Macmillan, 2007).

——, *The Norton Shakespeare*, ed. Stephen Greenblatt et al., 2nd edn (New York: Norton, 2008).

——, and John Fletcher, *King Henry VIII*, ed. Gordon McMullan (London: Arden Shakespeare, 2000).

——, and ——, *The Two Noble Kinsmen*, ed. N.W. Bawcutt, introd. Peter Swaab (London: Penguin, 2009).

Sidney, Sir Philip, *The Countess of Pembroke's Arcadia*, ed. Maurice Evans (Harmondsworth: Penguin, 1977).

——, *The Four Foster Children of Desire* (1581), in Jean Wilson ed., *Entertainments for Elizabeth I* (Woodbridge: D.S. Brewer, 1980), pp. 61–85.

——, 'The Defence of Poesy', in *The Oxford Authors: Sir Philip Sidney*, ed. Katherine Duncan-Jones (Oxford: Oxford UP, 1989).

——, *The Lady of May*, in Arthur F. Kinney ed., *Renaissance Drama: An Anthology of Plays and Entertainments* (Oxford: Blackwell, 1999), pp. 35–44.

Spenser, Edmund, *The Shorter Poems*, ed. Richard A. McCabe (London: Penguin, 1999).

Stubbes, Phillip, *The Anatomie of Abuses* (London, 1583).

Taylor, John, *The Colde Tearme, Or, The Frozen Age, Or, The Metamorphosis of The River of Thames* (London, 1621).

Warning for Fair Women, A (London, 1599).

Webster, John, 'An excellent Actor', in *New Characters (Drawne to the Life)*, attrib. Sir Thomas Overbury (London, 1615).

——, *The Duchess of Malfi and Other Plays*, ed. René Weis (Oxford: Oxford UP, 1996).

Whitney, Isabella, Mary Sidney and Aemilia Lanyer, *Renaissance Women Poets*, ed. Danielle Clarke (London: Penguin, 2000).

Whitworth, Jr., Charles W. ed., *Three Sixteenth-Century Comedies: 'Gammer Gurton's Needle', 'Roister Doister', 'The Old Wife's Tale'* (London: Ernest Benn, 1984).

Wits Recreations. Selected from the Finest Fancies of Moderne Muses (London, 1640).

Wright, James, *Historia Histrionica* (London, 1699).

Wroth, Lady Mary, *The Countesse of Mountgomeries Urania* (London, 1621).

——, *Love's Victory: The Penshurst Manuscript*, ed. Michael G. Brennan (London: Roxburghe Club, 1988).

——, *The First Part of the Countess of Montgomery's Urania*, ed. Josephine A. Roberts (Tempe, Arizona: Renaissance English Text Society, 1995).

——, *The Second Part of the Countess of Montgomery's Urania*, ed. Josephine A. Roberts, Suzanne Gossett and Janel Mueller (Tempe, Arizona: Renaissance English Text Society, 1999).

SECONDARY WORKS

Adams, Henry Hitch, *English Domestic or Homiletic Tragedy, 1575 to 1642* (New York: Columbia UP, 1943).

Arshad, Yasmin, 'The enigma of a portrait: Lady Anne Clifford and Daniel's *Cleopatra*', *British Art Journal* 11.3 (Spring 2011), pp. 30–36.

Barker, Francis, *The Tremulous Private Body: Essays on Subjection* (Ann Arbor: U of Michigan P, 1995).

Barton, Anne, *Ben Jonson, Dramatist* (Cambridge UP, 1984).

Beadle, Richard ed., *The Cambridge Companion to Medieval English Theatre* (Cambridge: Cambridge UP, 1994).

Bellany, Alastair, *The Politics of Court Scandal in Early Modern England: News Culture and the Overbury Affair, 1603–1666* (Cambridge: Cambridge UP, 2002).

Braunmuller, A. R., and Michael Hattaway eds, *The Cambridge Companion to English Renaissance Drama*, 2nd edn (Cambridge: Cambridge UP, 2003).

Bray, Alan, *Homosexuality in Renaissance England* (1982; 2nd edn, London: Gay Men's Press, 1988).

Briggs, Julia, *This Stage-Play World: English Literature and Its Background, 1580–1625* (Oxford: Oxford UP, 1983).

British Humanist Association website, www.humanism.org.uk/home, accessed 16 April 2011.

Brooke, Nicholas, *Horrid Laughter in Jacobean Tragedy* (London: Open Books, 1979).

Burckhardt, Jacob, *The Civilization of the Renaissance in* Italy (1860), trans. S.G.C. Middlemore, introd. Peter Burke (London: Penguin, 2004).

Burnett, Mark Thornton, *Shakespeare and World Cinema* (Cambridge: Cambridge UP, forthcoming, 2013).

——, and Ramona Wray eds, *Screening Shakespeare in the Twenty-First Century* (Edinburgh: Edinburgh UP, 2006).

Burt, Richard, and Lynda E. Boose eds, *Shakespeare, The Movie, II* (London: Routledge, 2003).

Butler, Martin, *Theatre and Crisis 1632–1642* (Cambridge: Cambridge UP, 1984).

Catholic Encyclopedia, The, www.newadvent.org/cathen/, accessed 13 Aug 2012.

Chamber of Demonstrations, The: Reconstructing the Jacobean Indoor Playhouse, http://www.bristol.ac.uk/drama/jacobean/project1.html, accessed 13 Aug 2012.

Chambers, E.K., *The Elizabethan Stage*, 4 vols (Oxford: Clarendon, 1623).

Cheney, Patrick ed., *The Cambridge Companion to Christopher Marlowe* (Cambridge: Cambridge UP, 2004).

Cox, John D., and David Scott Kastan eds, *A New History of Early English Drama* (New York: Columbia UP, 1997).

Craig, D.H. ed., *Ben Jonson: The Critical Heritage* (London: Routledge, 1990).

Crockett, Brian, *The Play of Paradox: Stage and Sermon in Renaissance England* (Philadelphia: U of Pennsylvania P, 1995).

Cuddon, J.A., *A Dictionary of Literary Terms* (1977; rev. edn, Harmondsworth: Penguin, 1979).

Dobson, Michael, *The Making of the National Poet: Shakespeare, Adaptation and Authorship, 1660–1769* (Oxford: Clarendon, 1992).

Dollimore, Jonathan, *Radical Tragedy: Religion, Ideology and Power in the Drama of Shakespeare and his Contemporaries* (1984; 2nd edn, Hemel Hempstead: Harvester Wheatsheaf, 1989).

Donaldson, Ian, *Ben Jonson: A Life* (Oxford: Oxford UP, 2011).

Duncan-Jones, Katherine, *Ungentle Shakespeare: Scenes from his Life* (London: Arden Shakespeare, 2001).

——, *Shakespeare: Upstart Crow to Sweet Swan, 1592–1623* (London: Methuen, 2011).

Egan, Gabriel, 'Reconstructions of the Globe: a retrospective', *Shakespeare Survey* 52 (1999), pp. 1–16.

Eliot, T.S., 'Four Elizabethan dramatists', in *Elizabethan Essays* (London: Faber, 1934), pp. 7–20.

Dutton, Richard, *Ben Jonson: Authority: Criticism* (Basingstoke: Macmillan, 1996).

Findlay, Alison, and Stephanie Hodgson-Wright, with Gweno Williams, *Women and Dramatic Production 1550–1700* (Harlow: Pearson, 2000).

Gill, Roma, 'Christopher Marlowe', in Fredson Bowers ed., *Dictionary of Literary Biography: Elizabethan Dramatists* (Detroit: Gale, 1987), vol. 62, pp. 212–31.

Greenblatt, Stephen, *Renaissance Self-Fashioning: From More to Shakespeare* (Chicago: U of Chicago P, 1980).

——, *Hamlet in Purgatory* (Princeton: Princeton UP, 2001).

Griswold, Wendy, *Renaissance Revivals: City Comedy and Revenge Tragedy in the London Theatre, 1576–1980* (Chicago: U of Chicago P, 1986).

Gurr, Andrew, 'Who strutted and bellowed?', *Shakespeare Survey* 16 (1963), pp. 95–102.

——, *The Shakespearean Stage 1574–1642*, 3rd edn (Cambridge: Cambridge UP, 1992).

——, *The Shakespearean Playing Companies* (Oxford: Oxford UP, 1996).

Hackett, Helen, 'Dream-visions of Elizabeth I', in Katharine Hodgkin, Michelle O'Callaghan and S.J. Wiseman eds, *Reading the Early Modern Dream: The Terrors of the Night* (New York: Routledge, 2008), pp. 45–66.

——, *Shakespeare and Elizabeth: The Meeting of Two Myths* (Princeton: Princeton UP, 2009).

Hannay, Margaret P., *Philip's Phoenix: Mary Sidney, Countess of Pembroke* (Oxford: Oxford UP, 1990).

——, *Mary Sidney, Lady Wroth* (Farnham: Ashgate, 2010).

Happé, Peter, *English Drama Before Shakespeare* (London: Longman, 1999).

Harp, Richard, and Stanley Stewart eds, *The Cambridge Companion to Ben Jonson* (Cambridge: Cambridge UP, 2000).

Hazlitt, William, *Lectures on the Dramatic Literature of the Age of Elizabeth*, 2nd edn (London, 1821).

Heinemann, Margot, *Puritanism and Theatre: Thomas Middleton and Opposition Drama under the Early Stuarts* (Cambridge: Cambridge UP, 1980).

Hodgson-Wright, Stephanie, 'Jane Lumley's *Iphigenia at Aulis*: multum in parvo, or less is more', in S.P. Cerasano and Marion Wynne-Davies eds, *Readings in Renaissance Women's Drama: Criticism, History and Performance 1594–1998* (London: Routledge, 1998), pp. 129–41.

Honan, Park, *Christopher Marlowe, Poet and Spy* (Oxford: Oxford UP, 2005).

Hopkins, Lisa, *Christopher Marlowe, Renaissance Dramatist* (Edinburgh: Edinburgh UP, 2008).

Howard, Jean, *The Stage and Social Struggle in Early Modern England* (London: Routledge, 1994).

Hunt, Arnold, *The Art of Hearing: English Preachers and Their Audiences, 1590–1640* (Cambridge: Cambridge UP, 2012).

Kelly, Joan, 'Did Women Have a Renaissance?', in *Women, History and Theory: The Essays of Joan Kelly* (Chicago: U of Chicago P, 1984), pp. 19–51.

Kennedy, Dennis, 'Found in Translation', *Around the Globe* 50 (Spring 2012), pp. 2–4

Kerrigan, John, *Revenge Tragedy: Aeschylus to Armageddon* (Oxford: Clarendon, 1996).

Kewes, Paulina, '"A Fit Memorial for the Times to Come …": Admonition and Topical Application in Mary Sidney's *Antonius* and Samuel Daniel's *Cleopatra*', *Review of English Studies* 63.259 (April 2012), pp. 243–64.

Knights, L.C., 'How many children had Lady Macbeth?', in *Explorations: Essays in Criticism Mainly on the Literature of the Seventeenth Century* (London: Chatto & Windus, 1946), pp. 1–39.

Lamb, H.H., *Climate: Present, Past and Future*, vol. 2 (London: Methuen, 1977).

Langhans, Edward A., 'The theatre', in Deborah Payne Fisk ed., *The Cambridge Companion to English Restoration Theatre* (Cambridge: Cambridge UP, 2000), pp. 1–18.

Lever, J.W., *The Tragedy of State* (London: Methuen, 1971).

Levin, Harry, *The Overreacher: A Study of Christopher Marlowe* (London: Faber, 1954).

Levine, Laura, *Men in Women's Clothing: Anti-Theatricality and Effeminization, 1579–1642* (Cambridge: Cambridge UP, 1994).

MacCulloch, Diarmaid, *Reformation: Europe's House Divided* (2003; London: Penguin, 2004).

MacLure, Millar ed., *Marlowe: The Critical Heritage, 1588–1896*

McManus, Clare, *Women on the Renaissance Stage: Anna of Denmark and Female Masquing in the Stuart Court, 1590–1619* (Manchester: Manchester UP, 2002).

McMullan, Gordon, and Jonathan Hope eds, *The Politics of Tragicomedy: Shakespeare and After* (London: Routledge, 1992).

Manley, Lawrence, *Literature and Culture in Early Modern London* (Cambridge: Cambridge UP, 1995).

Massai, Sonia ed., *World-Wide Shakespeares: Local Appropriations in Film and Performance* (London: Routledge, 2005).

Montrose, Louis Adrian, 'Gifts and reasons: the contexts of Peele's *Araygnement of Paris*', *English Literary History* 47.3 (Autumn 1980), pp. 433–61.

Mulryne, J.R., and Margaret Shewring eds, *Shakespeare's Globe Rebuilt* (Cambridge: Cambridge UP, 1997)

Nicholl, Charles, *The Reckoning: The Murder of Christopher Marlowe* (1992; paperback, London: Picador, 1993).

Nichols, John ed., *The Progresses and Public Processions of Queen Elizabeth*, 3 vols (London, 1823).

Orgel, Stephen, *The Illusion of Power: Political Theater in the English Renaissance* (Berkeley: U of California P, 1975).

Oxford Dictionary of National Biography (Oxford: Oxford UP, 2004; online edn, Jan 2011), www.oxforddnb.com.

Oxford English Dictionary [*OED*] (Oxford: Oxford UP, 2011), www.oed.com.

Palfrey, Simon, and Tiffany Stern, *Shakespeare in Parts* (Oxford: Oxford UP, 2007).

Picard, Liza, *Elizabeth's London: Everyday Life in Elizabethan London* (London: Weidenfeld & Nicholson, 2003).

Rawlings, Peter ed., *Americans on Shakespeare 1776–1914* (Aldershot: Ashgate, 1999).

Revenger's Tragedy, The, press reviews, National Theatre website, https://www.microsites.nationaltheatre.org.uk/?lid=35417 &dspl=reviews, accessed 21 Aug 2012.

Rowse, A.L., *Christopher Marlowe: A Biography* (London: Macmillan, 1964).

Sanders, Julie, Kate Chedgzoy and Susan Wiseman eds, *Refashioning Ben Jonson: Gender, Politics, and the Jonsonian Canon* (Basingstoke: Macmillan, 1998).

Scott, Sarah K., and M.L. Stapleton eds, *Christopher Marlowe the Craftsman: Lives, Stage, and Page* (Farnham: Ashgate, 2010).

Shapiro, James, *1599: A Year in the Life of William Shakespeare* (London: Faber, 2005).

Shapiro, Michael, *Gender in Play on the Shakespearean Stage: Boy Heroines and Female Pages* (Ann Arbor: U of Michigan P, 1994).

Shell, Alison, *Catholicism, Controversy and the English Literary Imagination, 1558–1660* (Cambridge: Cambridge UP, 1999).

——, *Shakespeare and Religion* (London: Arden, 2010).

Singh, Jyotsna G., *Colonial Narratives/Cultural Dialogues: "Discoveries" of India in the Language of Colonialism* (London: Routledge, 1996).

Smith, Bruce R., *Homosexual Desire in Shakespeare's England: A Cultural Poetics* (1991; pbk, Chicago: U of Chicago P, 1994).

Smith, David Lawrence, *A History of the Modern British Isles, 1603–1707: The Double Crown* (Oxford: Wiley-Blackwell, 1998).

Smith, Emma, 'Chettle, Henry (d. 1603x7)', *Oxford Dictionary of National Biography* (Oxford: Oxford UP, 2004), http://www.oxforddnb.com/view/article/5245, accessed 30 June 2011.

Southern, Antonia, *Player, Playwright and Preacher's Kid: The Story of Nathan Field, 1587–1620* (London: Athena Press, 2009).

Spencer, Charles, *The Revenger's Tragedy*: the enduring appeal of nastiness and perversity', *The Telegraph*, 6 June 2008, http://www.telegraph.co.uk/journalists/charles-spencer/3553709/The-Revengers-Tragedy-the-enduring-appeal-of-nastiness-and-perversity.html, accessed 21 Aug 2012.

Stern, Tiffany, *Making Shakespeare: From Stage to Page* (London: Routledge, 2004).

——, *Documents of Performance in Early Modern England* (Cambridge: Cambridge UP, 2009).

Stewart, Alan, *The Cradle King: A Life of James VI and I* (London: Chatto and Windus, 2003).

Strehler, Giorgio, 'Notes on *The Tempest*', trans. Thomas Simpson, *PAJ: A Journal of Performance and Art*, 24.3 (Sept 2002), pp. 1–17.

Stribrny, Zdenek, *Shakespeare and Eastern Europe* (Oxford: Oxford UP, 2000).

Taylor, Gary, *Reinventing Shakespeare: A Cultural History from the Restoration to the Present* (London: Hogarth, 1990).

Thorndike, Ashley H., 'The relations of *Hamlet* to contemporary revenge plays', *PMLA* 17. 2 (1902): 125–220.

Tomlinson, Sophie, '"My brain the stage": Margaret Cavendish and the fantasy of female performance', in Clare Brant and Diane Purkiss eds, *Women, Texts and Histories 1575–1760* (London: Routledge, 1992), pp. 133–62.

——, *Women on Stage in Stuart Drama* (Cambridge: Cambridge UP, 2005).

Trill, Suzanne, Kate Chedgzoy and Melanie Osborne eds, *Lay By Your Needles, Ladies, Take the Pen: Writing Women in England, 1500–1700* (London: Arnold, 1997).

Trivedi, Poonam and Dennis Bartholomeusz eds, *India's Shakespeare: Translation, Interpretation and Performance* (Newark: U of Delaware P, 2005).

Vaughan, Virginia Mason and Alden T. Vaughan eds, *Shakespeare in American Life* (Washington, D.C.: Folger Shakespeare Library, 2007).

Vickers, Brian ed., *Shakespeare: The Critical Heritage: Vol. 2: 1693–1733* (London: Routledge, 1974).

—— ed., *Shakespeare: The Critical Heritage: Vol. 5: 1765–1774* (London: Routledge, 1979).

——, *Shakespeare, Co-Author: A Historical Study of Five Collaborative Plays* (Oxford: Oxford UP, 2002).

Ward, Joseph P., 'The Taming of the Thames: Reading the River in the Seventeenth Century', *Huntington Library Quarterly* 71.1 (March 2008), pp. 55–75.

Ward, Victoria, 'William Shakespeare is voted Britain's greatest national treasure', *The Mirror*, 3 Jul 2009, http://www.mirror.co.uk/news/uk-news/william-shakespeare-is-voted-greatest-404099, accessed 21 Aug 2012.

Weis, René, *Shakespeare Revealed: A Biography* (London: John Murray, 2007).

Wilson, Jean, *Entertainments for Elizabeth* I (Woodbridge: Boydell and Brewer, 1980).

Wiseman, Susan, *Drama and Politics in the English Civil War* (Cambridge: Cambridge UP, 1998).

Wood, Michael, *In Search of Shakespeare* (London: BBC Worldwide, 2003).

Index

Figures in bold indicate illustrations.